To our parents, who taught us the
love of travel and the joy of discovery

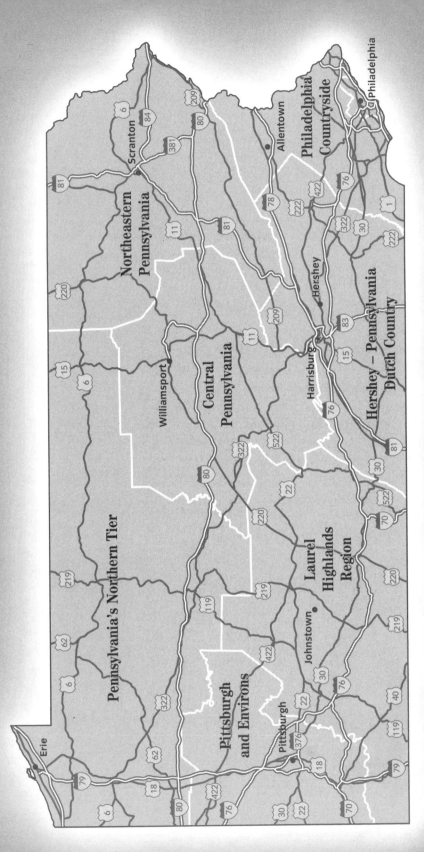

PENNSYLVANIA

Erie

Pennsylvania's Northern Tier

Scranton

Northeastern Pennsylvania

Williamsport

Central Pennsylvania

Allentown

Philadelphia Countryside

Philadelphia

Hershey

Harrisburg

Hershey – Pennsylvania Dutch Country

Johnstown

Laurel Highlands Region

Pittsburgh

Pittsburgh and Environs

6
84
209
80
81
387
11
81
78
222
422
76
1
322
30
222
220
15
6
11
209
83
15
322
522
22
80
220
219
70
522
30
119
219
220
422
219
30
76
219
322
62
22
376
18
40
119
79
80
76
30
22
70
79
18
62
6

INSIDERS' GUIDE®

FUN WITH THE FAMILY™ SERIES

fun WITH the Family™

PENNSYLVANIA

HUNDREDS OF IDEAS FOR DAY TRIPS WITH THE KIDS

FAITH

AND

EMILY PAULSEN

FIFTH EDITION

INSIDERS' GUIDE®

GUILFORD, CONNECTICUT
AN IMPRINT OF THE GLOBE PEQUOT PRESS

The prices, rates, and hours listed in this guidebook
were confirmed at press time. We recommend, however, that you
call establishments to obtain current information before traveling.

To buy books in quantity for corporate use
or incentives, call **(800) 962–0973, ext. 4551,**
or e-mail **premiums@GlobePequot.com.**

INSIDERS' GUIDE®

Copyright © 1996, 1998, 2000, 2003, 2005 by The Globe Pequot Press

Insiders' Guide is a registered trademark of The Globe Pequot Press.
Fun with the Family is a trademark of The Globe Pequot Press.

Text design by Nancy Freeborn and Linda Loiewski
Maps by Rusty Nelson © The Globe Pequot Press
Spot photography throughout © Photodisc and © RubberBall Productions

ISSN 1539-8730
ISBN 0-7627-3687-9

Manufactured in the United States of America
Fifth Edition/First Printing

Contents

Acknowledgments

Our names may be on the cover, but there are a lot of people who have helped make this book possible. We'd like to thank all the people at the tourist boards and sites who took extra time to answer our questions and point us in the right direction. We'd also like to thank our husbands, Martin Livezey and Bart Sacks; Faith's children, Judah, Seth, and Gideon Paulsen-Sacks; and Emily's children, Eli and Maya Livezey, for their enthusiasm and support.

Introduction

Pennsylvania's history reflects America's history. Today it is more important than ever for families to learn about the background, and the responsibilities, of the freedoms we cherish.

In Pennsylvania it is easy to take our historical sites for granted, but this is a great time to explore Old City Philadelphia, Independence Hall and the Lights of Liberty sounds and lights show, as well as places like Valley Forge, Washington's Crossing, and Gettysburg National Military Park. Historic landmarks and living-history sites can be found in every corner of the state. There's no better time to discover them than now.

But liberty is not just something from the past; it is a living legacy that requires regular care. The National Liberty Museum and the new National Constitution Center get kids thinking in new ways about the responsibilities of citizenship.

When we first visited Pennsylvania on a family vacation in 1969, neither of us realized that someday we would each adopt the state as our home, and we certainly never dreamed we would write a book about it. As children then, we saw the Liberty Bell and the Franklin Institute with our parents and our brother, Bruce. Now we take our own children to these places and many more.

Between us, we have five children, three dogs, and four cats. Together and separately, we've enjoyed many family adventures here. But until we began to write it all down, we never fully appreciated the richness of this state.

Whether you're looking for a place to hike, bike, camp, ski, horseback ride, or just take a Sunday afternoon drive, Pennsylvania has a park for you. We've tried to cover the highlights of the state park system in this book, but to devote the space each deserves, we'd have to write another book on the subject. If you want more information about Pennsylvania state parks, call their special toll-free number, (888) PA–PARKS, or check the Web site www.dcnr.state.pa.us.

Pennsylvania has nine major caves open to the public, including the only water-filled cave in the country. Many of the caves offer educational programs on such topics as geology, bats, and Native American history—all geared especially for children.

In 1969, when we walked through the beating heart at the Franklin Institute, it was exciting because it was our first experience with hands-on, interactive science education. Today, the Franklin Institute Science Museum is only one example of "user-friendly" science centers; others include the Carnegie Science Center, Williamsport's Children's Discovery Workshop, Erie's expERIEnce Children's Museum, and Harrisburg's Whitaker Center, to name just a few. Some of the best family adventures can be adventures in learning.

Many parents are afraid to take kids to art museums, but we've found that our children respond well to art museums as long as they experience them in small doses. Sometimes we visit the gift shop first, pick up a few postcards, then see who can find the pictured artworks in the galleries. Pennsylvania has some first-rate art museums, large and small, from the Philadelphia Museum of Art to the Carnegie Museum of Art.

Pennsylvania also has places to go for just plain fun, with no hidden agenda. Amusement parks include Sesame Place, Dorney Park & Wildwater Kingdom, Hersheypark, Idlewild, Kennywood, Sandcastle, and many more. New for this edition are not one but two indoor waterpark resorts, Great Wolf Lodge and Splash Lagoon, in which families can enjoy all the thrills and fun of a waterpark—no matter what the weather.

No matter what the season, whether you like your adventures indoors or outdoors, Pennsylvania is a wonderful destination for families. We're certainly enjoying what the state has to offer, and we hope you will, too. Looking for a place to start? The Web site at www.experiencepa.com is a great jumping-off point for your adventure in Pennsylvania.

Please note that some sections of Pennsylvania have "ten-digit dialing." In these areas it is necessary to dial the area code before dialing any telephone number, even if you're only calling next door. This is true in the 610, 215, 412, 724, 878, 267, 445, 484, and 835 area codes. Another note: Exit numbers on major roads throughout the state are being changed. Check recent road maps or call ahead to avoid confusion.

Lodging, Restaurant, and Attraction Fees

Each chapter in this book gives a list of accommodations and restaurants for the area. This list is not meant to be complete, and we also recommend checking with the local tourist bureaus for other options. In general, we recommend advance reservations. Lodging prices can vary depending on the season and other factors, so make sure you understand in advance how much you'll be expected to pay.

Because admission fees change frequently, we offer a general idea of the prices charged by each attraction. Keep in mind that even though many preserves and museums offer **free** admission, a donation is often expected to help the facility with the costs of keeping the lands and buildings open to the public.

Rates for Attractions

$	under $5
$$	$5.01 to $10
$$$	$10.01 to $20
$$$$	over $20

Attractions Key

The following is a key to the icons found throughout the text.

SWIMMING		DINING	
BOATING / BOAT TOUR		LODGING	
HISTORIC SITE		CAMPING	
HIKING / WALKING		MUSEUMS	
FISHING		PERFORMING ARTS	
BIKING		SPORTS/ATHLETICS	
AMUSEMENT PARK		PICNICKING	
HORSEBACK RIDING		PLAYGROUND	
SKIING / WINTER SPORTS		SHOPPING	
PARK		PLANTS / GARDENS / NATURE TRAILS	
ANIMAL VIEWING		FARMS	

Help Us Keep This Guide Up to Date

Every effort has been made by the authors and editors to make this guide as accurate and useful as possible. However, many changes can occur after a guide is published—establishments close, phone numbers change, hiking trails are rerouted, facilities come under new management, and so on.

We would love to hear from you concerning your experiences with this guide and how you feel it could be improved and be kept up to date. While we may not be able to respond to all comments and suggestions, we'll take them to heart, and we'll make certain to share them with the authors. Please send your comments and suggestions to the following address:

The Globe Pequot Press
Reader Response/Editorial Department
P.O. Box 480
Guilford, CT 06437

Or you may e-mail us at: editorial@GlobePequot.com

Thanks for your input, and happy travels!

Philadelphia

On January 17, 2006, the world celebrates the 300th birthday of Philly's own Benjamin Franklin. The centerpiece of *Franklin 300* will be *Benjamin Franklin: In Search of a Better World,* an exhibit that will travel the nation after debuting at the National Constitution Center. This exhibit will contain the largest collection of Franklin materials ever assembled and include Franklin's walking stick, his signed copy of the *Treaty of Paris,* and pages from *Poor Richard's Almanac.* There will also be copies of the five founding documents, all of which Franklin signed, and more than forty interactive kiosks and hands-on displays. Philadelphia also plans a summerlong heritage tourism festival, re-enactments and tours, and much more in honor of the first Founding Father to reach 300. For details, check www.benfranklin300.org.

Faith & Emily's
FavoriteAttractions in Philadelphia

1. Liberty Bell Center

2. Independence Hall

3. National Constitution Center

4. Lights of Liberty

5. Philadelphia Heritage Park at Franklin Square

6. National Liberty Museum

7. Franklin Institute

8. Academy of Natural Sciences

9. Betsy Ross House

10. Philadelphia Zoo

PHILADELPHIA

If you visited Philadelphia's Independence National Historical Park even just a few years ago, it's time to come back. It is truly a new experience. The new Liberty Bell Center opened on October 9, 2003, featuring groundbreaking new exhibits that showcase the Bell's significance in richly meaningful ways. The Independence Visitor Center provides a comprehensive gateway to the park, the city, and the region. And the National Constitution Center brings the Constitution alive through dramatic and interactive learning experiences. Down the street, families will soon enjoy a completely remade Heritage Park in Franklin Square.

The Liberty Bell's move to its newest home became the occasion for a history project for the people of the City of Brotherly Love. Philadelphians have always cherished the Liberty Bell as a symbol of American freedom. It has also become an icon of freedom to abolitionists, feminists, and figures from Nelson Mandela to the Dalai Lama.

But recent archaeological research unearthed a startling fact: The new Liberty Bell Center was being built above the remains of the quarters where President George Washington once housed his slaves. The discovery precipitated lively discussion involving local newspapers and radio talk programs as well as negotiations between historians, community groups, the National Park Service, and the general public.

In the end, it was decided that our painful history could not and should not be "buried" but embraced as a teaching opportunity. Today's new Liberty Bell Center examines the Liberty Bell in its historical context, with the freedom it symbolizes seen as a process, as a goal both attained and not yet attained.

Faith & Emily's
Favorite Events in Philadelphia

- **Mummer's Day Parade** (January 1, summer version in June), (215) 336–3050

- **Philadelphia Flower Show** (late February or early March), (215) 988–8800; www.theflowershow.com.

- **Philadelphia International Children's Festival** (April or May), (215) 898–6791 or (215) 898–6683; www.pennpresents.org.

- **Philadelphia Orchestra Concerts at Mann Music Center** (outdoor summer series), Fifty-second and Parkside Avenue, (215) 893–1995 or (215) 893–1999; www.philorch.org.

- **Summer concerts at Penn's Landing** (June through August), (215) 928–8801; www.pennslandingcorp.com.

- **Sunoco Welcome America! Celebration** (July), (215) 683–2200; www.americasbirthday.com.

- **Army-Navy Game** (December), Lincoln Financial Field, (215) 336–2000; www.PhillyLovesArmyNavy.com.

The new Liberty Bell Center offers a video presentation and exhibits focusing on the Liberty Bell's origins and its modern-day role as an international icon of freedom. Taped presentations about the history of the Liberty Bell are offered in a dozen languages for the convenience of foreign visitors. The Liberty Bell itself is displayed in a magnificent glass chamber with Independence Hall in the background. Visitors can also view a new film on the Liberty Bell produced for the National Park Service by the History Channel.

The National Constitution Center, opened in 2003, features *Freedom Rising,* an excellent dramatic presentation, as well as exciting interactive exhibits that bring the Constitution to life in all its grandeur and complexity.

A new Heritage Park in Franklin Square is due to open in Memorial Day weekend 2005, and will be open seasonally, featuring a Philadelphia-themed miniature golf course, living history storytellers, the Liberty Carousel, and much more.

You can do some great research on the Internet before your visit. Check out the Web site of the Independence Visitor Center at www.independencevisitorcenter.com. The Greater Philadelphia Cultural Alliance has a Web site called www.phillyfunguide .com, which offers a great deal of useful information. The Web site of the Greater Philadelphia Marketing Corporation, www.gophila.com, offers itineraries, events, tours for special interests, and much more.

Philadelphia **Tours**

Two new kinds of Philadelphia tours have recently begun. The Neighborhood Tourism Network offers immersion tours through some of Philadelphia's most vibrant neighborhoods. Themes include Urban Oases, Latin Soul, Latin Flavor, Voices of Chinatown, Philadelphia's Civil Rights Struggle, Taking a Stand for Freedom, and The Sound of Philadelphia. Philadelphia Neighborhood Tours depart from the Independence Visitor Center at 10:00 A.M. most Saturdays in May, June, September, and October and are recommended for ages eight and up. Price includes trolley transportation, refreshments, and performances. Call (215) 599–2295 or check www.gophila.com.

The Mural Arts program has also introduced four alternating tours of some of Philadelphia's most wonderful murals. The Mural Arts bus tours depart every Saturday, April through October, from the Independence Visitor Center. Each Saturday of the month, you may tour the murals of a different Philadelphia neighborhood. There are also tours some Wednesdays. Advance reservations are recommended. Call (215) 685–0754 or check out the Web site at www.muralarts.org.

The Web site of the Philadelphia Convention and Visitors Bureau is www.pcvb .org. For travel and lodgings try http://philadelphia.citytravelguide.com. Another worthwhile site is http://philadelphia.about.com. You can take a virtual tour of the historic section at www.ushistory.org/tour and of City Hall at www.geocities.com.

If you're visiting Philly for several days, we recommend the CityPass, which gets you into six attractions for one price and with no ticket lines. You can save about 50 percent off the combined box-office prices for The Franklin Institute, Philadelphia Trolley Tour, the Philadelphia Zoo, The Academy of Natural Sciences, Independence Seaport Museum, and the new National Constitution Center. Tickets are valid for nine days from first date of use. You can purchase CityPass at any participating attraction, the Independence Visitor Center, or in advance at www.citypass.com.

Philadelphia is a great walking city. Most attractions are an easy jaunt from hotels and from each other. And when the feet get sore or the kids get cranky, the purple PHLASH bus, which travels in a loop from Penn's Landing to the Art Museum, is one of the best deals in town. To get to some of the attractions in the outskirts of the city, a car can be handy, but the one-way streets in Center City and cost of parking can be frustrating. Public transportation or walking is your best bet.

There are lots of companies that offer tours of Philadelphia, on everything from a reproduction of an old-time trolley or a horse and buggy to a streamlined coach. Here are some companies to contact: American Trolley Tours/Choo-Choo Trolley, (215) 333–2119; Big Bus Tour, (215) 965–7676, or (800) 537–7676, '76 Carriage Co., (215) 923–8516 (tours begin at Independence National Park); Riverboat Queen Fleet, (215) 923–4778 (cruises leave from Penn's Landing); Philadelphia Trolley Works, (215) 925–TOUR; PHLASH bus, (215) 4–PHLASH.

Historic Philadelphia

When most people think of Philadelphia, they think of its place in U.S. history. You'll hear the word *first* a lot while touring this historic city. In fact, the area that makes up Independence National Historic Park (from Second to Sixth Street along Walnut Street) is called "America's most historic square mile." Here, you'll meander the streets walked by Benjamin Franklin, Thomas Jefferson, Betsy Ross, George Washington, Dolley Madison, John Adams . . . the list goes on and on.

Independence National Historical Park (all ages) 🏛
www.nps.gov/inde.

Forty-five acres in Center City containing more than forty different historic buildings make up Independence National Historical Park. Here you can visit the Liberty Bell Pavilion, Independence Hall, Congress Hall, Old City Hall, Second Bank of the United States, Carpenters' Hall, New Hall Military Museum, Franklin Court, Christ Church, Bishop White House, Todd House, Declaration House, and other sites.

Independence Visitor Center (all ages) 🏛

Sixth and Market Streets; (215) 597–8974 or (800) 537–7676; www.independence visitorcenter.com. Most park buildings are open 8:30 A.M. to 5:00 P.M. daily. These hours are subject to some change, and in summer some buildings are open into the evening. Admission is free.

The brand-new Independence Visitor Center is not just a spectacular new building; it's the perfect introduction to the greater Philadelphia region.

Start by parking your car in the underground Autopark at Independence Mall. Inside the visitor center, make sure you visit its state-of-the-art theater for a brief video that gets you oriented. A second theater shows the excellent film *Independence!* directed by John Huston. Afterward, if you wish to tour Independence Hall, pick up a free dated-and-timed ticket here. You can also make reservations for restaurants in the area here, purchase tickets, or sign up for a Philadelphia heritage tour. You can even print out your own itinerary in visitor computer stations. You can get a snack at the Old Capital Coffee Bar or browse through the gift and book shop. A seventy-two minute AudioWalk tour is available for rent.

Be sure to pick up a copy of the *Historic Philadelphia Gazette,* a free newspaper that lists events, demonstrations, and current hours for many sites in Philadelphia. (At home, check www.HistoricPhiladelphia.org.)

Most buildings within the park are free and open to the public, but a guide is required to tour some, and for others, such as the Todd House and the Bishop White House, tickets are required. There is an admission fee ($) for persons aged sixteen and older to enter the Second Bank of the United States. The urban park rangers of the National Park Service obviously love their jobs, and they'll make history come alive with their stories of colonial Philadelphia.

Also making history come alive are the Town Criers and other actors in period costumes that help transport visitors back in time. A special-events list distributed by the Town Criers gives a schedule of presentations, such as "General Washington's Call to Arms." Families are encouraged not only to watch these events, but also to participate. Most events take place on weekends, with daily performances in summer. For more information call (925) 372–7721 or check the Web site, www.ushistory.org.

Liberty Bell Center (all ages) 🏛

Sixth and Market Streets; (215) 597–8974. The Liberty Bell Pavilion is open from 9:00 A.M. to 5:00 P.M., with extended hours in summer. Admission is free. Wheelchair accessible.

Contrary to popular belief, the Liberty Bell's famous crack was not the result of overzealous ringing on July 4, 1776. In 1846, a thin crack was detected. It was repaired but cracked again when rung on George Washington's birthday. It has not rung since. To read the whole story, check www.ushistory.org/libertybell/. In October

2003 the Liberty Bell moved to a new home. This new center puts the Bell into context with interpretive exhibits that examine the Bell as an international symbol of liberty—both liberties attained and those not yet attained. The Liberty Bell first achieved iconic status during the 1840s, when it was adopted as a symbol of the abolitionist movement. Since then it has come to represent freedom and civil rights for many groups both in the United States and abroad. Viewing these exhibits makes seeing the bell, with Independence Hall in view just across the street, a moving experience.

New Security Procedures at
Independence Square and Liberty Bell

In March 2004, a secure area was created so that visitors will have to be screened only once during their visit to Independence National Historical Park. At the time of this writing, new security procedures were in effect for the Independence National Historical Park area. These are subject to change, so if you have any questions, please contact the Independence National Historical Park or Independence Visitor Center at (800) 537–7676.

First, pick up your free, timed-and-dated tickets to tour Independence Hall at the Independence Visitor Center. There are no restrooms in the secure area, so have the kids go to the bathroom at the visitor center. (The visitor center is outside of the secure area. A port-o-potty has been placed on the northwest corner of Fifth and Chestnut, but this also is outside the screening area.) Since security procedures may take some time, it's a good idea to arrive forty-five minutes to one hour before your scheduled tour. The fewer personal items your bring, the faster you will move through security.

Under new security procedures, visitors enter the screening facility on Market Street between Fifth and Sixth Streets. Here, you are directed through the Liberty Bell Center. After viewing the Liberty Bell, you will cross the street to Independence Square. Once on the square you may visit the buildings there at your own pace, or you may leave the secure area if you choose not to see the other buildings.

You will not be able to return to the Liberty Bell once you cross Chestnut Street. You will be able to tour Independence Hall by timed, dated tickets only.

Amazing
Philadelphia Facts

Philadelphia is the largest city in Pennsylvania, the second largest on the East Coast (New York is first, but you knew that), and the fifth-largest city in the United States.

Congress Hall (ages 8 and up)
Sixth and Chestnut Streets.

If you have some time to spare after viewing the Liberty Bell Center and before your tour of Independence Hall, stop by some of the other interesting sites inside the secured area. Please note that after you have crossed Chestnut Street, you will not be permitted to return to the Liberty Bell Center. You must exit the secured area at a marked exit.

Congress Hall served as the meeting place for both houses of Congress during those early years when Philadelphia was the nation's capital. Well-informed Park Service interpreters are available to answer any questions.

Great Essentials (ages 8 and up)
Chestnut Street, next to Congress Hall.

While waiting for your tour of Independence Hall, take a look at this moving display of historic documents that played pivotal roles in our nation's history. Here you can see surviving copies of the Declaration of Independence, the Articles of Confederation, and the Constitution. If you look closely, you can see handwritten notes in the margins, reminding us of the debates that shaped the final drafts. Here you can also see the Syng inkstand, which was probably used by signers of both the Declaration of Independence and the Constitution.

Old City Hall (ages 10 and up)
Fifth and Chestnut Streets.

Next to Independence Hall is Old City Hall, home of the first U.S. Supreme Court.

Independence Hall (ages 6 and up)
Chestnut Street between Fifth and Sixth Streets; (215) 597–8974. Open by tour only. Admission is free, but between March 1 and December 31, tickets are still required for all persons touring Independence Hall, including infants. The free tickets are timed and dated. You may get "walk-up" tickets at the Independence Visitor Center on the day of your visit. For a service charge of $1.50 per ticket, you may order tickets in advance through Spherix ticket reservation service at (800) 967–2283 or http:// reservations.nps.gov. Each individual may reserve up to six tickets.

It goes without saying that Independence Hall is a must-see for all ages. This building was originally known as the Pennsylvania State House, but in 1824 when General Lafayette returned to Philadelphia, he called it "the hall of independence," and the name stuck. The Declaration of Independence was adopted here, and the U.S. Constitution was written here. The Assembly Room has been restored to look exactly as it did in 1776.

Between 1790 and 1800, when Philadelphia was the capital of the United States, the Congress met in Congress Hall next door. On the other side of Independence Hall is Old City Hall, where the U.S. Supreme Court met from 1791 to 1800. Unlike many historic buildings, Old City Hall is wheelchair accessible.

Second Bank of the United States and Carpenters' Hall
(ages 10 and up) 🏛

Second Bank is located on Chestnut Street between Fourth and Fifth Streets; (215) 597–8974; open daily 9:00 A.M. to 5:00 P.M. Admission $ for 16 and older. Carpenters' Hall is open Tuesday through Sunday 10:00 A.M. to 4:00 P.M.; closed Tuesday in January and February. Admission is free. Carpenters' Hall information, (215) 925–0167.

The Second Bank of the United States and Carpenters' Hall, where the First Continental Congress met in 1774, are worth noting. Perhaps with kids you'd like to see the exterior only. Today Carpenters' Hall displays early carpenter's tools and chairs. The Second Bank houses the park's portrait gallery, featuring portraits of many Revolutionary War heroes. For information call the visitor center at (215) 597–8974.

New Hall Military Museum (ages 6 and up) 🐾

Carpenter's Court between Third and Fourth Streets on the south side of Chestnut Street; call the visitor center (215–597–8974) for information. Open daily 10:00 A.M. to 2:00 P.M., but hours may change seasonally. Admission is free. www.ushistory.org/tour/tour_milit.htm

The New Hall Military Museum offers a treasure trove for military buffs. On display are uniforms, dioramas, weapons, ship models, battle flags, and other memorabilia of the U.S. armed forces, going back to the Revolution. The museum features a gun deck preserved from an eighteenth-century naval ship, as well as interactive displays such as one that allows visitors to control a ship's sails and rudder, and an honor roll of Marines who gave their lives in battle.

Bishop White House and Todd House (ages 8 and up) 🏛

Walnut Street between Third and Fourth Streets; (215) 597–8974. The Todd House and Bishop White House are open daily from 9:00 A.M. to 4:30 P.M. Tickets are $ for adults over 16 and may be purchased at the Independence National Historic Park Visitor Center.

The Bishop White House and Todd House present an interesting opportunity to compare and contrast two different early American lifestyles.

Bishop White was the first Episcopal bishop of Pennsylvania and chaplain of the Continental Congress and of the new U.S. Senate, and this elegant home was built for him and his family in 1786. Children will enjoy the boys' and girls' bedrooms, where initials were carved into the wood more than 200 years ago.

The Todd House, on the other hand, represents a middle-class Quaker home from the same period. Although well-to-do, this family lived more simply. After the death of John Todd, Dolley Todd married James Madison and became one of the most famous U.S. First Ladies.

Historic Reenactments in and around Independence National Historical Park (all ages) 🎵

Schedules are available in the visitor center. Or call (215) 629–5801 or visit the Web site http://historic.philly.com.

Be inducted into the Continental Army. Hear strolling singers perform colonial ditties. The colonial actors from Historic Philadelphia, Inc. bring the past to life at selected sites in the historic district.

National Constitution Center (ages 8 and up) 🧑‍💻

Arch Street, between Fifth and Sixth Streets; www.constitutioncenter.org. Open seven days a week, 9:30 A.M. to 5:00 P.M., Sunday through Friday, and 9:30 A.M. to 6:00 P.M. Saturday. *Freedom Rising*, the theater show that begins the visitor experience, runs every half hour.

The National Constitution Center, opened in 2003, features *Freedom Rising*. This dramatic presentation uses both a live actor and a surround-screen to explore the meaning of the words of the Constitution and how they have been interpreted throughout our history. When you exit the Kimmel Theater, you'll enter the DeVos exhibit hall where you may enjoy interactive exhibits. Your children can enter a voting booth and vote for their all-time favorite president. Here's your chance to take a photo of your child being sworn in as President of the United States. In Signers' Hall, your child can mingle with life-size bronze sculptures of the signers of the Constitution. There's also a brand-new restaurant. This stirring experience will help you "enter as a visitor, leave as a citizen."

Declaration House (Graff House) (ages 8 and up) 🏛️

Seventh and Market Streets; (215) 597–8974. Declaration House is open daily 9:00 A.M. to 1:00 P.M. Hours may change seasonally, so call ahead for information. Admission is free. Wheelchair accessible.

A couple of blocks away from the Liberty Bell is Declaration House (or Graff House), also part of the National Historic Park. In 1776 the Virginia delegate (Thomas Jefferson) to the Second Continental Congress rented rooms in this building, and it was in these rooms that he wrote a little document called the Declaration of Independence. School-age kids will be especially interested to see the exact place where the Declaration of Independence was penned.

City of **Murals**

On the corner of Seventh and Market, across the street from the visitor center, you can see the mural *Tree Walk*. Driving on Interstate 95 you can see the spectacular *Hanging Garden of I–95*. Philadelphia is the proud home of the largest collection of public murals in the country. Over 2,400 indoor and outdoor murals adorn the city, some sporting mosaic, sculptural, or fresco elements, some abstract, and many celebrating heroes both local and universal. This is all due to Philly's exceptional Mural Arts Program, begun in 1984 as the Philadelphia Anti-Graffiti Network.

This city-funded effort has not only brought art to the cityscape, turning graffiti-scarred walls into colorful vistas, but has also been a community-building experience. Each mural has its own story. Local communities get involved from the ground floor, requesting the mural, cleaning the space, choosing the artist and subject matter, often even picking up paintbrushes and getting hands dirty.

As you tour the city on your own, keep your eyes open. There may be a colorful surprise behind the next corner. If you want to see more, the Mural Arts Program offers bus tours every Saturday, April through October, departing from the Independence Visitor Center. Each Saturday of the month, you may tour the murals of a different Philadelphia neighborhood. There are also tours some Wednesdays. Advance reservations are recommended. Call (215) 685–0754 or check out the Web site at www.muralarts.org. On the Web site, you can print out your own self-guided walking or driving-tour routes, which start at the Independence Visitor Center. You can also order books, gifts, and notecards featuring Philadelphia's murals.

Walk down Thirteenth Street from Market to Lombard for a nice concentration of about seven murals, all within easy walking distance of the visitor center.

Atwater Kent Museum (ages 6 and up) 🔖

15 South Seventh Street; (215) 685–4830; www.philadelphiahistory.org. Open daily except Tuesday 10:00 A.M. to 4:00 P.M. Closed on major holidays. Admission is $. Wheelchair accessible. Free admission on Saturday.

On the same block as Declaration House, but not part of the park, is the Atwater Kent Museum, which tells the history of Philadelphia, a city whose story parallels that of our nation as a whole. Children under twelve enjoy the low-tech, hands-on approach. Special family programs include hat making or a visit from the "candy man," as well as exhibitions such as the annual Toys of Holidays Past, Trains and Trolleys, and Children Turning the Centuries.

Lights of Liberty (ages 6 and up) 🏛️ 🎵

Shows depart from PECO Energy Liberty Center, Sixth and Chestnut Streets, and take place throughout Independence National Historic Park. Tuesday through Sunday dusk to 11:15 P.M., up to six shows per hour, May through October. Additional shows may be added during holiday seasons. Purchase tickets ($$$) at the PECO Energy Liberty Center, or reserve in advance by calling (215) LIBERTY or (877) GO–2–1776.

Your family can be a part of the Revolution! Lights of Liberty, the world's first walking sound and light show, uses the latest technology to immerse you in the Revolution as it happened and where it happened. Walking along these historic streets, you'll see five-story projections on historic buildings. Wireless headsets equipped with 3-D sound make you feel as if you're a member of the crowd surrounding Independence Hall as the Declaration is read. Headsets are available in a children's version, as well as several different languages. Since each person gets an individual headset, everyone can choose the version that's most appropriate. This is an excellent introduction to the city's historic district. There is some walking on cobblestone streets, which may be difficult for toddlers and parents using strollers.

U.S. Mint (ages 8 and up) 🏛️

Fifth and Arch Streets; (215) 408–0114; www.usmint.gov, www.phil.frb.org/money_in _motion/index.html. September through May open 9:00 A.M. to 4:30 P.M. Monday through Friday; June through August open Monday through Friday 9:30 A.M. to 4:30 P.M., Saturday and Sunday 10:00 A.M. to 4:00 P.M. Closed major holidays. Admission is free.

The U.S. Mint is the world's largest coinage operation. Visitors can take a forty-five-minute self-guided audiovisual tour and watch money in the making from a glass-enclosed gallery.

African-American Museum in Philadelphia (all ages) 🔖

701 Arch Street; (215) 574–0380; www.aampmuseum.org. Open Tuesday through Saturday 10:00 A.M. to 5:00 P.M. and Sunday noon to 5:00 P.M. Admission is $$ for adults, $ for seniors, students, and the physically challenged.

The African-American Museum houses 500,000 objects, images, and documents, including fine arts, folk art, photography, and more. Call for information about current exhibitions.

Betsy Ross House (ages 6 and up)

239 Arch Street; (215) 686–1252; www.ushistory.org/betsy. Open seven days a week, Memorial Day through Labor Day, 10:00 A.M. to 5:00 P.M. In the off-season, open Tuesday through Sunday 10:00 A.M. to 5:00 P.M. Open on Monday holidays including Martin Luther King Day, Presidents' Day, Columbus Day, and Veterans Day. Closed Thanksgiving, Christmas, and New Year's Day.

Just 2 blocks away from the U.S. Mint, on Arch between Second and Third Streets, is the Betsy Ross House. Yes, Betsy Ross really lived here at 239 Arch Street. And yes, she really did sew flags for the Continental Congress, although nobody is certain how active a role she played in the design of the American flag. Her renovated house is an excellent example of a colonial artisan's home. Greeters are in colonial garb, and tours are self-guided, with kid-friendly signs. The tour itself is brief, but there is continuous family-friendly entertainment on the stage in the courtyard. For example, you might meet Betsy Ross, Ben Franklin, or an eighteenth-century magician.

Elfreth's Alley (all ages)

Between Arch and Race Streets on Second Street in Old City; (215) 574–0560; www .elfrethsalley.org. Mantua Maker's House Museum and Windsor Chairmaker's House are open Tuesday through Saturday 10:00 A.M. to 4:00 P.M. and Sunday noon to 4:00 P.M. Admission is $ for adults and children 5 to 18; kids under 5 are free. Maximum admission per family, $$.

To get an idea of what Philadelphia may have looked like in the 1700s, take a walk down Elfreth's Alley, the oldest residential street in America. Families still inhabit this cobblestone alley tucked between Arch and Race streets on Second Street in Old City. Walking down this charming street, you can imagine what life must have been like when these thirty houses were built between 1728 and 1836, when carpenters and other artisans lived here.

Number 126, the 1762 Mantua Maker's House Museum, and Number 124, the Windsor Chairmaker's House, are open to the public. (A mantua was a type of gown made by the house's first residents, a pair of seamstresses.) A guide will show you around. Other houses are open during special open-house events. On weekends in summer there are demonstrations of traditional crafts, such as basket weaving, broom making, needlework, and candle dipping. In June, the Elfreth's Alley Association hosts Fête Days, when many of the houses and gardens are opened to the public, and colonial crafts are demonstrated. On the second Friday of December, the alley hosts "Deck the Alley," a candlelight open-house tour. The garden and Windsor Chairmaker's House are wheelchair accessible. People still live in these houses, so remind your children to use their manners.

Amazing
Philadelphia Facts

Philadelphia is America's number-one city for African-American tourism.

Mum Puppet Theatre (all ages)

115 Arch Street; (215) 925–8686; e-mail: mum@libertynet.org. Productions run from October through April. Admission varies with productions.

The remarkable Mum Puppet Theatre has built a reputation for fun and innovative puppet performances. Some productions are aimed at younger children; others are more sophisticated. Call ahead for specifics.

Fireman's Hall (all ages)

147 North Second Street; (215) 923–1438. Open Tuesday through Saturday 9:00 A.M. to 5:00 P.M. Admission is free.

Just about every family has somebody who wants to be a firefighter when he or she grows up. Fireman's Hall will fascinate that somebody. Ever since Benjamin Franklin founded the city's first fire department in 1736, Philadelphia has had fire equipment and firefighters. You'll see old-fashioned leather buckets, hand pumpers, three fire wagons that date from 1730, a spider hose reel from 1804, fire helmets from around the world, and a memorial wall for firefighters who died in the line of duty. Aspiring firefighters can try out the re-created living quarters of real firefighters or take the helm of a fireboat. Fireman's Hall is in the historic district, half a block from Elfreth's Alley.

Christ Church (ages 8 and up)

Second Street between Arch and Market Streets; call (215) 922–1695 to check winter hours and for group reservations; www.christchurchphila.org. The church is open to the public from 9:00 A.M. to 5:00 P.M. Monday through Saturday and from 1:00 to 5:00 P.M. on Sunday. In January, the church is closed on Monday and Tuesday.

At Christ Church you can find the pews formerly occupied by George Washington, Benjamin Franklin, Betsy Ross, and other characters out of your history books. Kids will be interested to learn that this is also the birthplace of a character from a children's book: Amos, the mouse who befriended Ben Franklin in the classic *Ben and Me.* "The Nation's Church" is now celebrating 300 years as an active Episcopal parish, with Sunday morning services at 9:00 and 11:00 and communion services on Wednesday at noon. All are welcome to attend.

National Liberty Museum (ages 6 and up) ⊞

321 Chestnut Street; (215) 925–2800; www.libertymuseum.org. Open Tuesday through Saturday 10:00 A.M. to 5:00 P.M. and Sunday 12:00 noon to 4:00 P.M. Closed on Monday in the winter. Admission is $$ for adults and $ for seniors and students.

The National Liberty Museum was created to celebrate our nation's history of freedom and the wonderfully diverse society it has produced. After your family has seen the places where our liberty was born, bring them here to learn what we all must do to preserve our liberty.

Using artwork, dioramas, displays, and hands-on experiences, visitors are encouraged to think about the responsibilities we all share. Visitors can "vote" on real contemporary issues and learn about more than 350 modern-day heroes of all backgrounds. They can see a model of Nelson Mandela's cell or Anne Frank's attic. (For parents of younger children, it is easy to bypass the more disturbing images.) First, view the introductory film, and then go up to the third floor and work your way down. Doing this, you'll end your experience at the shredder machine, where kids are encouraged to write down "mean words" they've heard or used and put them into the shredder, where they are ripped into colorful shards. A walk across the "Bridge of Forgiveness" completes the experience.

Highlighted in the museum are many beautiful glass sculptures. Glass is used as a metaphor for, and illustration of, liberty because once broken, it cannot be put back together the same way. This is an inspiring trip, especially for older children who are beginning to be aware of social issues.

Franklin Court (ages 6 and up) ⊞

Market Street between Third and Fourth Streets; (215) 597–8974. Open Monday through Friday 10:00 A.M. to 4:00 P.M., Saturday and Sunday 10:00 A.M. to 5:00 P.M.

Historians know very little about the appearance of Franklin's house, which once stood on this site. Today an oversized "Ghost Structure," designed by world-famous architect Robert Venturi marks the spot. Here you can also see the Franklin Print Shop, U.S. Postal Service Museum, and the Franklin Museum.

Amazing
Philadelphia Facts

Fairmount Park is the nation's largest landscaped city park.

Seeing Independence National Historic Park **with Limited Time**

If you have only time for a half-day visit, use your time wisely. Don't miss these highlights:

- Independence Visitor Center
- Independence Hall and Congress Hall
- Liberty Bell Pavilion

If you have a little more time, we recommend these sites:

- Declaration House
- Bishop White House
- Todd House

"Ben Franklin" and Franklin's Friends (all ages) 🎵

For details contact "Ben Franklin" at P.O. Box 40178, Philadelphia 19106; call (215) 238–0871, fax (215) 238–9102, or e-mail Ben1776@aol.com. For Franklin's Friends, call (215) 238–0871; www.ben1776.com. Free.

"Ben Franklin" performs at Franklin Court daily, Memorial Day through Labor Day, at 11:00 A.M. His "Friends" perform a program called "Meet America's Founders" from Carpenter's Hall Tuesday through Sunday, Memorial Day through Labor Day, from noon to 2:00 P.M. Another friend demonstrates the music of the glass armonica, which Franklin invented, Tuesday through Sunday, Memorial Day through Labor Day also at Carpenters Hall. For information on the glass armonica musician, visit www.Skyglassmusic.com.

City Tavern (ages 6 and up) 🍴

138 South Second Street; (215) 413–1443. Open Sunday through Thursday 11:30 A.M. to 10:00 P.M., Friday and Saturday 11:30 A.M. to midnight.

Now that you're completely steeped in history, why not eat a historic meal? Don't make the mistake of assuming City Tavern is just a restaurant with a colonial theme. Dining here gives a real feeling of the past. This historic gathering place, now part of the Independence National Historic Park, was opened in 1774. Paul Revere came here in May of that year to announce that the Port of Boston was closed. General Washington set up headquarters here, and Benedict Arnold slept here. John Adams called it "the most genteel tavern in America."

The building was rebuilt in 1975 to look exactly as it did in colonial times. The tavern serves Thomas Jefferson Ale, brewed exclusively by the Dock Street Brewing Company, along with colonial specialties such as turkey-thigh stew and beef and pork pie. More tame entrees are also available, but this is not the place to bring picky eaters.

City Tavern is in the heart of the Historic District, a short walk from Elfreth's Alley.

ALSO IN THE HISTORIC DISTRICT

Other sites within the Historic District include **Congregation Mikveh Israel** and the **National Museum of American Jewish History** at 55 North Fifth Street, which tells the story of the American-Jewish experience. Open daily except Saturday and Jewish holidays. Admission is $. (215) 923–3811 or www.nmajh.org for more information.

The Waterfront/Penn's Landing

New things are happening all over Philadelphia, and the site that once hosted William Penn's arrival in 1682 bustles with activity. A new Hyatt Regency hotel has just opened, as well as a state-of-the-art amphitheater with new festival space encompassing the area from Walnut to Market Streets along Columbus Boulevard.

On the Philadelphia side of the river, you can enjoy RiverRink (in season), the Independence Seaport Museum, Dave & Buster's, and lots of shops. A new Family Entertainment Center is under construction.

April to September, you can take the RiverLink ferry across the river to Camden, New Jersey, to see the Camden Aquarium and Children's Garden or attend a concert at the Tweeter Center. To find out more about these attractions, check the Web site www.pennslandingcorp.com. For information on RiverLink, call (215) 925–LINK or visit http://riverlink.org.

The Spirit of Philadelphia cruises leave from Penn's Landing at Lombard Circle, near the Chart House Restaurant. For information call (866) 211–3808 or check www.spiritcitycruises.com/philly/index.html.

Independence Seaport Museum and Historic Ships (all ages) 🏛️

211 Columbus Boulevard at Walnut Street; (215) 925–5439; http://seaport.philly.com. Open daily 10:00 A.M. to 5:00 P.M. Admission to the Museum and Historic Ship Zone (*Olympia* and *Becuna*) is $$ for adults; $ for children ages 5 to 12. Children under 5 enter free. The museum offers free admission on Sunday mornings from 10:00 A.M. to noon.

Start your visit to Penn's Landing with the Independence Seaport Museum, which uses exciting family-oriented interactive exhibits to tell the story of four centuries of maritime history. The collection of nautical artifacts and ship models that were formerly housed in the old Philadelphia Maritime Museum have been incorporated into a panorama and are enlivened at every turn by audiovisuals and multimedia computers. Kids can try out an immigrant's steerage bunk or a rowing machine, or learn about the history of underwater exploration. This is a great place for any folks with a taste for the nautical.

In exhibits like Home Port Philadelphia, children can chart a course for Penn's Landing and navigate underneath the three-story replica of the Benjamin Franklin Bridge. Protecting the Nation features the bridge of the guided-missile destroyer USS *Lawrence,* most recently used in the Persian Gulf Conflict. Divers of the Deep explores the development of diving technologies such as helmets and scuba gear.

The Independence Seaport Museum also includes Historic Ship Zone, where you can see two real vessels: the *Olympia* and the *Becuna* (319 Delaware Avenue, at Spruce Street; 215–922–1898). Step aboard the *Olympia,* flagship of Admiral Dewey's Asiatic fleet, and see the bronze impressions of the admiral's feet in the exact spot where he stood in 1898 and said, "You may fire when you are ready, Gridley." Then take the kids aboard the *Becuna,* a guppy-class submarine from World War II, where sixty-six men shared the tight living quarters.

If you purchase a RiverPass, it includes round-trip fare on the River Link ferry from Penn's Landing to Camden, New Jersey, plus admission to both the New Jersey State Aquarium (closed until May 2005) and the Independence Seaport Museum. The aquarium is worth a visit, especially if you have school-age kids. They can even pet a shark (a small, harmless one, of course). A Children's Garden is adjacent to the aquarium.

Dave & Buster's (ages 6 and up before 10:00 P.M.)

Pier 19 North, 325 North Columbus Boulevard (formerly Delaware Avenue); (215) 413–1951. Open to children 11:30 A.M. to 10:00 P.M.

Older children or young adults will probably enjoy Dave & Buster's. This unusual attraction bills itself as a family entertainment center with something for everyone. New attractions include Virtual World and Eyework, a turbo-ride theater.

Parents should be aware, however, that not all activities are appropriate for all ages. For example, many of the video games have violent content. There are also bars here. Dave & Buster's has taken over all 70,000 square feet of Pier 19 on the Philadelphia waterfront and filled it with skee-ball, hoop toss, video games, a variety of bars and restaurants for different tastes, music, and virtual-reality games. You can even play golf on a virtual golf course. There are billiards, shuffleboard, and an outdoor deck with a view of the Ben Franklin Bridge.

All games are activated by a "power card." The only additional charges are for food, beverages, billiards, and the turbo-ride. No one under twenty-one is permitted unless accompanied by a parent. Clean and neat clothing required; no tank tops. No more than three children to one guardian over twenty-five years of age.

Parkway Attractions

Philadelphia has a tradition of excellence in museums. On Benjamin Franklin Parkway, sometimes called "Philadelphia's Champs-Elysées," there's something for everyone—from toddlers to teenagers. We've found that for most of the museums on the parkway, it's best to beat the crowd by arriving in the morning right when the museum opens.

Academy of Natural Sciences (all ages)

Nineteenth Street and Ben Franklin Parkway; (215) 299–1000. Open Monday through Friday 10:00 A.M. to 4:30 P.M., weekends and selected holidays 10:00 A.M. to 5:00 P.M. Admission is $$; under 3, free. Wheelchair accessible.

You really should not miss the butterfly exhibit, which can only be described as "magical." On one family visit, our six-year-old insisted on walking through *twice!* On the third floor Outside In is a hands-on exhibit for children twelve and under. Kids can touch mice, snakes, "legless lizards" (skinks), frogs, turtles, and enormous cockroaches from Madagascar. Enthusiastic and well-informed volunteers are available to answer questions. Near Outside In is a robotic dinosaur not to be missed. It roars! (Very little children may be frightened.)

The Academy of Natural Sciences is the oldest continuously operating natural-history institution in the Western Hemisphere, but to our kids, it will always be "the dinosaur museum." Dinosaur Hall features *Tyrannosaurus rex* and *Gigantosaurus,* one of the largest meat-eating dinosaurs ever discovered. In The Dig, visitors can be paleontologists and dig for real fossils with real tools.

Make sure you check the schedule when you arrive at the academy, because there are live animal shows and films at regular intervals. Family memberships are available.

Amazing
Philadelphia Facts

Founded in 1812, Philadelphia's Academy of Natural Sciences is the oldest scientific research institution in the Western Hemisphere.

Franklin Institute (ages 5 and up)

Twentieth Street and Benjamin Franklin Parkway; (215) 448–1200; www.fi.edu. The Science Center is open daily 9:30 A.M. to 5:00 P.M. The Mandell Center is open daily 9:30 A.M. to 5:00 P.M. The Tuttleman IMAX Theater is open museum hours, plus until 9:00 P.M. on Friday and Saturday evenings. Call for prices and Imax and planetarium show times. Admission starts at $$ for children 4 to 11, $$$ for adults.

If you visited the Franklin Institute as a child, as we did in 1969, you'll probably remember walking through the model of the human heart, following the path that the blood vessels take, hearing the sound of the heartbeat. In celebration of its fiftieth anniversary, the model heart has received a complete renovation and upgrade. Now, the heart has more elaborate sounds and special effects. It is also accompanied by exhibits such as video footage of actual heart surgery!

The Franklin Institute was founded in 1824, and exhibits such as the heart pioneered the idea of hands-on museum displays. The museum has continued its tradition of forward-looking exhibits. Several new exhibits were added in 2000 and 2001. The Sports Challenge uses interactive devices and virtual-reality technology to teach kids about the physics, physiology, and material science behind their favorite sports. In Kidscience, children ages five to eight can explore a cave, turn the crank of a water wheel, and have a lot of fun while learning basic science concepts. In The Tram Factory, you can visit the Franklin Institute's beloved Baldwin steam locomotive in its new home, as the centerpiece of a brand-new Railroad Hall.

Be sure to also check out the Science Center, which includes exhibits about flight, optical illusions, and the Fels Planetarium.

The Tuttleman IMAX Theater showcases very special movie experiences on its huge screen, giving a 180-degree field of view. Check to see what movie is currently playing, but the short feature *Philadelphia Symphony,* which usually precedes the main show, presents an excellent introduction to Philly.

The gift shops offer an unusual assortment of educational and scientifically oriented toys, books, posters, and so forth.

Please Touch Museum (ages 2 to 8)

210 North Twenty-first Street. For details call (215) 963–0666; www.pleasetouch museum.org. Hours are 9:00 A.M. to 4:30 P.M. daily, 9:00 A.M. to 5:30 P.M. from July 1 to

Labor Day. Admission is $$ for ages 1 and over; children under 1 are free. In the future, the museum is expected to move to a new location in Memorial Hall in Fairmount Park.

Named one of the best children's museums in the world by the *Observer* of London, and rated one of the "Top 50 Attractions By Child Appeal" by Zagat's *U.S. Family Travel Guide,* the Please Touch Museum is a Philadelphia treasure. Other museums may be for older children but the Please Touch Museum is perfect for kids ages one to seven. Your child can visit again and again, always discovering something new.

There are nine major exhibit areas. *Sendak* presents an ingenious landscape of settings and characters from the beloved books of Maurice Sendak, *Where the Wild Things Are* and *In the Night Kitchen.* Your kids can climb into Max's 10-by-6-foot bed and make their own "wild rumpus" filled with Wild Things.

In *The SuperMarket,* kids push pint-sized shopping carts through a fully-stocked market complete with a cafe, bakery, and cash registers. *Barnyard Babies* features a scarecrow to dress, chickens to feed, and vegetables to pick, all aimed at children under three.

Please Touch offers many annual events. Every February, visitors can enjoy the sounds of Junior Jazz. In mid-August things get sporty with ABC Games. In October, the museum hosts ghosts, wizards, and potions. The day after Thanksgiving, the museum displays scenes from the original Enchanted Colonial Village. Each year ends with a New Year's Countdown Celebration on December 31 at 12:00 noon, instead of 12:00 midnight, for those who can't stay up that late!

Adults must accompany children into the museum and are encouraged to play just as much as their young companions. Wheelchair accessible. Strollers are not permitted on the gallery floor.

A Paulsen **Family Adventure**

It was obvious from the moment we entered the main floor of the Please Touch Museum for the first time, with three-year-old Judah and infant Seth, that this was a pretty stimulating place.

The large open space had been divided into different environments to attract young visitors. There were children building with blocks, playing with puppets, trying on costumes, petting a rabbit, and climbing in and out of the cab of a SEPTA bus. The voices of play surrounded us.

We looked down and Judah was missing. We checked all the exciting places that we thought he'd gravitate toward. No Judah.

We finally found him in the reading corner curled up with a book.

Wachovia Science Park (all ages)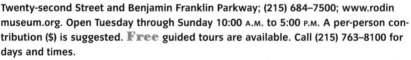

Twenty-first Street, between Winter and Race Streets; (215) 448–1200. Admission through Please Touch Museum or Franklin Institute. Open May through September, seven days a week, 10:00 A.M. to 3:00 P.M., weather permitting.

The Franklin Institute teamed up with the Please Touch Museum to build the Science Park, a family-centered outdoor learning area including more than twenty elements, such as miniature golf, swings, sundials, sand pendulums, hide-and-seek tunnels, and more. Admission is **free** with admission to either museum.

Free Library of Philadelphia (all ages) 🏛

Nineteenth and Vine Streets. Call (215) 686–5322 for hours; www.library.phila.gov. Admission is free.

The Free Library of Philadelphia stands across Logan Square from the Franklin Institute and the Academy of Natural Sciences and down the parkway from the Art Museum and Rodin Museum. It houses more than six million books, magazines, newspapers, and other printed items and frequently hosts special events and exhibits. The library is open daily in winter, closed Sunday in summer. On Sunday there are tours of its remarkable rare books department.

Rodin Museum (ages 6 and up)

Twenty-second Street and Benjamin Franklin Parkway; (215) 684–7500; www.rodin museum.org. Open Tuesday through Sunday 10:00 A.M. to 5:00 P.M. A per-person contribution ($) is suggested. Free guided tours are available. Call (215) 763–8100 for days and times.

Everybody knows Rodin's *Thinker.* You can see this popular sculpture at the Rodin Museum, along with the most complete collection of Auguste Rodin's work outside Paris. This museum is administered by the Philadelphia Museum of Art, down the parkway.

Philadelphia Museum of Art (ages 6 and up)

Located at the end of Benjamin Franklin Parkway at Twenty-sixth Street; (215) 684–7500; www.philamuseum.org. Open Tuesday through Sunday 10:00 A.M.to 5:00 P.M., on Wednesday until 8:45 P.M. Admission is $$ for adults and students age 13 and up; children to age 12, free. Special admission is charged on Sunday, when the rule is "Pay what you wish, all day." Free guided tours are conducted hourly between 11:00 A.M. and 3:00 P.M. Tours are also available in foreign languages (215–684–7923) and sign language (215–684–7601). The Museum Restaurant is open for lunch Tuesday through Sunday 11:30 A.M. to 2:30 P.M. and for dinner Wednesday 5:00 P.M. to 7:30 P.M. Sunday brunch is available from 11:00 A.M. to 3:30 P.M. The cafeteria is open 10:00 A.M. to 4:30 P.M. Wheelchair accessible.

At the far end of the parkway, on the other side of Eakins Oval, are some steps that many people will recognize. Who can forget that memorable scene from *Rocky* when the boxer runs up all these steps? But the collection inside the Philadelphia Museum of Art is even more memorable—with a permanent collection of some 300,000 works, including one of the largest and most important collections of European art in the United States. The art museum takes a somewhat unusual approach, juxtaposing the painting, sculpture, furniture, ceramics, textiles, and architectural elements from the same period to convey a sense of that time. The museum is also known for its outstanding collection of rural Pennsylvania crafts and works by Thomas Eakins. We know a seven-year-old boy who could spend all day in the Arms and Armor collection.

The art museum's neoclassical facade stands at the end of Benjamin Franklin Parkway at Twenty-sixth Street, within walking distance (unless your children's legs are very short) of the Franklin Institute, Free Library of Philadelphia, Please Touch Museum, Logan Circle, and other parkway sites.

"Something every Sunday" is how the museum describes its family activities. Different programs are offered, usually on a walk-in basis, for families with children ages three to thirteen. Most of the programs take place on Sunday at 10:15 A.M. or 1:30 P.M. Programs range from storytelling to hands-on art activities, with titles like Tales and Treasures, Try a Technique, and Gallery Games. Many of these programs are free, and the rest are $. Accompanying adults are free. Children especially like the Japanese teahouse, Chinese palace hall, and the thirteenth-century French cloister. Every day of the week you can pick up a family-oriented, self-guided tour brochure at the West Information Desk. The museum's automated information line is (215) 684–7500. For information about family activities and children's art classes, call (215) 684–7605. Wheelchair accessible, with changing tables in the restrooms.

Fairmount Park Waterworks Interpretive Center

640 Waterworks Drive; (215) 685–0723; www.fairmountwaterworks.org.

If you've ever driven the Schuylkill Expressway in Philly, you may have noticed the striking building below the Art Museum. This is the Waterworks, the nation's first municipal water center. The Waterworks Interpretive Center, brand new in fall 2003, is an exciting combination of environmental education, architectural history, and cultural heritage. Combine a visit here with a walk along Boathouse Row, a stroll through the Azalea Garden, and a tour of the Art Museum.

Eastern State Penitentiary (ages 7 and up)

Fairmount Avenue at Twenty-second Street, 5 blocks from the Philadelphia Museum of Art and the parkway; (215) 236–3300; www.EasternState.org. Open April through November, Wednesday through Sunday, 10:00 A.M. to 5:00 P.M.; closed Monday and Tuesday, and the months of December through March except for private tours. Guided tours are available every hour from 10:00 A.M. to 4:00 P.M. Children under 7 are not admitted. Admission: adults, students, and seniors $$; children ages 7 to 17, $.

When Charles Dickens visited the United States in 1842, there were two sights he didn't want to miss: Niagara Falls and the Eastern State Penitentiary. It has been called the most influential prison in the world, because its design was grounded on the nineteenth century's most modern ideas about civic responsibility and criminal behavior. Instead of using physical punishment, this prison was designed to encourage solitude and penitence.

A nationally broadcast special on the History Channel and a full-page spread in the *New York Times* have focused on the prison, and the number of visitors has tripled in recent years.

Al Capone did time here, as did the "gentleman bandit" Willie Sutton. An operating prison for more than 140 years, until 1971, the building has been reopened as the Eastern State Penitentiary Historic Site Society makes plans for its future. At present there are special art exhibits here, and sometimes dramatic productions.

The building has been made safe for tours but has otherwise been left "as is." Visitors must wear hard hats and stay with tour groups. Most people won't have to be reminded; the decaying plaster, dampness, and remnants of prison life make this a pretty eerie place—great for teenagers! The Halloween Ghost Tours are very popular; call (215) 763–NITE. The gift shop offers T-shirts, posters, and books with a prison theme.

Fairmount Park

At 8,700 acres, Philadelphia's Fairmount Park is one of the world's largest city parks and an amazing source of activities. The park includes: Andorra Natural Area, Bartram's Gardens, Boathouse Row, Japanese House and Garden, Smith Playground and Playhouse, and the Philadelphia Zoo. Of lesser interest to families with children are the following sites: Horticultural Center, Memorial Hall, Ryerss Library and Museum, and the ten colonial mansions of Fairmount Park. Although the Philadelphia Museum of Art and the Fairmount Park Waterworks are technically part of Fairmount Park as well, we have included it in our discussion of "Parkway Attractions."

The Fairmount Park Information Center is located at Memorial Hall, North Concourse Drive near Forty-second Street and Parkside Avenue; (215) 685–0000 (yes, those zeros are correct). You can also check www.phila.gov/fairpark. For a guided tour of the mansions, please contact Mansions of Fairmount Park, Park House Guides Office, Philadelphia Museum of Art, or call (215) 684–7926. There are also trolleys that circulate around the park, stopping at all the historic mansions so that you may tour the houses on your own. For information about these trolleys (and also Philadelphia City Trolley Tours), please call (215) 925–TOUR.

Andorra Natural Area (all ages) 🏕️ 🌿

Between Ridge and Germantown pikes on Northwestern Avenue; (215) 685–9285. The park is open daily dawn to dusk. The visitor center is usually open on weekends noon to 4:00 P.M. Free; some educational programs have fees.

Andorra Natural Area offers many wonderful programs for children including nature trails, exhibits, and special events. Most activities begin at Treehouse Visitor Center, a one hundred-year-old home where you can explore a touch table and other exhibits. Even when the visitor center is closed, there are maps, activity sheets, program calendars, and other information available.

Two annual festivals emphasize hands-on participation. In October you can pick apples and make them into apple butter at the Harvest Festival, and in February you can tap a tree at the Maple Sugar Festival.

Historic Bartram's Garden (gardens: all ages; house: ages 8 and up)
🏕️ 🌿

Fifty-fourth Street and Lindbergh Boulevard; (215) 729–5281; www.bartramsgarden.org. The garden is open daily from dawn to dusk; admission is free. The home is open Tuesday through Sunday noon to 4:00 P.M. There is a charge ($) for the house tour.

The oldest surviving botanical garden in the country includes the pre-Revolutionary home of botanist John Bartram, as well as forty-four acres of gardens.

Boathouse Row (all ages) 🚣

A lovely place for a stroll along the Schuylkill River, Boathouse Row consists of twelve nineteenth-century buildings where Philadelphia's rowing clubs keep their boats. The outline of each boathouse is trimmed with lights to create a luminous view of the boathouses from across the river at night.

Amazing Philadelphia Facts

More Revolutionary War battles were fought within a 50-mile radius of Philadelphia than in all the New England states combined. It was also the capital during the Revolution, except for nine months when it was occupied by the British. It then served as the nation's capital from 1790 to 1800.

Japanese House and Garden (ages 5 and up) 🍁 ❄

Near the Horticultural Center, at Belmont and Montgomery Avenues; (215) 878–5097; www.shofuso.com. Open May 1 through October, Tuesday through Sunday 10:00 A.M. to 4:00 P.M. Admission is $; children under 6 enter free.

Having celebrated its fiftieth anniversary in 2004, the Japanese House and Garden offers many events that your family might enjoy, including a Japanese tea ceremony presented in the Japanese House. At the annual Children's Festival, held in May, kids can learn about origami, kimonos, Japanese crafts, dolls, and armor. They can also see a traditional tea ceremony, hear traditional music and stories, and try Japanese food. This event is modeled after the Japanese celebrations of Boys' Day and Girls' Day. At the Summer Festival in June, kids can participate in the beautiful custom of launching lantern boats.

Smith Memorial Playground and Playhouse (ages 2 to 12) 🍁 🎡

Kelly Drive; (215) 765–4325; www.smithplayhouse.org. Enter the park at the statue of Ulysses S. Grant on Kelly Drive and follow the signs to the playground. The playhouse is open year-round Monday through Saturday 10:00 A.M. to 3:30 P.M. Available on Sunday for birthday parties. The playground is open 9:00 A.M. to 4:45 P.M. daily. It closes one hour earlier in winter. The playhouse is open to children ages 5 and under, and the playground is open to ages 12 and under. Admission is free.

Smith Memorial Playground and Playhouse in Fairmount Park has hosted an average of 1,000 children daily every summer for nearly 105 years! The playground was closed in May 2003 so that Smith could improve and recreate the facilities—no official opening has been announced.

Inside the playhouse there are three floors of activities for preschoolers. The train on the first floor was donated by the group Boyz II Men, whose members played here as children. The foam-block room has been expanded, and a reading room with books, cozy corners, and a puppet stage has been added. In Smithville (on the basement level), little kids climb into the kid-size cars and "drive" on kid-size roads, with delightful details like traffic lights and parking meters.

A Paulsen **Family Adventure**

Typical first-time parents, we doted on everything Judah did. At the Smith Memorial Playground, we coaxed our three-year-old up the ladder to the slide. Every rung was greeted with cheers. We applauded him as he cautiously shuffled across the catwalk and slid down the slide.

We were so busy encouraging Judah we didn't pay any attention to seven-month-old Seth, who crawled up the ladder and across the catwalk and slid down the slide all by himself!

During the summer months, there is an outside carousel for preschoolers, two swimming pools (including a wading pool for little ones), and a concession stand. Adjacent to Smith Memorial, on its property, is the only Frisbee golf course in the city. Free and open to all ages.

Winner of several "Best of Philly" awards for birthday parties and the Giant Slide and dubbed "Best Playground for Children," Smith's is partially wheelchair accessible. There are restrooms in the house, and a concession stand is open seasonally. There is also plenty of free parking.

The Rest of Center City

Former Philadelphia mayor Edward G. Rendell realized the importance of tourism to his city. One of his first actions upon taking office was to start renovating the amazing City Hall (at the intersection of Broad and Market Streets, the dead center of William Penn's original plan for the city) and open it for free tours.

City Hall (observation deck, all ages; tour, ages 8 and up) 🏛

Broad and Market Streets; (215) 686–2840. Tours available daily at 12:30 P.M. Tours are free, but donations are welcome. The observation deck is open daily 9:30 A.M. to 4:15 P.M.

Philadelphia's City Hall celebrated its one hundredth birthday in 2001. See the courtroom where the film *Philadelphia* was made and the 548-foot-tall tower that is topped by a statue of William Penn. The bronze statue was designed by Alexander Milne Calder, grandfather of the twentieth-century mobile creator Alexander Calder. The statue is 37 feet tall. Billy Penn's nose alone is 18 inches long.

A virtual tour is available on the Web site at www.geocities.com/Athens/Delphi/2115. Volunteer guides from the Foundation for Architecture conduct real tours departing from Room 121, the Tour Office, Monday through Friday at 12:30 P.M. There are tours of the tower only Monday through Friday every fifteen minutes from 9:30 A.M. to 4:30 P.M. All tours are free.

The observation deck (at William Penn's feet) affords a spectacular view of the city.

Claes Oldenburg's Clothespin (all ages)
Located in Centre Square Plaza at Fifteenth and Walnut Streets.

Either you love it or you hate it. Either way, Claes Oldenburg's public sculpture of a giant clothespin is one you're not likely to forget.

Robert Indiana's Philadelphia *Love* (all ages)
Located at Kennedy Plaza, Fifteenth Street and JFK.

This public sculpture became famous in the 1960s and 1970s. It has been cleaned and looks better than ever.

Pennsylvania Academy of the Fine Arts (ages 8 and up)

118 North Broad Street at Cherry; (215) 972–7600; www.pafa.org. The museum is open Tuesday through Saturday 10:00 A.M. to 5:00 P.M. and on Sunday 11:00 A.M. to 5:00 P.M.; closed Mondays and New Year's Day, Thanksgiving, and Christmas. Admission is $$ for adults, seniors, and students with ID; $ for children under 5 to 12; and free to members and children under 5.

Walking up Broad Street near Cherry, 1 block from City Hall and the Convention Center, you can't miss the graceful facade of the Pennsylvania Academy of the Fine Arts, home of the nation's first art museum and its first art school, the Academy School. The building, with its Gothic arches and lacy ironwork, is a masterpiece of High Victorian Gothic architecture. Thanks to a grant from the Richard C. von Hess Foundation, the galleries of the historic landmark building are currently under renovation. The museum collection includes works by Benjamin West, Charles Willson Peale (one of the academy's founders), Thomas Eakins (who served as the academy's director during the 1880s), Mary Cassatt, Winslow Homer, Horace Pippin, Andrew Wyeth, Alexander Calder, Louise Nevelson, and many others.

You can make your visit more lively with Family Inform, an audio-guide system. Look around the galleries to find numbers that you key into the audio machine's keypad, and you can hear messages about the works of art.

Academy of Music (ages 10 and up)

Broad and Locust Streets; call (215) 893–1935 for information or to make reservations. Tickets available through www.anytickets.com or www.rpac.org.

That spectacular opera house seen in the movie *The Age of Innocence* is Philadelphia's own Academy of Music. You can see the landmark if you attend a concert by the Philadelphia Orchestra or a performance by the Opera Company of Philadelphia. But by reservation only, you can take a one-hour afternoon tour of this beloved building on Broad and Locust Streets, including a peek backstage and into the artists' dressing rooms.

The Kimmel Center for the Performing Arts (ages 3 and up)

260 South Broad Street on the Avenue of the Arts; (215) 790–5800; www.rpac.org.

The Kimmel Center, opened in December 2001, joins the Academy of Music to become one of the nation's largest performing arts complexes. The Kimmel Center and Academy of Music are home to eight of Philadelphia's premier ensembles: The Philadelphia Orchestra, The Opera Company of Philadelphia, the Pennsylvania Ballet, American Theater Arts for Youth, The Chamber Orchestra of Philadelphia, PHILADANCO, The Philadelphia Chamber Music Society, and Peter Nero and the Philly Pops.

Avenue of **the Arts**

Broad Street south of City Hall has been renamed the Avenue of the Arts. Already home to the Academy of Music, Kimmel Center, the Merriam Theater, and the University of the Arts, several new theaters are planned for the street.

Tickets to any of the theaters in Kimmel Center and Academy of Music are available at the Web site above.

The Philadelphia Orchestra offers outstanding children's concerts at reasonable prices. The Sound All Around series is aimed at three- to five-year-olds, and the Family Concert series is for ages six to twelve.

Reading Terminal Market (all ages)

Twelfth and Arch Streets; (215) 922–2317. Open Monday through Saturday 8:00 A.M. to 6:00 P.M. year-round. The Amish merchants occupy the northwest corner of the market and are open Wednesday 8:00 A.M. to 3:00 P.M. and Thursday through Saturday 8:00 A.M. to 5:00 P.M.

If you're hungry and you don't know what to eat, or if you're planning a picnic, stop by the Reading Terminal Market, where farmers and merchants from around the Philadelphia area (many of them Amish) sell very fresh produce, cheese, fish, meats, baked goods, and much more. There are over forty different restaurants and lunch stands, offering everything from cheesesteaks to sushi.

While you're in the area, head across the street and up the stairs to the old **Reading Terminal,** which has been converted as part of the Pennsylvania Convention Center. This cavernous hall was at one time the main train station in downtown Philadelphia.

Chinatown (all ages) 🍴

Between Arch and Vine Streets, Eleventh to Eighth Streets. For information about Chinatown call (215) 922–2156.

Go 1 block east of the Reading Terminal, and you're in the heart of Philadelphia's Chinatown. Stop here for authentic Chinese cuisine and products.

Amazing
Philadelphia Facts

There are more than one hundred museums in Philadelphia alone.

Edgar Allan Poe National Memorial (ages 10 and up)

532 North Seventh Street; (215) 597–8780; www.nps.gov/edal. Open November through May, Wednesday through Sunday 9:00 A.M. to 5:00 P.M.; June through October, daily 9:00 A.M. to 5:00 P.M. Closed Thanksgiving, Christmas, and New Year's Day. Admission is **free.**

A couple of long blocks north of Chinatown is the house where Edgar Allan Poe lived with his wife and mother-in-law in 1843–44. There is a brief slide presentation about the author's life.

Rosenbach Museum and Library (ages 10 and up)

2010 Delancey Place, on Rittenhouse Square; (215) 732–1600; www.rosenbach.org. Open Tuesday through Sunday 11:00 A.M. to 4:00 P.M. (last tour, 2:45 P.M.). Closed Monday, national holidays, and the period from August 1 to the second Tuesday after Labor Day. Admission is $$; seniors and students (including children) $.

To get a feeling of a traditional, stately Philadelphia neighborhood, stroll around the blocks surrounding Rittenhouse Square. On Rittenhouse Square, the Rosenbach Museum and Library houses an astounding collection of rare books, manuscripts, antique furniture, silver, porcelain, and works of art in the beautiful home of the Rosenbach brothers, who lived here from 1948 until their deaths in 1952 and 1953. This wonderful museum is more suited to older children and literary folks, although occasionally there are special exhibits of illustrated books that may appeal to youngsters.

Among the more than 30,000 rare books and 300,000 manuscripts are letters penned by George Washington, Thomas Jefferson, Benjamin Franklin, and Abraham Lincoln. You may also see Lewis Carroll's own copy of *Alice's Adventures in Wonderland,* the manuscript for James Joyce's *Ulysses,* and the notes for Bram Stoker's *Dracula.* The museum also owns more than 3,000 original drawings by Maurice Sendak, noted author of classic children's books.

For information about wheelchair accessibility, call (215) 732–1600, ext. 25 or e-mail maw-rml@libertynet.org.

Civil War Library and Museum (ages 10 and up)

1805 Pine Street; (215) 735–8196; www.netreach.net/~cwlm/library.html. Open Thursday through Saturday 11:00 A.M. to 4:30 P.M. Admission: $$ for adults, $ for seniors and students with ID.

A couple of blocks away from the Rosenbach Museum, the Civil War Library and Museum houses artifacts from that tumultuous era in our history.

North Philadelphia

Philadelphia is home to a huge number of colleges and universities. Besides adding to the rich cultural diversity of the city, these institutions offer some unusual museums.

Temple University Dental Museum (ages 8 and up)

Broad Street and Allegheny Avenue; (215) 707–2816; www.temple.edu/dentistry/museum.htm. Open by appointment only.

The Victorian dental office, on the third floor of the dental school, is open full time, no appointment necessary. By appointment only, you can also tour an unusual collection of dental memorabilia going back to the 1700s. Its best-known piece is the first dental chair in the United States, dating from the 1790s.

Wagner Free Institute of Science (ages 8 and up)

1700 West Montgomery Avenue; (215) 763–6529; www.wagnerfreeinstitute.org. Open Tuesday through Friday 9:00 A.M. to 4:00 P.M. for self-guided tours. Occasional Saturday openings; call for schedule. Admission is free.

The Wagner Free Institute of Science presents an unusual opportunity to visit a science museum that looks pretty much the way it did in about 1890. This is a great place for amateur naturalists and paleontologists.

Amateur scientist William Wagner founded the institute in 1855 to provide free science education to all, regardless of race, gender, or financial resources. He used his personal collections to illustrate the lectures, and these objects now form the core of the museum's exhibits, which were given their present arrangement after Wagner's death in 1885.

More than 100,000 specimens, including fossils, minerals, shells, mounted animals, skeletons, and insects, are displayed in the Victorian cherrywood cases. (Very young children may have difficulty seeing into some of the cases.) All children under eighteen must be accompanied by an adult. The institute also offers evening and Saturday-morning science classes (off-site) for ages twelve and up.

Shoe Museum (ages 10 and up)

Eighth and Race Streets, at the Temple University School of Podiatric Medicine. Free tours must be arranged in advance by calling (215) 625–5243; podiatry.temple.edu/shoe_museum.

A unique diversion, the Shoe Museum at the Temple University School of Podiatric Medicine displays footwear belonging to celebrities such as Ringo Starr, Julius Erving, Lucille Ball, Mamie Eisenhower, and Ronald and Nancy Reagan. There are also shoes from around the world, tiny Chinese shoes for bound feet, huge shoes for circus giants, tap shoes, ballet slippers, and many more.

Mutter Museum and College Gallery of the College of Physicians of Philadelphia (ages 10 and up)

19 South Twenty-second Street, between Chestnut and Market Streets; (215) 563–3737; www.collphyphil.org. The Mutter Museum and College Gallery are open Monday through Saturday 10:00 A.M. to 4:00 P.M. Admission is $$ for adults, seniors, students, and children 6 to 18; children under 6 enter free.

For years the College of Physicians of Philadelphia (not an educational institution, but the nation's oldest private medical society) has maintained the Mutter Museum of medical anomalies. Begun as a teaching collection for medical students in a time when students had little access to clinical situations, it has become known for its wall of more than one hundred skulls, the tumor removed from President Cleveland's jaw, and the preserved body of an eighteenth-century woman.

The college's exhibits, however, are now moving into the twenty-first century by taking on some of the hottest issues in current medicine. The new College Gallery features temporary exhibits that examine important issues. The C. Everett Koop Community Medical Information Center (CHIC) is a free library on health, with books, CD-ROMs, Internet access, and videos.

West Philadelphia

There is also an abundance of learning opportunities throughout West Philadelphia. The University of Pennsylvania and Drexel University are just two of the must-see sights in the area.

The Philadelphia Zoo (all ages)

3400 West Girard Avenue; (215) 243–1100; www.philadelphiazoo.org. Open daily 9:30 A.M. to 5:00 P.M.; closed major holidays. Admission: adults $$$, seniors and children ages 2 to 11 $$, members and children under 2 free. Additional fee for Zooballoon.

That tethered hot-air balloon you see rising over the Schuylkill Expressway is the Philadelphia Zoo's newest attraction: the Channel 6 Zooballoon. For an additional fee, you can ride up 400 feet above the trees and view the animals from above. Each voyage lasts fifteen minutes.

One annual feature is not to be missed. From April to October, weather permitting, the Birds of Australia exhibit is open. Even bigger kids are wide-eyed with wonder when these colorful birds drink nectar from the children's hands.

The zoo offers a treat for all ages—a chance to meet more than 1,800 animals housed in naturalistic settings, all surrounded by beautiful trees and plantings. Other highlights include the white lions, tigers, elephants, rhinos, bears, and more.

University of Pennsylvania Museum (ages 8 and up) 🐾

Thirty-third and Spruce Streets; (215) 898–4000; www.upenn.edu/museum. Open Tuesday through Saturday 10:00 A.M. to 4:30 P.M. and Sunday 1:00 to 5:00 P.M. Closed Sunday in summer. Admission is a donation of $$ for adults, $ for students and children; children under 6 are free. For information on Family Fun Days, call (215) 898–4890. For children's workshops call (215) 898–4015.

The University of Pennsylvania Museum is a treasure trove for your budding archaeologist or anyone interested in sphinxes, mummies, African sculpture, or ancient Mayan, Greek, or Polynesian culture. The three floors of this museum are loaded with a wealth of artifacts unearthed by the University of Pennsylvania Museum's own world-renowned archaeological and ethnographic expeditions.

Kids will be awe-struck by the genuine Sphinx of Ramesses II, weighing in at twelve tons of solid granite. They will be mystified, and perhaps a little unnerved, by the real mummies. The huge Chinese crystal ball is a favorite with our kids. Other ongoing exhibits include Raven's Journey: World of Alaska's Native People.

The annual Chinese New Year celebration and the Celebration of African Cultures, both popular family events, are held in the winter. Please note that while the large marble halls keep pretty cool, the building is only partially air-conditioned. The Cafe offers a kid-friendly multicultural menu, especially on weekends. The Pyramid Gift Shop has educational and inexpensive items for children. Wheelchair accessible, with diapering facilities in some bathrooms.

ALSO IN THE AREA

Also on the Penn campus, kids might enjoy a look at **College Hall,** one of two Philadelphia structures reputed to be a model for the *Addams Family* house. (Charles Addams went to Penn and was well acquainted with this building. The other candidate is the Ebeneezer Maxwell Mansion in Chestnut Hill.) There are also some interesting sculptures on this campus, such as Claes Oldenburg's oversized button and the statue of Benjamin Franklin.

Philadelphians Get Two
Great New Stadiums

In 2003 and 2004, Philadelphia sports fans celebrated inaugural years for two new stadiums. The Phillies now play in the new Citizens Bank Park, which is fun for families because you can see from nearly any seat. Additional concessions make the experience more accessible to kids. For tickets, call (215) 463–1000 or go to www.phillies.com.

The Eagles' new home is Lincoln Financial Field. For Eagles tickets, please call (215) 463–5500.

South Philadelphia

South Philadelphia is home to many of the city's ethnic neighborhoods, as well as the world's largest outdoor market, the Italian Market.

Italian Market (all ages) 🍴🏠

Ninth Street, between Wharton and Christian Streets; (215) 334–6004 for Italian Market tours. Open Tuesday through Sunday 9:00 A.M. to 4:00 P.M.

The country's largest daily outdoor market, the Italian Market is a great place to find unusual cheeses, fresh fruits and vegetables, homemade pasta, exotic spices, and unusual kitchen wares.

Mummers Museum (ages 8 and up)

1100 South Second Street; (215) 336–3050; www.mummers.com. Open Tuesday through Saturday from 9:30 A.M. to 4:30 P.M., and Sunday from noon to 4:30 P.M. It is closed on Monday, and on Sunday in July and August. Admission is $; guided tours are available by reservation.

No Philadelphian can hear the tune of "Golden Slippers" without picturing the sequined costumes, the feathers, and, of course, the distinctive strut of the mummers. But non-Philadelphians may need a word of explanation.

Philadelphians have created a mummers tradition all their own in the annual Philadelphia New Year's Day Parade, when the string bands, fancy brigades, and clowns strut up Broad Street. The Mummers Museum surrounds you with the spangles, the colors, the history, and the music of the mummers. You can see videos of past parades, learn how the costumes are made, and practice your "Mummers' Strut." In nice weather, the string bands appear for concerts on selected Tuesday evenings at 8:00 P.M.

Fort Mifflin on the Delaware (ages 8 and up) (icon)

Fort Mifflin Road; (215) 492–1881. Open April through November, Wednesday through Sunday 10:00 A.M. to 4:00 P.M. Closed Monday and Tuesday. During the off-season pre-booked tours may be available. Admission is $$ for adults, $ for seniors and children 2 to 12, and free for children under 2.

Fort Mifflin played a strategic role in the Revolutionary War. In 1777, more than 200 British warships sailed up the Delaware River with needed supplies for British troops occupying Philadelphia. For seven weeks the little fort held back the mightiest navy in the world. Although it was almost completely destroyed in the process, Fort Mifflin never surrendered.

On Sunday afternoons, in addition to tours, there are militia-guard drills. A blacksmith also demonstrates how weapons were made in this period.

Manayunk and Chestnut Hill

Although located within Philadelphia's city limits, the Manayunk and Chestnut Hill sections feel more like small towns than urban neighborhoods. Manayunk, one of the country's oldest villages, has a reputation as an artists' community. Main Street in Manayunk is lined with art galleries, boutiques, and unusual shops. Chestnut Hill has a different atmosphere, with its beautiful old homes and elegant shops. Both offer wonderful restaurants (see the Where to Eat section of this chapter).

Ebeneezer Maxwell Mansion (ages 8 and up) (icon)

Greene and Tulpehocken Streets, Chestnut Hill; (215) 438–1861. Open Friday through Sunday 1:00 to 4:00 P.M.

Rumor has it that the Ebeneezer Maxwell Mansion is the model for the *Addams Family* house, as depicted by Philadelphia's own Charles Addams. It is unclear how much the cartoonist Charles Addams was influenced by the Victorian buildings he saw, but it is known that he was familiar with both College Hall (on the Penn campus) and the Ebeneezer Maxwell Mansion, and both may have shaped the architecture of the *Addams Family* house. This eighteen-room Victorian mansion in the Chestnut Hill section was built in 1859. Young children will love the children's bedroom, filled with games and toys of the period. The gadgets are also wonderful, including an apple corer and a sausage stuffer. The gardens include a grape arbor and a small lake. At Christmas there's a Dickensian Christmas celebration and in fall a ghost walk.

Morris Arboretum (all ages) (icon) (icon)

Germantown Pike at 100 Northwestern Avenue, Chestnut Hill; (215) 247– 5777; www.upenn.edu/arboretum. Open Monday through Friday 10:00 A.M. to 4:00 P.M., Saturday and Sunday from November through March 10:00 A.M. to 4:00 P.M., and April through October 10:00 A.M. to 5:00 P.M. During June, July, and August, the Gardens offer extended hours on Thursday evenings until 8:30 P.M. Guided tours are given Saturday and Sunday at 2:00 P.M. Admission: adults $$, students $, and children under 6 free.

The Morris Arboretum, the botanical garden of the University of Pennsylvania, is filled with exotic plants and picturesque vistas. The arboretum fills ninety-two acres in Chestnut Hill, including Japanese gardens, rose gardens, the only Victorian fernery in the United States, and a charming pond complete with swans.

For kids, the real highlight of the Morris Arboretum is definitely the new Garden Railway, open from mid-June until early October. This delightful G-scale model railroad has six trains and three trolley lines, operating on a layout of thirty-four miniature buildings including Independence Hall, Betsy Ross House, and many more. The buildings are replicated to scale and constructed out of acorns, moss, bark, twigs, leaves, seeds, and honeysuckle. The ten bridges and trestles are made of logs and railroad ties. There's even a waterfall.

In season, the Garden Railway display is open daily 10:00 A.M. to 4:00 P.M. and until 8:00 P.M. on Thursday. It is wheelchair accessible. Nearby, the Cafe by Bruno's is open daily 11:00 A.M. to 2:30 P.M., from April 30 through October 31.

Northeast Philadelphia

Insectarium (all ages) 🐞

8046 Frankford Avenue in Northeast Philadelphia; (215) 335–9500 or (215) 338–3000 (to inquire about educator availability); www.insectarium.com. Open 10:00 A.M. to 4:00 P.M. Monday through Saturday. Admission is $$ per person. It is free for anyone younger than 2 with a paying adult.

Named "Philly's Best Kid's Attraction, Repulsive" in 2001, the Insectarium has been featured in *Life* magazine. Steve's Bug-Off Exterminating Co. has assembled the Insectarium, a collection of live insects in naturalized settings, mounted specimens, and interactive displays. This one-of-a-kind museum is designed to teach the importance of insects as part of the diversity of nature—but mostly it's a lot of fun. You won't be able to forget the "cockroach kitchen," the "glow-in-the-dark" scorpion, the live termite tunnel, or the tarantulas (no matter how hard you try). A new outdoor Learning Garden includes a butterfly tent.

Amazing Philadelphia Facts

The Benjamin Franklin Parkway has been called "Philadelphia's Champs-Elysées."

John Heinz National Wildlife Refuge (all ages) 🏕️ 🧺

8601 Lindbergh Boulevard, in the Tinicum section; call (215) 365–3118 for information; http://heinz.fws.gov. The Cusano Environmental Education Center (CEEC) is open 8:30 A.M. to 4:00 P.M. daily. The trails are open 8:00 A.M. to sundown daily. The programs, facility, and grounds are free.

The 1,200-acre John Heinz National Wildlife Refuge is managed by the U.S. Fish and Wildlife Service for conservation of habitat and promotion of environmental education. The refuge is alive with 281 species of birds and healthy populations of mammals, reptiles, and amphibians. Ten miles of hiking and biking trails meander along the Tinicum Marsh and Darby Creek. Don't forget your binoculars to enhance the view from the Observation Tower.

The Cusano Environmental Education Center (CEEC) was built using sustainable design techniques. The building includes a resource center, classrooms, Tinicum Treasures Bookstore, and a "living marsh machine." The center houses many interactive exhibits and displays highlighting wetlands and wildlife.

Where to Eat

IN PHILADELPHIA

City Tavern, 138 South Second Street; (215) 413–1443; www.citytavern.com. Award-winning children's menu, booster seats. In the heart of the Historic District.

Italian Market, Ninth Street between Christian and Dickinson; (215) 922–5557.

KatManDu, 417 North Columbus Boulevard; (215) 629–7400. High chairs, booster seats, children's menu. Great view of the Ben Franklin Bridge. Voted best restaurant in Philadelphia by the *City Paper.*

Magnolia Cafe, 1602 Locust Street; (215) 546–4180. Cajun/Creole food. Booster seats, children's menu.

Mulberry Market, 236 Arch Street; (215) 928–9064. Deli-style food, sandwiches, hoagies. Across the street from the Betsy Ross House.

Pizzeria Uno, 509–511 South Second Street; (215) 592–0400. Located in South Street area. High chairs, booster seats, children's coloring menu with crayons.

Reading Terminal Market, Twelfth and Arch Streets; (215) 922–2317.

IN MANAYUNK

Le Bus, 4266 Main Street; (215) 487–2663. Children's menu, high chairs, casual atmosphere.

Sonoma, 4411 Main Street; (215) 483–9400. "Italifornia" food. High chairs, booster seats; babies and toddlers welcome.

Where to Stay

IN PHILADELPHIA

Best Western Center City Hotel, 501 North Twenty-second Street; (215) 568–8300 or (800) 528–1234. Convenient to major museums and other attractions. Restaurant, outdoor pool.

Crown Plaza—Center City, 1800 Market Street; (215) 561–7500; www.crownplaza .com/philadelphia-centercity.

Holiday Inn—Express Midtown, Thirteenth and Walnut; (215) 735–9300.

Holiday Inn—Independence Mall, (Historic Area), 400 Arch Street; (215) 923–8660 or (800) HOLIDAY. Seasonal outdoor rooftop pool.

Sheraton Society Hill, 1 Dock Street; (215) 238–6000.

For More Information

Greater Philadelphia Tourism Marketing Corp., (888) 999–3790; www .gophila.com.

Philadelphia Convention and Visitors Bureau, (800) 537–7676 or (215) 636–1666; www.pcvb.org.

Amazing
Philadelphia Facts

Philadelphia is known for its distinctive foods, including cheese steaks, scrapple, snapper soup, and soft pretzels with mustard.

Philadelphia
Countryside

The countryside surrounding Philadelphia offers many opportunities for family fun and learning. For sheer fun with little or no hidden educational agenda, our picks are Sesame Place, the Crayola Factory, Giggleberry Fair, and Dorney Park. In 2005, Dorney Park introduces its $13 million-floorless roller coaster, Hydra The Revenge. Sesame Place, an amusement park based on the beloved PBS TV show, offers rides and activities designed for the whole family, and waterslides that even older children will enjoy along with their younger brothers and sisters. The Crayola Factory gives young imaginations a place to run wild. And Giggleberry Fair offers a

Faith & Emily's
FavoriteAttractions
in the Philadelphia Countryside

1. Sesame Place, Langhorne

2. Crayola Factory, Easton

3. Giggleberry Fair, Lahaska

4. Valley Forge National Historical Park, Valley Forge

5. Dorney Park and Wildwater Kingdom, Allentown

6. Mercer Museum, Doylestown

7. Tubing at Point Pleasant (Bucks County River Country)

8. Elmwood Park Zoo, Norristown

9. Colonial Pennsylvania Plantation, Media

10. Discovery Center of Science and Technology, Bethlehem

PHILADELPHIA COUNTRYSIDE

colorful, six-level climbing structure and thousands of soft foam "berries." If you prefer nature's roller coasters, try tubing at Point Pleasant with Bucks County River Country outfitters.

There are plenty of opportunities for more serious fun as well. Younger children especially love the friendly Elmwood Park Zoo, with its playful otters and prairie dogs. School-age children on up will appreciate the quirky Mercer Museum and the exciting Discovery Center of Science and Technology.

Other opportunities for family adventure beckon at living-history sites such as Hopewell Furnace, Colonial Pennsylvania Plantation, and Peter Wentz Farmstead. Historic parks such as the Brandywine Battlefield, Washington Crossing, and Valley Forge offer a great combination of history and outdoor fun, all in the beautiful Pennsylvania countryside.

Faith & Emily's
FavoriteEvents
in the Philadelphia Countryside

- **Mercer Museum Folkfest** (May); (215) 345–0210; www.mercermuseum.org/folkfest.

- **Pennsylvania Fair,** Bensalem (May); (215) 633–0404 or (215) 639–9000; www.pennsylvaniafair.com.

- **Devon Horse Show** (ten days surrounding Memorial Day weekend); (610) 964–0550; www.thedevonhorseshow.org.

- **Musikfest,** Bethlehem (August); (610) 861–0678; www.musikfest.org.

- **Great Allentown Fair** (starts on the Tuesday before Labor Day); (610) 433–7541; www.allentownfairpa.org.

- **Philadelphia Folk Festival** (weekend before Labor Day); (215) 242–0150, (215) 247–1300, or (800) 556–FOLK; www.folkfest.org.

- **Scarecrow Competition and Display** at Peddler's Village (September); (215) 794–4000; www.peddlersvilage.com.

- **Great Pumpkin Carve** in Chadds Ford (October); (610) 338–7376; www.chaddsfordhistory.org.

- **Longwood Gardens Christmas Display** (November to January 1); (610) 388–6741; www.longwoodgardens.org. Considered the "best Christmas display in the world" by London's *Financial Times*.

Art can be fun too, and the Barnes Foundation's collection of Impressionist art is dazzling, and its building has been recently restored. The streets of New Hope teem with art—in galleries, craft shops, and the new second location for the James A. Michener museum.

The following Web sites introduce you to this area:

- Bucks County Conference and Visitors Bureau, Inc.: www.buckscountycvb.org

- Valley Forge: www.valleyforge.org

- Lehigh Valley Convention and Visitors Bureau: www.lehighvalleypa.org

- Chester County Conference and Visitors Bureau: www.brandywinevalley.com

- Brandywine Valley Guide: www.thebrandywine.com

Brandywine Valley

For a trip that includes historic homes and battlefields, art, and gardens, all within easy distance of one another, contact the Chester County Tourist Bureau (800–228–9933). You may wish to make a weekend visit to the towns of Kennett Square and Chadds Ford. The Web site for the Chadds Ford Historical Society is www.chaddsford history.org.

The fields, mills, and farms of rural Pennsylvania have found their way into the art of Chadds Ford's most famous artist, Andrew Wyeth. Here you're surrounded by Wyeth's landscapes and his art. You can visit the historic Brandywine Battlefield, eat lunch in a historic inn, shop, and take a walk along the Brandywine River.

Longwood Gardens (all ages) 🏛️ 🌺

Route 1 in Kennett Square; (610) 388–1000; www.longwoodgardens.org. The outdoor gardens and conservatory open at 9:00 and 10:00 A.M., respectively, every day of the year. Both close at 5:00 P.M. from November through March and at 6:00 P.M. from April through October, although both are frequently open later for special events and holiday displays. Call ahead for a complete schedule. Admission is $$$ for adults ($$ on Tuesday), $$ for youths ages 16 to 20, $ for children 6 to 15, and free under age 6. Prices subject to change.

Longwood Gardens is a place to enjoy the variety of nature, both indoors and out. In a four-acre conservatory, Longwood's visitors can see orchids, roses, bonsai, exotic jungle plants, and waterfalls, even on the coldest winter days. And on warmer days, you can tour the outside gardens and the fountains. No matter what the weather, don't miss the annual holiday display.

Longwood's completely redesigned and expanded Children's Garden is due to open in late 2006. In the meantime, children can enjoy the Bee-Amazed Children's Garden, which features: the Honeycomb Maze, Flower Fountain, and Buzz Trail. The garden focuses on the busy honeybees and their important role in pollination. The Honeycomb Maze is full of surprises: tunnels, a beehive arbor, and the Queen Bee's Throne.

The Garden Railway, open seasonally, depicts the Brandywine Valley, including the duPont farm that became Longwood Gardens. Look closely and you'll see that architectural details are made of cinnamon sticks, beech seedpods, and other garden findings.

Longwood's admission rate structure varies fees seasonally. All admission fees are discounted on Tuesday. The Terrace Restaurant includes both a cafeteria and a sit-down dining room. Reservations are recommended for the dining room.

Brandywine River Museum (ages 6 and up)

U.S. Route 1; (610) 388–2700; www.brandywinemuseum.org. Open daily 9:30 A.M. to 4:30 P.M. Admission is \$\$ for adults; \$ for senior citizens, students with ID, and children 6 to 12; free for children under 6. N. C. Wyeth House and Studio open April through November; \$ additional admission.

Andrew Wyeth came from a family of distinguished artists. The Brandywine River Museum, in a converted gristmill on Route 1 in Chadds Ford, has the world's largest collection of Andrew Wyeth's work, as well as that of his father, N. C. Wyeth; his son, Jamie Wyeth; and other family members.

Children especially go for Jamie Wyeth's painting *Portrait of Pig* and the life-size animal sculptures along the riverbank. Many visitors will recognize the illustrations of N. C. Wyeth for such swashbuckling classics as *Treasure Island* and *Kidnapped.* The Brandywine River Museum has a children's audio tour of its permanent collection as well as selected exhibitions. This lively tour answers questions such as, "How did Jamie Wyeth convince a pig to pose for a painting?" Works by other artists from the Brandywine region hang near still-life paintings, landscapes, and an unparalleled collection of American illustration.

Surrounding the museum are stands of wildflowers, trees, and shrubs indigenous to the Greater Brandywine Valley. For an additional fee, visitors may tour the N. C. Wyeth House and Studio. In 2004, the Brandywine Museum introduced tours of the Kuerner Farm, inspiration for over 1,000 of Andrew Wyeth's paintings.

John Chads House (ages 8 and up)

Route 100; (610) 388–7376; www.chaddsfordhistory.org. Open May through September, Saturday and Sunday from noon to 5:00 P.M. Admission is \$\$ for adults, \$ for children. Combination ticket to both John Chads House and Barns–Brinton House is \$\$ for adults and \$ for children.

Often you can watch bread being baked in the beehive oven. On the weekend after Labor Day, the Chadds Ford Historical Society, which administers both John Chads House and Barns–Brinton House, hosts the annual Chadds Ford Days. The event features pony rides, music, Brandywine Valley art, games, and crafts. People often come for the sausage sandwich.

Chadds Ford Village (ages 6 and up)

US 1; (610) 388–7361. **Free.**

Chadds Ford Village is a charming place to browse in craft shops or to enjoy a meal at the Chadds Ford Inn, which has been serving travelers since 1736.

Barns–Brinton House (ages 8 and up)

US 1; (610) 388–7376; www.chaddsfordhistory.org. **Same hours and admission fees as the John Chads House.**

At the Barns–Brinton House, guides in period costume demonstrate colonial crafts and give tours of this early eighteenth-century home and tavern. Just past the herb garden, you'll find the Chaddsford Winery.

Brandywine Battlefield Park (ages 8 and up)

US 1; (610) 459–3342. **The battlefield park grounds are open, free, year-round Tuesday through Saturday 9:00 A.M. to 5:00 P.M. and Sunday noon to 5:00 P.M. The visitor center is open Tuesday through Saturday 9:00 A.M. to 5:00 P.M. and Sunday noon to 5:00 P.M. Closed Monday. Admission for house tour only: $. A family rate ($$) is available.**

After retreating at the Battle of Brandywine, George Washington's troops moved on to camp at Valley Forge. At Brandywine Battlefield Park you can tour the house where Washington and Lafayette set up their headquarters. The visitor center offers an audiovisual introduction to the park, along with maps for a self-guided driving tour that includes twenty-eight historic points of interest. A reenactment of the battle is held every September. There is a museum shop, and picnic areas are available.

Elverson

Hopewell Furnace (ages 8 and up)

2 Mark Bird Lane; (610) 582–8773, TDD 582–2093; www.nps.gov/hofu/. **Open daily 9:00 A.M. to 5:00 P.M., except New Year's Day, Martin Luther King Jr. Day, Presidents' Day, Veterans Day, Thanksgiving, and Christmas. Entrance fee is $ per person. For living-history events an additional fee ($) per person is charged. Annual passes, family passes, and senior passes are available.**

Watch a real blacksmith hammer a shape from white-hot iron. Visit a cast house where iron weapons were made for the Continental Army. Learn how colonists prepared food and clothing. Hopewell Furnace National Historic Site gives you a chance to see what life was like in a colonial iron-making town. As you take your self-guided walking tour, taped messages give you a first-hand feeling for the experiences of the people who lived and worked here. Although open year-round, the site is most active in summer, when authentically costumed artisans demonstrate their crafts. Mother's Day is sheep-shearing day. The visitors center and restrooms are wheelchair accessible. Some of the historic structures are accessible. Call for more details about wheel-chair accessibility. A Junior Ranger program is available.

ALSO IN THE AREA
Nearby, **French Creek State Park** offers outdoor family adventures such as hiking, fishing, swimming, and camping, as well as winter sports. You may wish to have lunch or do some shopping in **Victorian St. Peter's Village.**

Chester Springs

Where nature brought forth yellow water with medicinal properties, man has brought forth *The Blob*. Some would say Chester Springs's attractions have run "from the sub-lime to the ridiculous."

Historic Yellow Springs (ages 8 and up) 🏛
Art School Road; (610) 827–7414. Open for self-guided tours Monday through Friday 9:00 A.M. to 4:00 P.M., weekends by reservation. Closed major holidays. A donation is suggested.

For centuries, starting with indigenous peoples and, later, colonial settlers, presi-dents, and entertainers, people have come to Yellow Springs in hopes of finding a cure for their illnesses. In 1722 there was a health spa here. From 1916 to 1952 the Pennsylvania Academy of Fine Arts ran a landscape school on these beautiful grounds. And later still, Valley Forge Films made movies here, including the 1958 Steve McQueen classic *The Blob* and *4-D Man*.

At present this site is operated as Historic Yellow Springs, Inc. Visitors may take a self-guided tour of the grounds and eighteenth- and nineteenth-century buildings, but it's most fun to come during special events such as art shows, classes, and work-shops or to attend annual events such as the Frolicks.

West Chester

QVC Studio Tours (ages 6 and up)
1200 Wilson Drive; (800) 600–9900; www.qvctours.com. Tours are conducted daily, every hour on the hour, 10:00 A.M. to 4:00 P.M. Reservations are not required. Not rec-ommended for children under 6.

The QVC cable home-shopping channel conducts a tour of its large studio complex. If you're a fan of QVC, this tour is a must. If you're not a QVC shopper, the tour offers an interesting look behind the scenes of TV production. The guided tour follows the path of a QVC product from sourcing, testing, and TV presentation to home delivery. Overnight event packages available.

Amazing
Pennsylvania Facts

> Battered by defeats throughout the fall of 1777, Gen. George Washington and his troops retreated to Valley Forge for the winter. By February 1778 he had lost nearly half his men to death, disease, and desertion.

Valley Forge

Valley Forge National Historical Park (all ages) 🏛️ 🏕️

Visitor center at Route 23 and North Gulph Road; (610) 783–1077; www.nps.gov/vafo. Park buildings are open daily except Christmas from 9:00 A.M. until 5:00 P.M. Admission is $ for Washington's Headquarters. Children 16 and under are free. Park grounds are open to the public free.

After viewing the eighteen-minute introductory film and exhibits at the visitor center, you can get information about touring the park. The visitor center also displays various exhibits and artifacts that help you get more out of your visit.

In the summer of 2004, Valley Forge National Historical Park introduced bus tours three times per day, from Memorial Day through Labor Day. To reserve a seat, call (610) 783–7503.

From June to October tour buses take a regular route, allowing visitors to get off when a particular site sparks their interest and then catch the next bus. A map allows families to take a self-guided driving tour accompanied by a narrated audiotape, if desired.

Trails are available for visitors who prefer to see the park by bike, on foot, or on horseback. Pick up a brochure at the visitor center for more information about the trails. There are fields perfect for kite flying and three different picnic areas.

Your kids will not want to miss the re-created encampment where Washington's troops spent the winter of 1777–78. Boys are especially interested in the Artillery Park, reconstructed fortifications, and the Grand Parade Grounds, where the troops trained for battle. General Washington set up his temporary headquarters in Isaac Potts's House (also known as Washington's Headquarters), now restored to look as it did during that famous winter. Costumed interpreters appear at the Muhlenberg Brigade daily from June through August, 10:00 A.M. to 4:00 P.M., weekends year-round in good weather.

The American Revolution Center at Valley Forge, expected to open in 2007, will be a joint venture between the National Park Service and its private partner, the American Revolution Center. This partnership has already produced the new Encampment Gift Shop in the visitor center. The new center will be the first and only museum devoted to educating and inspiring people about the period of the American Revolution. It will be built into the quarry bluff at the far end of the main visitor parking lot adjacent to the current visitor center.

ALSO IN THE AREA

For another kind of family adventure in the Valley Forge area, contact **United States Hot Air Balloon Team,** P.O. Box 490, Hopewell Road, St. Peters 10470; (610) 469–0782 or (800) 763–5987; www.ushotairballoon.com.

The nation's second largest shopping mall, the **Plaza and Court of King of Prussia,** is only minutes from Valley Forge Park, on Route 202.

Audubon

Although John James Audubon lived at Mill Grove for only three years, it was his first home in America (he arrived here in 1803), and the perfect place to inspire his career as a painter of birds.

Mill Grove (house, ages 6 and up; grounds, all ages) 🚗 🏛 🚶
**Audubon and Pawlings Roads; (610) 666–5593; www.montcopa.org/historicsites.
House open Tuesday through Saturday 10:00 A.M. to 4:00 P.M.; Sunday 1:00 to 4:00 P.M.;
Grounds open Tuesday through Sunday 7:00 A.M. to dusk. Free.**

One hundred and seventy-five acres of greenery, 175 species of birds, and 400 species of flowering plants surround the house, built in 1762. This is a lovely spot to stroll in the woods or enjoy a peaceful view of Perkiomen Creek. Inside the home you may tour eleven rooms filled with Audubon's collection of paintings, stuffed birds, and birds' eggs. The museum also owns a complete set of Audubon's greatest work, *The Birds of America,* with each bird painted in actual size. Call for a calendar of events and programs.

Amazing
Pennsylvania Facts

Although he founded Pennsylvania, William Penn lived here for only a total of four years.

Paoli

What is it about the Philadelphia area that seems to breed unforgettable characters? Doylestown has Henry Mercer, Merion has Albert Barnes, and Paoli has Wharton Esherick.

Wharton Esherick Studio (ages 8 and up)

Horseshoe Trail Road. For directions and reservations call (610) 644–5822 or log onto www.levins.com/esherick.html. Reservations are required for one-hour tours of Esherick's home and studio. Tours are available March through December, Saturday 10:00 A.M. to 5:00 P.M. and Sunday 1:00 to 5:00 P.M. Admission is $$ for adults, $ for children under 12.

Wharton Esherick started out as a painter, but after moving in 1913 to a stone farmhouse near Paoli, he became fascinated with wood. The Wharton Esherick Studio reflects this fascination. Everywhere you look, you discover some whimsical wooden object: wooden sculptures, wooden picture frames, wooden furniture.

Esherick was also entranced by what is now called "found objects." The handrail of his astounding double-spiral staircase is a real mastodon tusk! The artist created chairs out of hammer handles or wagon wheels.

Phoenixville

Water World (all ages)

On Route 724; (610) 935–1290; www.waterworldrec.com. Open daily May through September noon to 9:00 P.M. Admission is $$ per person. Access to waterslides is $$.

Water World is a relaxing place to cool off on a sticky summer day, with two waterslides, a rope swing, a large pool, and a wading pool for the little ones. There is a small snack bar and picnicking facilities.

Norristown

Elmwood Park Zoo (all ages) 🐘🍴

1661 Harding Boulevard; (610) 277–DUCK; www.elmwoodparkzoo.org. Open daily 10:00 A.M. to 5:00 P.M. (gates close at 4:00 P.M.). Call for current admission rates.

Enter the aviary, and you are surrounded by a naturalistic wetland environment filled with waterfowl, beaver, and two fun-loving river otters. The murky Bayou Building houses alligators, snakes, and armadillos. The Tom Kimmel Conservation Kingdom is an imaginative playground that teaches kids about conservation while they have fun. They can even crawl through a giant prairie dog tunnel at William's Prairie Dog Town. In all there are more than 200 animals representing forty species, including jaguars, cougars, timber wolves, and a peregrine falcon.

The youngest children still love feeding the ducks in the duck pond and petting the sheep and goats in the Petting Barn (open seasonally). There is also a snack shop, a gift shop, and pony rides. Wheelchair accessible, with diapering facilities in the restrooms.

Media

Media is the home of Ridley Creek State Park, where you can see the Colonial Pennsylvania Plantation.

Colonial Pennsylvania Plantation (ages 6 and up) 🏛

Located in Ridley Creek State Park; (610) 566–1725; www.colonialplantation.org. Open weekends, April to November, 10:00 A.M. to 4:00 P.M. Usually closed for rain.

On an eighteenth-century farm, animals were left to graze freely, not penned up as they are today. In the root cellar the farmer's family stored carrots, onions, and potatoes; in the springhouse, flowing water cooled milk and eggs. The clothing was made by hand, spun of natural fibers. All these details are meticulously re-created at Colonial Pennsylvania Plantation.

This is actually a working farm where 120 acres of crops are grown, using methods that date back more than 200 years. Here you can observe the staff demonstrating cooking, spinning, weaving, sheep shearing, planting, and harvesting. Even the clothing worn by interpreters is authentic—right down to the fibers. School groups get a chance to dip candles or cut firewood in the authentic manner.

Also in the park, the adjacent Tyler Arboretum has an extensive collection of native and nonnative plants. Highlights include a giant sequoia with a circumference of 9 feet and a unique fragrant garden designed specifically for the visually impaired. The arboretum is open daily and admission is **free,** 8:00 A.M. until dusk. Call (610) 566–5431.

Swarthmore

Scott Arboretum (all ages) 🏛️ 🌿

Swarthmore College campus; (610) 328–8025; www.scottarboretum.org. Open daily from dawn to dusk; free.

One hundred and ten acres surrounding Swarthmore College constitute the college's Scott Arboretum. Come here for a quiet stroll through collections of flowering cherries, roses, conifers, daffodils, dogwoods, lilacs, hollies, rhododendrons, and more. Specialty gardens include the Theresa Long Garden of Fragrance, the Dean Bond Rose Garden, and the Winter Garden, which provides longed-for colors in the gray of winter.

Merion

The Barnes Foundation (ages 8 and up) 🎨

300 North Latches Lane; (610) 667–0290; www.barnesfoundation.org. Open Friday, Saturday, and Sunday 9:30 A.M. to 5:00 P.M., September through June, by advance reservation only. During the months of July and August, the galleries are open Wednesday through Sunday 9:30 A.M. to 5:00 P.M. Admission: $$ per person. Audio tour: $$ per person.

The art lovers in our family have always been awestruck by the paintings at The Barnes Foundation, one of the nation's most amazing private collections of Impressionist and post-Impressionist art. This collection remained one of the art world's best-kept secrets until a national tour took many of its masterpieces to several major museums.

Dr. Albert C. Barnes was a physician and businessman by vocation, but art and education were his great loves, and he held very definite opinions about them. He collected more than 180 Renoirs, seventy Cézannes, and many Matisses, including a mural specifically commissioned for the gallery. The wall ensembles explore light, line, color, and space in an amazing multicultural array that includes works by van Gogh, Picasso, El Greco, Soutine, and Glackens, as well as Greek, Roman, Egyptian, and Native American artists.

Audio tour and gift shop available. Wheelchair accessible, with diapering facilities in the ladies' bathroom. The Barnes is within fifteen minutes of Suburban Square, Ardmore, for shopping or a bite to eat at Ruby's Diner.

Amazing
Pennsylvania Facts

In 1930 Dr. Albert Barnes commissioned the artist Henri Matisse to paint a mural for The Barnes Foundation in Merion. However, the measurements for the wall space were incorrectly translated from inches to centimeters, so when the mural arrived from France, it was 5 feet too short! Although he had spent more than a year on the first version, Matisse started all over again. The second version now decorates three arches above the main gallery in The Barnes Foundation.

Glenside

Keswick Theater (ages 6 and up) 🎵
Easton Road and Keswick Avenue; (215) 572–7650; www.keswicktheater.com.

The Keswick Theater offers concerts, plays, and other productions year-round. Ticket prices vary.

Churchville

Churchville Nature Center (ages 6 and up) 🏕🍁
501 Churchville Lane; (215) 357–4005; www.churchvillenaturecenter.org. The nature center is open Tuesday through Sunday 9:00 A.M. to 5:00 P.M. The grounds are open dawn to dusk. Admission is free.

Trails at the Churchville Nature Center are open from sunup to sundown daily. Inside the nature center you can view dioramas depicting local wildlife. There are also children's programs, such as nature crafts, junior naturalist hikes, and activities centered on the Lenape Native Americans. The paths are wheelchair accessible and wheelchairs are available.

Langhorne

Sesame Place (all ages) 🎡
100 Sesame Road, US 1 to Oxford Valley exit; (215) 752–7070; www.sesameplace.com. Operating days and hours vary, with the park opening in May for weekends only; starting in mid-May daily 10:00 A.M. to 5:00 P.M.; staying open later after Memorial Day

and returning to weekend-only hours after Labor Day until mid-October, when it closes for the season. Single-day admission (ages 3 to 54) costs $$$$. Discounts are available for families of four or more or during late-afternoon hours. Holders of Passport tickets receive unlimited admission for the season, plus special benefits.

Just about any kid will have fun at Sesame Place. We've found that even kids too grown up for Cookie Monster can't help but enjoy many of the water rides and physical play environments.

You can walk down Sesame Street, a full-size replica of the thoroughfare seen on the popular TV show, and take pictures of your kids in front of Bert and Ernie's house. You'll love the Rock Around the Block parade and shows such as "Big Bird's Beach Party" starring *Sesame Street* characters. There are more than fifty kid-powered physical play elements, such as Nets and Climbs and Ernie's Bed Bounce.

The park has thirteen water attractions, and most will appeal to all members of your family. Rambling River is a winding, relaxing circular tube ride your kids can go around and around all afternoon. Even very young children have no fear on Teeny Tiny Tidal Waves and the Rubber Duckie Pond. Sky Splash is filled with giant-size water adventures including an 8-foot-tall rubber duckie and huge tinker toys that spray water.

Sesame Place is located in Langhorne about thirty minutes from Philadelphia at exit 29A on Interstate 95 North. Most areas are accessible to the disabled, and special events include some designed for disabled children. Bathing suits are required for all water attractions.

Morrisville

Pennsbury Manor (ages 6 and up) 🏛
400 Pennsbury Memorial Road; (215) 946–0400; www.pennsburymanor.org. Open Tuesday through Saturday 9:00 A.M. to 5:00 P.M. and Sunday noon to 5:00 P.M. Last tour begins 3:30 P.M. Admission is $$ for adults and $ for seniors and children 5 to 12; children under 5 enter free. Family rate $$$.

Pennsylvania was William Penn's "holy experiment," a colony founded on Quaker moral principles. Although he only lived here for a total of about four years, Pennsbury Manor was never far from his thoughts. Today his home has been restored, complete with icehouse, stable, smokehouse, garden, and livestock. The boathouse contains a replica of the vessel Penn used to commute to Philadelphia. The oven in the bake-and-brew house can bake up to thirty loaves of bread at a time.

On Sunday afternoons from April to October, Pennsbury Manor offers living history just for families. It has an activity room and a worker's cottage where kids can try seventeenth-century skills, such as writing with a quill pen. Geese, peacocks, sheep, and Red Devon cattle—authentic breeds wherever possible—populate the farm. In December, the farm is lit by glowing candles and roaring yule logs.

Amazing Pennsylvania Facts

The *New York Times* recently included Sesame Place on its list of best water parks in the United States.

ALSO IN THE AREA

When William Penn was living at Pennsbury Manor, he attended Quaker Meeting at Falls Meeting in Fallsington, a town built around its meetinghouses. Guided tours start at the Gillingham Store and include several restored historic buildings: Moon–Williamson House, Burges–Lippincott House, and the Stagecoach Tavern. Fallsington is located on Route 13 off I–95. For details contact Historic Fallsington, Inc. at (215) 295–6567; www.historicfallsington.org.

Washington Crossing

We picture "Washington's crossing" as in the famous painting by Emanuel Leutz, with George Washington standing heroically in the small boat as his troops row across the Delaware to surprise the Hessians on Christmas Day.

The German artist had never seen Washington Crossing when he painted it in the nineteenth century. It may not be safe to stand up in a small boat, but the image depicts an artist's impression of a historic event. In the Memorial Building at Washington Crossing National Historic Park, you can see a copy of the painting. It's larger than life in more ways than one—the painting is 20 feet long, 12 feet tall.

Washington Crossing National Historic Park and Bowman's Hill Tower (ages 8 and up) 🏛️ 👥

Routes 32 and 532, 3 miles north of I–95 exit 31; (215) 493–4076; www.spiritof76.net. The visitor center and historic buildings are open Monday through Saturday 9:00 A.M. to 5:00 P.M. and on Sunday noon to 5:00 P.M. There is a fee for the buildings ($). The park grounds, however, are open at no charge from 8:00 A.M. until sunset. Free.

A thirty-minute film at the visitor center describes the events of December 25, 1776, which led to the turning point of the Revolution. Washington planned his surprise attack from his headquarters in the Thompson–Neely House, and he ate dinner before the crossing at the Old Ferry Inn. In the Durham Boat House, you can see the boats that were actually used for the crossing.

Every year on Christmas Day the park hosts a reenactment of Washington's crossing. Other special events here include Gingerbread Days, Tavern Nights, and special activities in honor of Washington's birthday. Gazebo Games, another special event, lets kids try out the games and toys enjoyed by eighteenth-century children.

Bowman's Hill Wildflower Preserve (ages 8 and up) 🏛 🏕

Located on the grounds of Washington Crossing Park but managed separately; (215) 862–2924; www.bhwp.org. Grounds open daily 8:30 A.M. to sunset, visitor center open daily 9:00 A.M. to 5:00 P.M. Admission $ for adults, seniors and children. Members and children under 4 free. Closed major holidays.

Surrounding Bowman's Hill Tower but managed separately and with its own admission fee, Bowman's Hill Wildflower Preserve offers a breathtaking variety of wildflowers. Check the Web site for information, directions, and bloom lists. From mid-March through October guided walks are offered at 2:00 P.M. daily. At any other time, there are self-guided nature walks. The Wildflower Preserve also has a children's reading program, a weeklong summer day camp and many children's programs. The third Saturday in July is Community Open House Day, a free event with guided tours offered all day, as well as music, nature crafts, and face-painting.

New Hope

In summer the streets of New Hope bustle with people drawn to the more than 200 art galleries, craft shops, restaurants, and history this town offers. But New Hope welcomes visitors any time of the year. You can get more information about bed-and-breakfasts in New Hope by stopping by the New Hope Information Center, 1 West Mechanic Street. For brochures about New Hope, call (215) 862–5880. To talk to a staff member about New Hope, call (215) 862–5030.

James A. Michener Art Museum—New Hope (all ages) 🖼

Located in Union Square complex on Bridge Street; (215) 862–7633; www.michenerart museum.org. April 1 through December 31, open Tuesday through Thursday 11:00 A.M. to 5:00 P.M., Friday and Saturday 11:00 A.M. to 8:00 P.M., Sunday 11:00 A.M. to 5:00 P.M. January 2 through March 31, open Thursday 11:00 A.M. to 5:00 P.M., Friday and Saturday 11:00 A.M. to 8:00 P.M., Sunday 11:00 A.M. to 5:00 P.M. Closed major holidays.

Doylestown's Michener Museum has recently opened a satellite location in the artistic community of New Hope. On permanent display here is *Artists Among Us: Creative Bucks County: A Celebration of Art and Artists.*

Coryell's Ferry Historic Boat Rides (all ages) 🔺

Ferries leave Coryell's Ferry at Gerenser's Exotic Ice Cream, 22 South Main Street (215–862–2050; www.newhopepa.com/History/Coryells_Ferry. April through October starting at 11:00 A.M.

Coryell's Ferry began carrying passengers across the Delaware in canoes in 1733. Ferries still operate here for half-hour tours; only now they use more commodious paddleboats. The longest ride on the river, aboard a 65-foot Mississippi riverboat, leaves at 11:00 A.M. daily, May through September. Call for details or to find out about special kids' days on the ferry.

Colonial New Hope Walking Tours (ages 6 and up)

Gerenser's Exotic Ice Cream, 22 South Main Street; (215) 862–2050; www.spiritof76 .net. Tours of New Hope are available April through October, starting at noon.

General Washington visited New Hope at least four times. To learn more about the history of this town, you can take a walking tour. Tickets and schedules for walking tours of New Hope are available here.

New Hope Mule Barges (all ages)

New Street; (215) 862–2842 or (800) 59–BARGE. Open April through November. Boat fares $$ for adults, $ for children.

You can take a ride on a mule barge, sailing past eighteenth-century homes, gardens, and workshops. Many barges are equipped with folk singers or historians. The Delaware Canal became operational in 1840, and, at its height, mules hauled thousands of barges, carrying loads of coal and limestone. The canal includes 25 lift locks, 9 aqueducts, and 106 bridges.

Boat Rides at Wells Ferry (all ages)

At the end of Ferry Street on River; (215) 862–5965. Open May through October 11:00 A.M. to 6:00 P.M. Admission: adults $$, children $.

The Star of New Hope carries thirty-six passengers at a time on a guided tour. Tour guides offer a little history, as well as a glimpse at New Hope's varied architecture. Some tour guides play guitar music as well.

New Hope and Ivyland Railroad (all ages)

Station at Bridge and Stockton Streets; (215) 862–2332; www.newhoperailroad.com. Trains run daily April to November, weekends only January until March. In December, special Santa Claus rides are offered. Tickets are $$$ for adults, $$ for seniors and kids 2 to 11, and $ for children under 2. The train operates seasonally.

The New Hope and Ivyland Railroad, built in 1889, eventually made the canal obsolete. If you take this train on its forty-five-minute narrated trip to Lahaska, you will notice a curved trestle bridge. If this bridge looks like something right out of *The Perils of Pauline,* that's because this actually was the bridge that was used in the 1914 movie series.

ALSO IN THE AREA

The **Bucks County Playhouse** offers a series of plays for children on Friday and Saturday, at reasonable prices. Call (215) 862–2041 for a schedule, or check the Web site www.buckscountyplayhouse.com.

If you wish to take any kind of ride or tour, including walking tours, check at **Gerenser's Exotic Ice Cream** at 22 South Main Street, where tickets and schedules are available. You can purchase tickets for a **colonial walking tour** (215) 862–2050. This is also where you get tickets for **Coryell's Ferry** (see previous entry). Have some ice cream while you're here. To find out about **Ghost Tours,** call (215) 357–5637 or (215) 957–9988. You can also find out about different tours and boat rides by checking out the Web site http://bctc.org. We especially enjoy just strolling along the canal, watching the barges go by. Some of the restaurants here have views of the canal.

Lahaska

While in Peddler's Village, take a look at some of the unusual shops and restaurants.

Giggleberry Fair (all ages) 🎡

Peddler's Village, Routes 202 and 263; (215) 794–8960; www.peddlersvillage.com /pages/giggleberry.php. Open Monday and Tuesday 10:00 A.M. to 6:00 P.M., Wednesday and Thursday 10:00 A.M. to 8:00 P.M., and Friday and Saturday 10:00 A.M. to 10:00 P.M. Sunday 10:00 A.M. to 7:00 P.M. Discovery Land/Giggleberry Mountain Combination Pass $$ per person. Individual tickets for specific attractions are also available.

Giggleberry Fair opened its doors in June 2001 "to provide a wholesome, quality experience for children to be both educated and entertained." Comprising four children's attractions, Giggleberry Fair is 10,000 square feet of family fun.

Peddler's Village has recently restored its wonderful Grand Carousel, built in 1922 by the famous Philadelphia Toboggan Company. The carousel has been joined by Giggleberry Mountain, Discovery Land, and the Painted Pony Cafe to create Giggleberry Fair.

Giggleberry Mountain is the area's largest and most attractive indoor obstacle course, challenging for both children and adults. The colorful, two-story, six-level structure is filled with tens of thousands of soft foam "berries." Kids fill tote bags with as many berries as they can grab and climb up through netting mazes to different levels where they can "blast" berries at their friends or reach the top of two different slides. Even adults get right in there with their kids. It's loud, but it's a happy loudness.

In Discovery Land, kids can explore a variety of calmer play environments. There's a pretend farm and orchard, a mini climbing wall, a rubber-duck waterway, and plenty of games. All games are rated "green"—suitable for all ages—by the Coin-Operated Video Game Parental Advisory System.

The Painted Pony Cafe offers pizza, hot dogs, a salad bar, and other kid-friendly choices.

Point Pleasant

The signers of the Declaration of Independence had to sweat it out in the notorious Philadelphia humidity, but you don't have to. Point Pleasant, north of Lahaska and New Hope, offers some great ways to cool off in its inviting, kid-friendly rapids. Bucks County River Country rents canoes, tubes, and rafts from April through October. To make reservations (which are required) or to find out about prices and special Pedal and Paddle trips, call Bucks County River Country (215) 297–5000.

Bucks County River Country (ages 6 and up) ⚠

Route 32, Upper Black Eddy; (215) 297–5000; www.rivercountry.net. Call for days, hours, prices, and river conditions.

Our kids spent a carefree summer afternoon riding the current in tubes, occasionally dunking each other or taking time to see how deep the water was (not very). To protect your feet, remember to wear old sneakers that can get wet, and don't forget the sunscreen. Bucks County River Country also presents other events in the woods, such as the nation's largest haunted-woods hayride.

Our Tubing Trip

—by Seth Paulsen-Sacks, at age 10

We had to wait in a line and tell the people how much we weighed. Then they gave us the inner tubes. All the kids in my group tied their tubes together with a camp counselor. The current was strong. We had to paddle so the current wouldn't pull us away. Luke and Paul fell off their tubes so the counselor got off, held onto our tubes, and waited for them to get back on. When we were waiting, it felt like we were still moving because of the current.

We saw a hot dog guy on a motorboat with big balloons on a string. You could buy hot dogs from him if you had money.

When we got back we found little frogs the size of ants and I caught three.

Doylestown

A wonderful choice for a day trip, Doylestown will charm you with its cast-iron lamp-posts, neat nineteenth-century houses, and unusual shops and galleries. You can walk to the Mercer Museum and James A. Michener Museum. Also within walking distance is the County Theater, showing art and vintage, as well as first-run, movies; the picturesque Doylestown Inn; as well as many other restaurants and shops. A short drive out of town, you may also wish to visit Fonthill and the Moravian Pottery and Tileworks. For information about Historic Doylestown, call (215) 345–0788.

Mercer Museum (ages 6 and up)

84 South Pine Street, near Ashland; (215) 345–0210; www.mercermuseum.org. Open Monday through Saturday 10:00 A.M. to 5:00 P.M., Sunday noon to 5:00 P.M. On Tuesday, the museum closes at 9:00 P.M. Closed New Year's Day, Thanksgiving, and Christmas. Admission is $$ for adults, $ for youth ages 6 to 17; children under 6 enter free.

On Pine Street in the charming town of Doylestown stands what can only be described as a castle, not of stone but of poured concrete, brainchild of Henry Chapman Mercer (1856–1930).

In 1916 Mercer built what is now the Mercer Museum, with its turrets and parapets, to house his collection of more than 50,000 artifacts and tools of more than sixty different American trades. Entering the central court of the museum, you find yourself surrounded by odds and ends hanging over your head: a Conestoga wagon; a whaling skiff; wooden buckets. Then, take the elevator up to the top floor and walk down, working your way through the implements left behind by shoemakers, bakers, candlemakers, milliners, and farmers of America's past.

Several new features are of special interest to families. Look for the new "Go for the Green" tags that mark exhibits designed for kids to touch, to build things, to pull the reins, and more. Bright paw prints indicate clues on a family scavenger hunt around the collection, and the new audio guides feature a channel just for kids. The museum also offers family events such as sleepovers, "Summer Boredom Busters," and "Under the Stars" movies.

Our kids felt that the highlight of the collection was the vampire-killing kit. They also enjoyed hunting for the footprints left in the concrete by Mercer's pet dog. The museum is unheated, so bring a sweater. There are special children's programs, as well as FolkFest in May.

James A. Michener Art Museum (all ages)

138 South Pine Street; (215) 340–9800; www.michenerartmuseum.org. Open Tuesday through Friday 10:00 A.M. to 4:30 P.M., Saturday and Sunday noon to 5:00 P.M. Open until 9:00 P.M. on Wednesday in summer only. Admission is $$ for adults, $ for students; children under 12 are free. **Some exhibitions may require an additional fee.**

The James A. Michener Art Museum, across the street from the Mercer Museum, offers the finest collection of Pennsylvania Impressionist paintings, as well as other important examples of regional contemporary and figurative art. Housed in a renovated historic site that formerly served as the Bucks County Jail from 1884–1985, the museum features a permanent exhibit on James Michener himself and the Nakashima Reading Room, completely designed and furnished by wood artist George Nakashima. The family education center provides puzzles and discovery boxes for children to explore. Light snacks are available at the cafe. The Michener Museum has just opened a satellite location in New Hope. (See listing for James A. Michener Art Museum—New Hope earlier in this chapter.)

Moravian Pottery and Tile Works (ages 8 and up)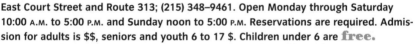

East Court Street; (215) 345–6722. Open daily, except major holidays, 10:00 A.M. to 4:45 P.M. Tours leave every thirty minutes, with the last tour departing at 4:00 P.M. Admission is $. The tile shop, open daily 10:00 A.M. to 4:45 P.M., can be entered without admission.

The Moravian Pottery and Tile Works is the legacy of Mercer's effort to preserve an American craft. You can purchase Moravian tiles here or take a tour to see how the tiles are made.

Fonthill (ages 8 and up)

East Court Street and Route 313; (215) 348–9461. Open Monday through Saturday 10:00 A.M. to 5:00 P.M. and Sunday noon to 5:00 P.M. Reservations are required. Admission for adults is $$, seniors and youth 6 to 17 $. Children under 6 are free.

Mercer's home, Fonthill, has forty-four rooms, eighteen fireplaces, and thirty-two staircases. Tours have recently been revamped to capture the interests of children. Be sure to check it out. Combination tickets are available for Mercer Museum and Fonthill.

ALSO IN THE AREA

Gardeners get a breath of fresh air at **Henry Schmieder Arboretum of Delaware Valley College** (on Route 202; 215–345–1500; www.delval col.edu/arboretum) and the nearby **Inn at Fordhook Farm** (a bed-and-breakfast; call 215–345–1766). The Burpee family (of Burpee Seeds) developed many well-known seed varieties in this area.

Another fun idea: Try ballooning. For information call Color the Sky, Inc. at (215) 340–9966; www.colorthesky.com.

Chalfont

Byers' Choice Ltd. (ages 6 and up) 🔒

4355 County Line Road; (215) 822–0150; www.byerschoice.com. The factory is open at no charge Monday through Saturday, 10:00 A.M. to 5:00 P.M. Sunday noon to 5:00 P.M. Closed major holidays.

At Byers' Choice Ltd. the Byers family and their employees hand-sculpt thousands of delightful Caroler figurines every year, giving a percentage of their profits to charity. They invite visitors to watch the delicate faces molded and painted and to tour their gallery of little carolers in various costumes and settings. Children's eyes grow wide when they see these tiny landscapes filled with doll-like figures, each one unique, each one singing a Christmas carol. There is also a gift shop and a short movie about the history of the company.

Hilltown

Green Hills Farm (Pearl S. Buck House) (ages 10 and up) 🏛

520 Dublin Road, 1 mile southwest of Route 313; (215) 249–0100, ext. 170 or (800) 220–BUCK; www.pearl-s-buck.org. Guided tours are available March through December, Tuesday through Saturday, at 11:00 A.M., 1:00 P.M., and 2:00 P.M. On Sunday, tours leave at 1:00 P.M. and 2:00 P.M. only. Admission is $$ for adults, seniors, and students; free for children under 6.

Perhaps you or your kids have read *The Good Earth* or other books by Pearl S. Buck. The author settled in this farmhouse at Green Hills Farm. In her office here she wrote more than one hundred novels. Buck was not only a writer but also a humanitarian. An early supporter of human rights, civil rights, and women's rights, her home still houses the offices of Pearl S. Buck International, "bringing hope to children worldwide."

The oldest section of the house was built in 1740, with sections added in 1825

Amazing
Pennsylvania Facts 🔍

Bucks County's fertile soil has nourished Broadway luminaries like George S. Kaufman, Moss Hart, Oscar Hammerstein II; writers like James Michener and Pearl S. Buck; and artists such as George Nakashima and Edward Hicks.

and 1935. The furniture, artifacts, and contemporary artwork represent a true blending of East and West.

Worcester

Peter Wentz Farmstead (ages 6 and up) 🏛

Off Route 73 at Schearer Road; (610) 584–5104; www.montcopa.org/historicsites. Open year-round Tuesday to Saturday 10:00 A.M. to 4:00 P.M. and Sunday 1:00 to 4:00 P.M.; closed Monday and major holidays. Admission is free. Donations are accepted.

The historians at Peter Wentz Farmstead have done an exceptional job researching and restoring this farm to its appearance in 1777, when General Washington occupied the house before and after the Battle of Germantown.

If you thought colonial farms were painted in subdued tones, you'll be amazed at the paint colors and wild patterns on the walls: dots, zig-zags, stripes, and more.

Special events are scheduled throughout the year, when you can watch costumed volunteers demonstrate colonial crafts using authentic techniques. You can watch spinning, weaving, candle making, and cooking, as well as unusual arts such as *scherenschnitte*, the German art of paper cutting. The kids especially like the farm animals. Annual events include a Market Day with Revolutionary War activities on the first Saturday in June, the Colonial Craft Festival on the first Saturday in October, and Candlelight House Tours on the first Saturday in December.

ALSO IN THE AREA

Only a few blocks away, on Weikel Road, you can see the **Morgan Log House,** built in 1695 and more than 90 percent intact. The Morgans, who lived here, had ten children, one of whom grew up to become the mother of Daniel Boone. Open April to November weekends only, noon to 5:00 P.M., or by appointment. Call (215) 368–2480.

Schwenksville

Pennypacker Mills (ages 8 and up) 🏛

Route 73 and Haldeman Road; (610) 287–9349; www.montcopa.org/historicsites. Open free of charge Tuesday through Saturday 10:00 A.M. to 4:00 P.M. and on Sunday 1:00 to 4:00 P.M. Last daily tour begins at 3:30 P.M. Closed Monday and major holidays.

Seven miles down Skippack Pike (Route 73) from the Peter Wentz Farmstead, you can see an excellent example of colonial revival architecture. Pennypacker Mills was owned by the Pennypacker family as early as 1747. In 1900 Samuel W. Pennypacker purchased it and added onto the home, making a turn-of-the-twentieth-century mansion. The mansion retains original furnishings. Pennypacker was governor of Pennsylvania from 1903 to 1907, as well as a respected historian, collector, and farmer. The home is surrounded by fifteen acres of gardens landscaped in the English "natural" style. At present the site is preserved by Montgomery County as a turn-of-the-twentieth-century country gentleman's estate.

Pennypacker Mills hosts special events for children, including a Halloween celebration with hayrides. Special children's events re-create the neighborhood parties once held by the Pennypacker daughters. There are also living-history events including a Civil War reenactment and Christmas holiday celebrations. Call for details about these events and others for adults, families, and young children.

ALSO IN THE AREA

The **Philadelphia Folk Festival,** which celebrated its fortieth birthday in 2001, is one of the oldest and best folk festivals in the country. The folk festival brings music, crafts, dancing, and thousands of people to Old Pool farm in Schwenksville every August. For information call (800) 556–FOLK or check out the Web site, www.folk fest.org. Children twelve and under enter any concert **free!**.

Alburtis

The anthracite iron industry played an important role in the development of this area, beginning in 1839.

Lock Ridge Furnace Museum (ages 6 and up) 🏛

Franklin Street; (610) 435–4664; www.lehighcountyhistoricalsociety.org. Open weekends May through September 1:00 to 4:00 P.M. Admission is free. Grounds open year-round.

Lock Ridge Furnace Museum operated as a furnace until 1914 and is now one of the sites administered by the Lehigh County Historical Society.

Breinigsville

Terry Hill Waterpark (all ages) 🌊

On Route 222 in Breinigsville; (610) 398–7555; www.terryhill.com. Open noon to 6:00 P.M. daily beginning in June. In July and August, open to 7:00 P.M. weekdays and noon to 8:00 P.M. weekends. Admission is $$$.

Terry Hill Waterpark has three pools, nine waterslides, refreshments, and more. The Kiddie Play Area and two child-size slides have recently been expanded.

In the fall, Terry Hill Waterpark becomes Terror Hill, offering family and group hayrides (www.terrorhill.com)

and in the winter, the slopes are dressed up for snowtubing for all ages and "kinder-tubing" for children three to five years old (www.pasports.com).

Allentown

On the waterfront in Allentown, long-quiet historic transportation and industrial buildings are being transformed into Lehigh Landing. The eleven-acre project will eventually include a visitor center for the region, playground, baseball field, riverfront walk, and more.

Lehigh Landing will be located immediately north of the Hamilton Street Bridge, a short walk east of downtown Allentown. Keep up-to-date on new developments by checking the Web site at www.americaonwheels.org.

Also in the planning stage is Bethlehem Works, a large entertainment complex to be built on the grounds of the former Bethlehem Steel. It is expected to include the National Museum of Industrial History as well as an ice-skating rink, swimming pool, hotels, restaurants, and shopping.

America On Wheels (all ages) 💷
718 Hamilton Street; (610) 432–4200; www.americaonwheels.org.

Due to open summer 2006 at Allentown's Lehigh Landing, America on Wheels explores the historical, economic, and social aspects of the development of over-the-road transportation in the Lehigh Valley and across America. The museum will include 23,000 square feet of exhibit space in its three main galleries, grand concourse, and lobby. Families can learn about carriages, wagons, bicycles, motorcycles, cars, and trucks through interactive stations focusing on the past, present, and future of transportation. The museum will also include an outdoor classroom where kids and adults can learn about transportation safety.

The Mack Truck Historical Museum (ages 6 and up) 💷
997 Postal Road; (610) 266–6767; www.macktrucks.com. Regular hours Monday, Wednesday and Friday 10:00 A.M. to 4:00 P.M. Hours subject to change. Please call ahead before you visit. Admission free.

The Mack Truck Museum has one of the original sightseeing buses built by Jack and Augustus Mack in the early twentieth century. You can also see a 1911 Mack Jr. that shared the streets with horse-drawn wagons as it delivered dry good and produce. The Museum is home to antique Mack trucks, a UPS tractor, and many photos and memorabilia related to the truck that epitomizes endurance on the road. Kids are allowed to climb into the driver's seat of a few of the trucks but others are for looking only. The Museum is staffed by retired Mack employees with great enthusiasm for the Museum and its research facility.

Museum of Indian Culture and Lenni Lenape Historical Society
(ages 5 and up)

2825 Fish Hatchery Road; (610) 797–2121; www.lenape.org. Open Friday through Tuesday noon to 3:00 P.M. Admission is $; special group rates are available. Wheelchair accessible.

As the saying goes, you can't understand another person until you've walked a mile in his moccasins. The Museum of Indian Culture and Lenni Lenape Historical Society gives kids just this kind of opportunity. Children will enjoy the many hands-on exhibits that illuminate Native American culture, as well as the exhibits of tools, baskets, and crafts. Three ceremonies are held annually: Corn Planting in May; Roasting Ears of Corn in August; and Time of Thanksgiving in October. There are also picnic facilities, two nature trails, and a fish hatchery.

Allentown Art Museum (all ages)

Fifth and Court Streets; (610) 432–4333; www.allentownartmuseum.org. Open Tuesday through Saturday 11:00 A.M. to 5:00 P.M. and Sunday noon until 5:00 P.M. Admission is $; free for kids under 12. Admission is also free on Sunday.

Parents and kids can enjoy hands-on art activities themed to the current exhibition at Art Ways, the Museum's interactive family gallery, open whenever the museum is open, except when a new installation is being set up. Entrance to this gallery is included in your museum admission. On Sundays from 1:00 to 4:00 P.M., museum educators host Sunday *Art*ventures in the Museum's Binney & Smith Learning Center. The museum also presents two family festivals per year, one in the fall and one in the winter, themed to current museum exhibitions. Many programs are available for school, and schoolgroups, homeschoolers, and birthday parties. Please call (610) 432–4333 ext. 32 for information about group visits.

Haines Mill (ages 8 and up)

3600 Haines Mill Road; (610) 435–9601; www.lehighcountyhistoricalsociety.org. Open weekends from May until September, 1:00 to 4:00 P.M. Admission is free.

The mill was built in 1760 and operated until 1956, after having been renovated in 1909 with a water-turbine power source.

Lehigh County Heritage Center (ages 10 and up)

432 Walnut Street; (610) 435–9601; www.lehighcountyhistoricalsociety.org. The museum and library are open 10:00 A.M. to 4:00 P.M., Monday through Saturday. Library is closed 12:30 to 1:00 P.M. Saturday. Admission is charged.

The Lehigh County Historical Society is scheduled to move into the Lehigh Valley Heritage Center, opening in mid-April 2005. Permanent exhibits explore the county's history from the Native Americans through the rich heritage of the pioneering Pennsylvania German settlers, to the developments that made the county an industrial powerhouse, attracting immigrants from all over the world. The Heritage Center also houses the historical society's library, an extensive collection of county, personal, business, and genealogical records.

The museum displays artifacts from the earliest inhabitants of the Lehigh Valley, the Lenni Lenape, as well as from the Pennsylvania Germans and other settlers who came to this area. The museum also includes the Scott Andrew Trexler II Memorial Library, an extensive collection of county and genealogical records.

Liberty Bell Shrine (ages 8 and up)

Zion Church at 622 Hamilton Mall; (610) 435–4664; www.geocities.com/Athens/Ithaca/ 1760. Open May through October, Monday through Saturday noon to 4:00 P.M. In November, December, February, March, and April open Thursday through Saturday noon to 4:00 P.M. Admission is free. Closed in January.

Did you know that during the Revolutionary War, when the British occupied Philadelphia, all the bells in the city were removed so that the British would not be able to melt them down for ammunition? From September 1777 to June 1778, the Liberty Bell was hidden under the floor of Allentown's Zion Church at 622 Hamilton Mall. At present the Liberty Bell Shrine includes an exact replica of the famous bell, as well as flags, maps, weapons, uniforms, and a 46-foot mural showing scenes from the Revolution.

Dorney Park and Wildwater Kingdom (all ages)

Near exit 16 on Route 309 South, at 3700 Hamilton Boulevard. For more information call (610) 395–3724. Hours for both parks vary according to season. Dorney Park is open weekends only in May and September, then daily from Memorial Day to Labor Day. Wildwater Kingdom is open mid-May to Labor Day and selected weekends in September. At the height of the season, tickets cost $$$$ for anyone 48 inches or taller, $$$ for anyone under 47 inches and seniors, and are free for children under 3. These prices include admission to both parks. There is a parking fee ($$).

According to ancient Greek legend, the hero Hercules defeated the nine-headed monster Hydra, but he was not able to kill all nine heads. There was one immortal head that could not be killed, so Hercules buried it under a huge boulder beside a lake.

But wait! What is that stirring by the edge of the lake at the feet of the sleeping Hercules? According to Dorney Park mythology, the Hydra has risen to take its revenge on Hercules, the wooden roller coaster the park retired after its 2003 season.

Hydra the Revenge is scheduled to make its monstrous debut in May 2005. Dorney Park officials describe the $13 million floorless coaster as "a one-of-a-kind experience." It will include seven inversions, a zero-gravity experience, several drops below ground level, and the jojo roll, the first-ever pre-lift inversion where riders twist upside-down after exiting the launch station.

Hydra the Revenge joins Dorney Park's line-up of coasters: Dominator, Steel Force, Laser, Meteor Thunderhawk, and Talon.

Wildwater Kingdom has eleven waterslides. Younger children will love meeting the Berenstain Bears, playing in the TotSpot, and cooling off in two water park areas specifically for small fry. Our kids could have spent the whole day in the giant wave pool.

In the fall, Dorney Park combines its rides with the frightening fun of Halloween to create Halloweekends.

ALSO IN THE AREA

The Lehigh County Historical Society administers a number of sites, including the Lehigh County Heritage Center and several historic homes. **Trout Hall** (414 Walnut Street; 610–435–9601) is Allentown's oldest home, built in 1770 by the son of the city's founder, William Allen. The **Troxell–Steckel House** in nearby Egypt (4229 Reliance Street; 610–435–9601) is an excellent example of a rural German-style farmhouse. Its barn contains a collection of old buggies and wagons. Trout Hall is open April through November, Tuesday through Saturday noon to 3:00 P.M. and on Sunday from 1:00 to 4:00 P.M. The Troxell–Steckel House is open weekends only 1:00 to 4:00 P.M.

Frank Buchman, founder of the worldwide Moral Rearmament Movement, who was nominated for two Nobel prizes, lived at 117 North Eleventh Street in Allentown. The **Frank Buchman House** displays some of Buchman's souvenirs from an extraordinary life. The house is open for tours weekends only 1:00 to 4:00 P.M.

Schnecksville

Game Preserve (all ages) 🐘

5150 Game Preserve Road; (610) 799–4171; www.gamepreserve.org. Open April through October, 10:00 A.M. to 5:00 P.M., last admission at 4:00 P.M. Admission: adults 13 to 64, $$; seniors 65 and older and children 2 to 12, $.

The Game Preserve is actually a zoo featuring a wide variety of wildlife in naturalistic habitats. There's a butterfly garden, pony rides, animal contact area, a birds of prey exhibit, and the zoo's newest residents: Arctic wolves. The Web site has fun animal puzzles for kids.

Claussville

Claussville One-Room Schoolhouse (ages 6 and up) 🏛

Route 100; (610) 435–9601; www.lehighcountyhistoricalsociety.org. Open on weekends from May through September 1:00 to 4:00 P.M. Admission is $ for adults; members and children free.

Children can picture what school must have been like in the Claussville One-Room Schoolhouse, in which children learned from 1893 until 1956. They can imagine kids sitting at these very desks, reading the very books displayed there. The schoolhouse is one of the Lehigh County Historical Society sites.

Hellertown

If your kids are fascinated by crystal formations, rocks, minerals, and stalagmites and stalactites, don't miss Lost River Caverns, located in Hellertown.

Lost River Caverns (ages 6 and up) 🍁 🐾

726 Durham Street, south of Bethlehem on Route 412, off Interstate 78 exit 21; (610) 838–8767; fax (610) 838–2961; www.lostrivercaverns.com. Open year-round. From Memorial Day to Labor Day, open 9:00 A.M. to 6:00 P.M.; the rest of the year, 9:00 A.M. to 5:00 P.M. Closed major holidays. Admission is $$ for adults and $ for children 3 to 12; children under 3 are free.

Yes, there is an actual lost river at Lost River Caverns. The clear water flows into the cavern from an unknown source, and then disappears just as mysteriously. Take an underground tour of a natural limestone cavern with crystal formations and a crystal chapel. There is also a museum, gift shop, and picnic grove.

Bethlehem

The Star of Bethlehem shines on Star Mountain every night of the year, watching over this city founded by Moravian settlers and named "Bethlehem" on Christmas Eve, 1741. You may wish to visit during Christkindlmarkt, in December, when lanterns are lit, or in August, when Musikfest is held. But no matter when you visit, start out at the visitors center, where you can see a film and multimedia presentation about the city. You can pick up a schedule of events and walking-tour map, or you can schedule a guided tour. The visitors center is in the Historic District, off Route 378, at 52 West Broad Street. Call (610) 868–1513, (610) 867–0173, or (800) 360–8687.

Moravian Museum (all ages) 🏛

66 West Church Street; (610) 867–0173. Open Tuesday through Sunday noon to 4:00 P.M. Closed in January. Admission: $$ for adults, $$ for children 6 to 12, free for children under 6.

A log cabin five stories tall, built entirely without nails, the Moravian Museum served as the Moravians' church when they first came to Bethlehem. It was also their sleeping quarters and workshop. Now it serves as a museum of Moravian history, exhibiting Moravian furniture, needlework, toys, and art.

Kemerer Museum of Decorative Arts (ages 8 and up) 🖼

427 North New Street; (610) 868–6868; www.historicbethlehem.org. Open Tuesday through Sunday noon to 5:00 P.M. Admission: $$ for adults, $ for children 6 to 12, free for children under 6.

The Kemerer Museum features eighteenth- and nineteenth-century decorative arts such as furniture, folk art, textiles, paintings, and toys. Call for a schedule of changing exhibits.

Burnside Plantation (all ages) 🏛

1461 Schoernersville Road, next to the Bethlehem Racquet Club; (610) 882–0450; www.historicbethlehem.org. Open for free self-guided tours Monday through Sunday 8:30 A.M. to 5:00 P.M.

Seven acres of James Burnside's original farm developed as a living-history museum to interpret farming between 1748 and 1848. You can see the restored farmhouse, 1841 bank barn, summer kitchen, and kitchen garden. The new 2-mile walking trail, the Monocacy Way, has recently opened. The Monocacy Way actually starts at Illick's Mill Park, crosses Burnside Plantation, and continues through the Colonial Industrial Quarter. The plantation hosts an annual Blueberry Festival on the last weekend in July.

The Discovery Center of Science and Technology (all ages) 🖼

511 East Third Street; (610) 865–5010; www.discovery-center.org. During the summer, the center is open to the public Monday through Saturday 9:30 A.M. to 4:30 P.M. Closed July 4 and Labor Day. During the school year, the center is open to the public Tuesday through Saturday 9:30 A.M. to 4:30 P.M., Sunday noon to 4:30 P.M. Admission is $. Children under 3 enter free. There are additional fees for the Laser Theater shows and for selected special exhibits and shows.

"Discover the fun of learning" is the slogan of the Discovery Center, where more than ninety hands-on interactive exhibits cover many science and technology topics. WaterWorks demonstrates water distribution, the water cycle, and natural water filters. The Tunnel challenges kids to navigate a 76-foot-long tunnel using only the senses of touch, smell, and hearing. There's also a Science Playground, Workbench, and more. The center offers educational programs, scout badge days, summer camp, birthday parties, and other activities. Fully wheelchair accessible.

Banana Factory (ages 5 and up) 🎵

25 West Third Street; (610) 332–1300; www.bananafactory.org. Open Monday through Thursday 8:30 A.M. to 9:00 P.M., Friday 8:30 A.M. to 7:00 P.M., and Sunday 9:00 A.M. to 5:00 P.M. Gallery hours subject to change. Admission is free.

The mission of the Banana Factory is "to kindle, support, and celebrate the artistic, cultural, and creative spirit of the Lehigh Valley." Located in a former warehouse for bananas, the Banana Factory offers classes for children and adults, as well as art exhibits. There are twenty-three artists' studios in the building, which is also home to the Pennsylvania Youth Theater and the Bethlehem Musikfest Association.

ALSO IN THE AREA

For ten days every August, the streets, plazas, and historic places of Bethlehem vibrate with music from all over the world. Bethlehem's Musikfest attracts hundreds of musicians and music lovers to performances at thirteen outdoor and six indoor venues. Specially for the children, clowns, jugglers, and magicians roam the streets. There is also an interactive theater for kids and parents. Hands-on crafts, an outdoor art studio called Muralplatz, and both regional and international foods, plus a fireworks display, complete the festivities.

Nazareth

Like Bethlehem, Nazareth was founded in the 1700s by Moravian settlers. At present Nazareth is also the home of Martin Guitars.

Martin Guitar Factory (ages 8 and up)

510 Sycamore Street; (610) 759–2837 or (800) 633–2060; www.martinguitar.com. Guided tours Monday through Friday at 1:00 P.M. except during holiday periods. For groups of ten or more, reservations are required and a per-person fee ($) is charged.

A small museum displays limited-edition guitars made for people like Gene Autry and Johnny Cash. The free tour takes about an hour and brings you close-up to the craftspeople who create the instruments.

ALSO IN THE AREA

Other sites in Nazareth include **Moravian Historical Society** (214 East Center Street; 610–759–5057; www.moravianhistoricalsociety.org), **Whitefield** (pronounced wit-field) **House Museum** (214 East Center Street; 610–759–5070), and **Nazareth Speedway** (located on Highway 191 in Nazareth; call 610–759–8000 for tickets).

Easton

Did you know that the average child in the United States will wear down 730 crayons by his tenth birthday? Your children won't want to miss out on the Crayola Factory at Two Rivers Landing, 30 Centre Square.

Crayola Factory (all ages) 🖐️🏛️🍴

30 Centre Square; (610) 515–8000; www.crayola.com/factory. Open Tuesday through Friday, 9:30 A.M. to 4:00 P.M.; Saturday 9:30 A.M. to 5:00 P.M., Sunday noon to 5:00 P.M. From July through Labor Day, Monday through Saturday 9:30 A.M. to 5:00 P.M., Sunday 11:00 A.M. to 5:00 P.M. Closed for two weeks in January—call ahead for dates. Closed Monday except for the following holidays: Martin Luther King Jr. Day; Presidents' Day; Memorial Day; Labor Day; Columbus Day; and the Monday after Christmas. Closed New Year's Day, Easter, Thanksgiving, Christmas Eve, and Christmas. Admission price includes access to the Crayola Factory and the National Canal Museum. Admission $$ for adults and children. Children under two admitted free.

Spend some time with your family at this hands-on discovery center filled with creativity and fun for children and adults alike. You'll be sure to leave with a bag of your child's own original souvenirs. Make your own artwork with melted crayon wax at Crayola Meltdown, or use Crayola Model Magic to create three-dimensional art in Super Sculptures. Dance in Cool Moves and see your image projected onto a screen. Even the youngest visitors can explore Color Park.

Don't miss the Crayola crayon and marker demonstrations, where staff show how these products are made, or Crayola Chronology, where information abounds on the over one-hundred-year history of Binney & Smith, makers of Crayola products.

National Canal Museum (ages 8 and up) 🖐️🏛️

30 Centre Square; reservations and information (610) 515–8000, office (610) 559–6613. Open Labor Day to Memorial Day Tuesday through Friday 9:30 A.M. to 4:00 P.M., Sunday noon to 5:00 P.M. From Memorial Day to Labor Day, open Monday through Saturday, 9:30 to 5:00 P.M. and Sunday 11:00 A.M. to 5:00 P.M. Closed Monday except for the following holidays: Martin Luther King Jr. Day, Presidents' Day, Memorial Day, Labor Day, and Columbus Day. Admission to the National Canal Museum and the Crayola Factory is $$; children under age 2 are free.

The Delaware Canal runs from Easton to Bristol, and its area has recently become a National Heritage Corridor. There are opportunities to learn about the canal's place in history in Bristol, New Hope, and other towns.

Here at the National Canal Museum, interactive exhibits allow you to operate a lock model or pilot your boat through the lock. Artifacts, photomurals, and life-size figures create a sense of "being there" as a canal boatman recounts tales of canal life interspersed with traditional canal songs.

The Anatomy Academy at the Weller Center (all ages) 🔊

325 Northampton Street; (610) 258–8500; www.wellercenter.org. Admission: $$ per person.

The Weller Center is the first interactive museum in the United States to focus on health education. Kids can walk through a giant model of the human brain. There's also a giant nose that actually sneezes. ("Oooh, gross!" they'll say, but they'll love it.) Other exhibits focus on nutrition, human growth and development, and drug abuse. Located adjacent to the Crayola Factory and the National Canal Museum, the Weller Center also has a very nice gift shop. The Web site offers lots of health information for kids and a section "For Teens Only."

Easton Museum of PEZ Dispensers 🔊

15–19 South Bank Street; (610) 253–9794, (888) THE–PEZ1; www.eastonmuseumofpez .com. September 1 through June 30, open Tuesday through Saturday 10:00 A.M. to 6:00 P.M., Sunday 10:00 A.M. to 5:00 P.M. July 1 through August 31, open Monday through Sunday 10:00 A.M. to 6:00 P.M. Open some Monday holidays.

Billed as "the Greatest Display of PEZ Dispensers in the World," the Easton Museum of PEZ Dispensers has literally thousands of the little plastic candy dispensers we remember from our childhoods. Cartoon character PEZ dispensers date back to 1948, and the first characters to be introduced were Mickey Mouse, Casper the Friendly Ghost, and Popeye. The most popular PEZ dispenser character is Winnie the Pooh. The Museum displays PEZ dispensers in creative ways, reenacting historic events and fantasy scenes such as a castle and a haunted house. There's also a PEZ gift shop, in case you need a refill for your own PEZ dispenser.

Josiah White II Canal Boat Rides and Hugh Moore Park (all ages) 🔺 👥

Hugh Moore Park (look for Canal Boat signs); (610) 559–6613. Rides available first Saturday in May to mid-June: Tuesday through Friday 9:45 A.M. to 2:20 P.M., Saturday, Sunday, and Memorial Day 1:30 to 4:30 P.M. From mid-June to Labor Day: Monday through Saturday 10:30 A.M. to 5:00 P.M., Sunday 12:45 to 5:00 P.M. Weekends in September: Saturday, Sunday, and Labor Day 1:30 to 4:00 P.M. Fares: adults, $$; children 3 to 15, $.

A costumed interpreter takes you on a forty-minute ride on a mule-drawn canal boat. Special evening rides with dinner and music are available, as are charter rides for groups.

While in Hugh Moore Park, you may wish to take advantage of the park's trails, pavilions, picnic areas, and playground. The Locktender's House Museum re-creates the life of a locktender and his family.

Upper Black Eddy

Ringing Rocks 🏕️

Ringing Rocks Road, west of Upper Black Eddy; (215) 757–0571; www.buckscounty.org.

This National Park includes an amazing three-and-one-half-acre field of boulders. If you (gently!) strike these rocks, they ring like bells! You might want to bring along some kind of hammer, but if you forget, you can even use smaller rocks to make the rocks ring.

Over the years legends grew up about the origins of Ringing Rocks. Maybe it was an Indian ceremonial site, some said, maybe a witches' meeting place, or a UFO landing site. But in reality, Ringing Rocks is the result of millions of years of geologic activity. But magical nonetheless.

Sneakers or rubber-soled shoes recommended. Please be careful not to chip or harm the rocks.

Where to Stay

IN BUCKS COUNTY

Best Western New Hope Inn, 6426 Lower York Road, Doylestown; (215) 862–5221. Country setting, pool, restaurant.

Holiday Inn Select—Bucks County, 4700 Street Road, PA Turnpike, exit 28, Trevose; (215) 364–2000 or (800) HOLIDAY. Indoor pool. Sesame Place packages available. Kids eat free.

IN MONTGOMERY COUNTY

Doubletree Guest Suites, Plymouth Meeting, 640 West Germantown Pike, Plymouth Meeting; (610) 834–8300 or (800) 222–TREE; www.doubletreeplymouth.com. Suite accommodations, restaurant, indoor pool.

The Inn at King of Prussia By Best Western, 127 South Gulph Road, King of Prussia; (610) 265–4500. Convenient to Valley Forge National Historic Park as well as King of Prussia shopping. Outdoor pool.

McIntosh Inn, 260 North Gulph Road, King of Prussia; (610) 768–9500 or (800)

444–2775. Next to King of Prussia mall. Great rates for families.

McIntosh Inn, US 1 and Route 352 South, Media; (800) 444–2775. Convenient to Brandywine River Museum, Brandywine Battlefield, Chadds Ford, etc.

The Philadelphia Marriott West, 111 Crawford Avenue, West Conshahacken; (610) 941–5600 or (800) 237–3639. Convenient to Valley Forge, Philadelphia, Main Line, and Manayunk.

For More Information

Bucks County, (800) 836–2825; www .bctc.org.

Bucks County Tourist Commission, Inc., (800) 836–BUCKS or (215) 345– 4552; www.bctc.org.

Chester County Tourist Bureau, Inc., (800) 228–9933 or (610) 280–6145; www.brandywinevalley.com.

Delaware County Convention and Visitors Bureau, Inc., (800) 343–3983 or (610) 565–3679; www.brandywine country.org.

Lehigh Valley Convention and Visitors Bureau, Inc., (800) 747–0561 or (610) 882–9200; www.lehighvalleypa.org.

Montgomery County Historic Sites, www.montcopa.org.

Nazareth Area Visitor Center, 201 North Main Street, Nazareth 18064; (610) 759–9174.

New Hope—Village of New Hope, Greater New Hope Chamber of Commerce, P.O. Box 633, New Hope 18938; (215) 862–3730; www.newhopepa.com.

Valley Forge Convention and Visitors Bureau, (800) 441–3549 or (610) 834– 1550; www.valleyforge.org.

New Hope Information Center, 1 West Mechanic Street, New Hope 18938; (215) 862–5880.

Hershey–
Pennsylvania
Dutch Country

H ershey–Pennsylvania Dutch Country beckons with amusement parks, historical sites, Pennsylvania Dutch arts and crafts, and lots of train rides. The year 2005 is the inaugural year of Lancaster's own new minor league baseball team, the Lancaster Barnstormers! Their beautiful new ballpark is located in downtown Lancaster on North Prince Street and Harrisburg Pike. This is the Keystone State's classic countryside, with Amish farms and roadside markets. It was also the site of the Battle of Gettysburg, where more American lives were lost than in any other single battle in U.S. history.

Harrisburg, the state capital on the shores of the Susquehanna, is a great place to visit. City Island, once abandoned, has been transformed into a family-entertainment

Faith & Emily's
FavoriteAttractions
in Hershey–Pennsylvania Dutch Country

1. Hersheypark, Hershey

2. Strasburg Rail Road, Strasburg

3. Railroad Museum of Pennsylvania, Strasburg

4. Whitaker Center for Science and the Arts, Harrisburg

5. State Museum of Pennsylvania, Harrisburg

6. *Pride of the Susquehanna* riverboat, Harrisburg

7. Fishing on the Yellow Breeches River, Boiling Springs

8. Herr Foods, Inc., Nottingham

9. Gettysburg National Military Park, Gettysburg

10. Middletown and Hummelstown Railroad, Middletown

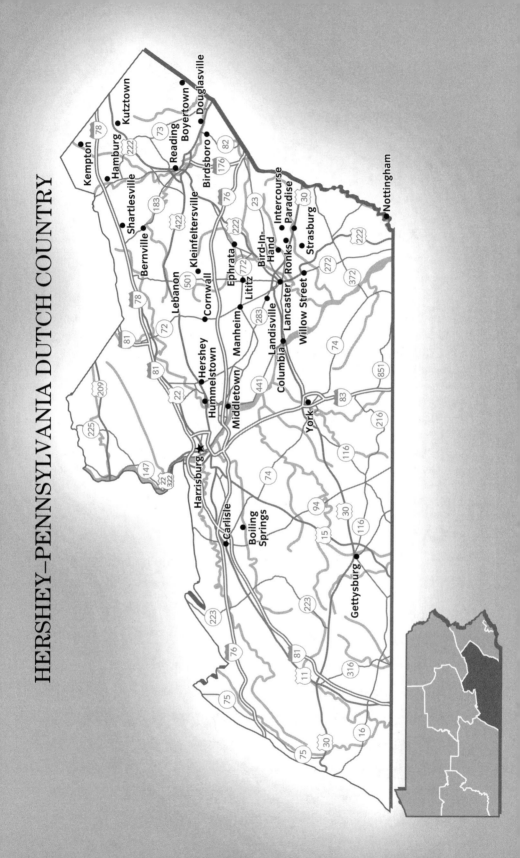

HERSHEY–PENNSYLVANIA DUTCH COUNTRY

spot, with miniature golf, the *Pride of the Susquehanna* riverboat, Class AA baseball, a children's railroad, and more.

Kids delight in Hershey, ChocolateTown USA, with its streetlights shaped like chocolate kisses and its triple helping of kid-friendly attractions—Hersheypark, ZooAmerica, and Chocolate World.

Some 70,000 Plain People live in Lancaster County, members of communities such as the Amish, Brethren, and Mennonites. Plain People appreciate it when tourists respect their privacy and dislike of cameras. Visits to The People's Place, the Amish Farm, and "The Amish Experience" will present important opportunities to teach your children sensitivity.

Families who visit Pennsylvania Dutch Country often comment on the food: It's abundant and inexpensive. Family-style restaurants abound, with diners seated at large tables and delicious, simple food passed around in large bowls.

A reader asked about driving on country roads in Lancaster County. If you take Route 772 starting in Intercourse and continuing toward Columbia, this well-marked road loops through the county, past Amish and Mennonite farms. You can stop at a farm stand and buy vegetables or preserves from an Amish child. You'll poke through

Faith & Emily's
FavoriteEvents
in Hershey–Pennsylvania Dutch Country

- **Greater Harrisburg Arts Festival** (Memorail Day weekend); (717) 238–5180.

- **Civil War Reenactments at Gettysburg National Military Park,** (717) 338–1525; www.gettysburgreenactment.com.

- **Kutztown Pennsylvania German Festival,** Kutztown Fairgrounds, Kutztown (nine days surrounding July 4); (888) 674–6136; www.kutztownfestival.com.

- **Pennsylvania Renaissance Faire** (late summer to early fall); (717) 665–7021; www.parenaissancefaire.com.

- **Fort Hunter Day** (September); (717) 599–5751.

- **Hersheypark Creatures of the Night** (October); (717) 534–3860 or (800) HERSHEY; www.hersheypa.com.

- **Dickens of a Christmas** (November through December); (717) 665–7021.

- **Hersheypark Christmas Candylane** (November through December); (717) 534–3860 or (800) HERSHEY; www.hersheypa.com.

little towns like Lititz, stumble upon quilt and craft shops, and admire scenic overlooks. The staff at the Pennsylvania Dutch Convention and Visitors Bureau can help
you map out your own route, taking into consideration your own interests and the
season.

The Pennsylvania Dutch area is a great place for a farm vacation. For more information on a vacation of any type in Pennsylvania Dutch Country, call the Pennsylvania
Dutch Convention and Visitors Bureau at (717) 299–8901. To learn about farm vacations, write to the Pennsylvania Farm Vacation Association, Pennsylvania Department
of Agriculture, Marketing Department, 2301 North Cameron Street, Harrisburg
17110–9408. A list of farm B&Bs is included in this chapter.
Here are some useful contacts:

- **Gettysburg Convention and Visitors Bureau** (Adams County); (800) 337–5015
  or (717) 334–6274; www.gettysburg.com.

- **PA Capital Regions Vacation Bureau, Inc.** (Cumberland, Dauphin, Franklin,
  Lebanon, and Perry Counties); (877) PA–PULSE; or (717) 231–7788; www.pa
  capitalregions.com.

- **Pennsylvania Dutch Convention and Visitors Bureau** (Lancaster County);
  (800) PA–DUTCH or (717) 299–8901; www.padutchcountry.com.

- **Reading and Berks County Visitors Bureau;** (800) 443–6610 or (610) 375–
  4085; www.readingberkspa.com.

- **York County Convention and Visitors Bureau;** (888) 858–YORK or (717) 848–
  4000; www.yorkpa.org.

- **The Pennsylvania Dutch Country Welcome Center;** www.800padutch.com.

Kempton

Hawk Mountain Sanctuary (ages 8 and up) 🏛 🐦

**Five miles east of Route 61, north of Hamburg, off Route 895; (610) 756–6000; www
.hawkmountain.org.The visitor center is open daily year-round 9:00 A.M. to 5:00 P.M.;
extended hours in fall. Admission is $$ for adults, $ for seniors and children 6 to 12.**

Every year about 75,000 visitors "flock" to Hawk Mountain nature-observation area to
watch the many species of hawks and eagles that pass through the area on their
annual migrations. During busy fall weekends, as many as a dozen very helpful
interns, volunteers, and staff members are available to interpret the spectacle of
migration for visitors.

Wind and weather conditions have a great impact on the birds, so plan your visit
based on the weather. Before you go, be sure to check the Web site for weather con-
ditions, directions, and specific information on which species you are likely to see

that day. Bring binoculars (very important), wear a jacket, and pack a lunch because there's no snack bar. But remember that you'll be carrying home all your trash; there are no garbage cans at the lookout and you are responsible for any food wrappers, cans, or bottles you bring along. You might also want to bring along something soft to sit on.

Children should be reminded that noise may frighten the birds. We recommend taking the kids on the rocky Escarpment Trail so that they can burn off some energy before arriving at North Lookout.

WK&S Railroad Line (all ages)

Take Route 143 North or 737 North into Kempton and follow signs to WK&S Railroad. For schedules and more information, call (610) 756–6469 or go to www.kempton train.com. The steam train runs on Sunday from May through October and on Satur- day during June, July, August, and October. The diesel train runs on Saturday in June and August. Fares are $$ for adults, $ for children ages 3 to 11. Children under 3 ride free.

The train ride on the Wanamaker, Kempton, and Southern is about 6 miles round-trip and takes about forty minutes. Pack a picnic and have the train drop you off at a trackside grove. You can ride all day if you like. A Santa Claus Special rides the rails in December; in October, it's time for the Harvest Moon Special. Please note that although the train is sometimes known as the Hawk Mountain Line, it does not actu- ally go to Hawk Mountain.

Kutztown

Crystal Cave (ages 8 and up) 🚌

Situated between Allentown and Reading off U.S. Route 222 at Crystal Cave and Valley Roads. For information and the schedule of guided tours, call (610) 683–6765; www.crystalcavepa.com. Admission: $$ for adults, $ for children ages 4 to 11.

Crystal Cave, discovered in 1871, is the oldest operating cave in Pennsylvania. Just use your imagination and you can see the ice-cream cone, the crystal ballroom, the giant's tooth, and the prairie dogs inside the geological formations here. After your underground adventure, try some of the free activities such as the nature trail, pic- nic area, and Amish buggy display.

This cave is probably less strenuous than some, with railings and walkways. No strollers are permitted in the cave, so put the baby in a backpack, if possible. The Main Inn has a large restroom and lounge, but no changing table. Picnic tables are available, some covered. You can eat at the Pennsylvania Dutch Fast Food Restau- rant, Sugar Shack, and ice-cream shop, open seasonally. Miniature golf is also avail- able for a fee.

Reading

In 2001 the Reading Phillies opened their Reading Phillies Pool Pavilion at GPU Stadium. Now, a day of AA baseball is even more fun for families and groups, with picnic tables, swimming, and cascading waterfalls. Water cannons erupt from the pool whenever the Phillies score a run. For details check www. readingphillies.com or call (610) 375–8469.

In 2001, the Sovereign Center opened, as well as the Sovereign Center for the Performing Arts. The Sovereign Center hosts many concerts and ice shows, and is also home to the newly franchised Reading Royals Ice Hockey team. For information check www.sovereigncenter.com or www.royalshockey.com.

The Reading Public Museum (610–371–5850, www.readingpublicmuseum.org) boasts an impressive collection of both art and science exhibits.

Reading Public Museum

500 Museum Road; (610) 371–5850; www.readingpublicmuseum.org. Adults $$, children 4–17 $, children under 4, free. Open Tuesday 11:00 A.M. to 5:00 P.M., Wednesday 11:00 A.M. to 8:00 P.M., Thursday through Saturday 11:00 A.M. to 5:00 P.M. and Sunday noon to 5:00 P.M. Closed Monday and major holidays.

The Reading Public Museum boasts an impressive collection of both art and science exhibits, as well as an arboretum.

Hamburg

To describe Cabela's as an outdoorsman's superstore doesn't begin to tell the story. In the first year of operations in Pennsylvania, Cabela's attracted nearly four million visitors.

Cabela's

100 Cabela Drive, near the intersection of Interstate 78 and Route 61; (610) 929–7000, www.cabelas.com. Open Monday through Saturday, 8:00 A.M. to 9:00 P.M., Sunday 10:00 A.M. to 8:00 P.M.

The largest of Cabela's retail stores and the only one in Pennsylvania, this 250,000-square-foot superstore has become a tourist destination in itself. Cabela's features a huge walk-through aquarium, an indoor mountain complete with waterfall, and more than 800 mounted wildlife specimens in museum-quality dioramas. It also has a shooting gallery, archery range, and a restaurant.

Shartlesville

Roadside America 🔲

109 Roadside Drive, near exit 23 off I–78/U.S. Route 22; (610) 488–6241; www. road sideamericainc.com. Summer (July through Labor Day): Open daily 9:00 A.M. to 6:30 P.M., weekends 9:00 A.M. to 7:00 P.M. Winter (September through June): Open daily 10:00 A.M. to 5:00 P.M., weekends 10:00 A.M. to 6:00 P.M. Admission is $. Children 5 and under enter free. Group rates available.

One of our readers recently wrote us a letter suggesting that we include a favorite destination of her family, Roadside America. This unique indoor miniature village is a wonderful piece of Americana. One man, Laurence Gieringer, created this scale model during more than sixty years of meticulous work. There are trains chugging through tunnels and over bridges, a gristmill, a trolley, and even a tiny fountain in the miniature zoo.

Young children may have to be lifted up to see some of the displays, but they'll love it anyhow.

Boyertown

Boyertown Museum of Historic Vehicles (all ages) 🔲

85 South Walnut; (610) 367–2090; www.boyertownmuseum.org; e-mail: museum@ enter.net. Open Tuesday through Sunday 9:30 A.M. to 4:00 P.M. Closed major holidays. Admission is $. Children under 6 enter free. Reservations are required for groups.

During the early days of the automobile industry, dozens of manufacturers built cars, trucks, and motorcycles right here in southeastern Pennsylvania. More than fifty of these rare automobile products can be seen in the Boyertown Museum of Historic Vehicles, along with examples of the horse-powered vehicles they eventually made obsolete.

Every Labor Day weekend for the past forty years, the museum has celebrated all "wheeled classicalia" at its annual Duryea Day event.

Douglassville

Mary Merritt Doll Museum and Merritt's Museum of Early Childhood (ages 10 and up) 🔲

Located between Pottstown and Reading on U.S. Route 422. Call (610) 385–3809 for the doll museum and (610) 385–3408 (www.merritts.com) for the museum of early childhood. Open Monday and Wednesday through Saturday 10:00 A.M. to 4:30 P.M.; Sunday and holidays 1:00 to 5:00 P.M. Closed holidays. Combination admission to both museums is $.

At the doll museum, your children can see thousands of antique dolls, the oldest dating from the 1660s. More than fifty dollhouses are on display. Just stroll around the toy trains, toy boats, rag dolls, pull toys, baby dolls, hobby horses, and paper dolls. We recommend that parents consider their children's maturity level; very little children might be frustrated that they can't touch the displays.

The museum of early childhood was designed to give other family members something to do while the doll enthusiasts were in the doll museum. It includes colonial and Victorian antiques. Each museum has its own gift shop. Wheelchair accessible.

Birdsboro

Daniel Boone Homestead (all ages) 🏛️ 🚐 ⛺

400 Daniel Boone Road; (610) 582–4900. Open Tuesday through Saturday 9:00 A.M. to 5:00 P.M., Sunday noon to 5:00 P.M. year-round. Admission is $. Family rate $$$.

Daniel Boone was born in 1734 and grew up in a log cabin at Daniel Boone Homestead. Only the foundation of the original cabin remains, but the oldest section of the log cabin that stands here now was built in 1750, around the time the Boones moved away. Here you can see a blacksmith's shop, smokehouse, bake oven, and sawmill. Children especially enjoy the horses and sheep. There are facilities available for picnicking and camping. The second floor of the house is not wheelchair accessible, but disabled visitors may view a video of it.

Bernville

Koziar's Christmas Village (all ages)

782 Christmas Village Road, 7 miles past the Reading Airport in Bernville, off Route 183; (610) 488–1110; www.koziarschristmasvillage.com. From November 1 to Thanksgiving, open Friday 6:00 to 9:00 P.M., Saturday and Sunday 5:30 to 9:30 P.M. From Thanksgiving to January 1, open Monday through Friday 6:00 to 9:00 P.M., Saturday and Sunday 5:00 to 9:30 P.M. Admission is $$ per person; children under 5 enter free.

Named "Best Outdoor Christmas Display in the World" by *Display World Magazine,* Koziar's Christmas Village is a holiday tradition—and every year it's new, improved, and all handmade. More than 500,000 lights sparkle on the lakeside house, along with its walkways, trees, and ten outbuildings including Santa's post office and toy shop. There are more than thirty buildings, about eight of which can be entered, but Koziar's is mostly an outdoor experience, so dress accordingly.

Kleinfeltersville

Middle Creek Wildlife Management Area (ages 8 and up)

Hopeland Road. Visitor center: (717) 733–1512; www.pgc.state.pa.us. Open February 1 to the day before Thanksgiving, Tuesday through Sunday 8:00 A.M. to 4:00 P.M. and Sunday noon to 5:00 P.M. **Free.**

Bundle up, bring your binoculars, and come to the Middle Creek Wildlife Management Area in February or March and you might see thousands of tundra swans and snow geese. In spring and fall there are many other species of migrating waterfowl. There are also 6,254 acres of state game land, with seven trails, plus fishing and hunting in designated areas only, including one trout stream that's accessible to the disabled. Picnic areas are available, but you must not feed the birds. Check the Web site to find out current migration patterns.

There are a number of annual events at Middle Creek. The first full weekend in August brings the annual art show. During the third full weekend in September, you can see an exhibit of woodcarving including decoys. Also in September is the annual Pennsylvania State Goose-Calling and Duck-Calling Championships.

Lebanon

The Daniel Weaver Company (ages 8 and up)

Located at the corner of Fifteenth and Weavertown Road, ½ mile off U.S. 422 in Lebanon. For more information call (717) 274–6100 or (800) WEAVERS; www.lebanon-bologna.com. Open Monday through Saturday 9:00 A.M. to 4:00 P.M.; **free** admission. Free tours also are available.

Lebanon is the one town where you can see how genuine Lebanon bologna is made. The Daniel Weaver Company, which produces both Weaver's famous Lebanon Bologna and Baum's Bologna, is the oldest commercial manufacturer of Lebanon bologna in the United States. Here you can see the outdoor smokehouses, visit exhibits, enjoy **free** samples, and visit their retail store.

Cornwall

Cornwall Iron Furnace (ages 8 and up)

Rexmont Road at Boyd Street, off Route 419; (717) 272–9711; www.phmc.state.pa.us. Open daily Tuesday through Saturday 9:00 A.M. to 5:00 P.M., Sunday noon to 5:00 P.M. from June through August. From September through May, open Tuesday through Saturday, 10:00 A.M. to 4:00 P.M., Sunday noon to 4:00 P.M. Open Memorial Day, Independence Day, and Labor Day. Admission is $.

The massive stone furnace, steam-powered air-blast machinery, and several related buildings survive intact. Cornwall Furnace cast cannon barrels for the Revolutionary and Civil Wars. Cornwall Iron Furnace operated from the 1740s until the 1880s. A guide takes you through the iron-making complex, the highlight of which is the 32-foot-tall furnace.

Mount Hope Estate, Pennsylvania Renaissance Faire (all ages) 🎵

Mount Hope Estate. Call (717) 665–7021 or check www.parenaissancefaire.com for details on schedules and admission.

On weekends from August through mid-October, join the raucous revelry of the Pennsylvania Renaissance Faire. Meet sixteenth-century knaves and wenches, jesters, pirates, princesses, and knights who will immerse your family in a spectacle of living theater. Events include jousting, human chess, children's games, crafts, short plays such as Robin Hood, and dancing. From the end of October through mid-November, you can be mystified at "Edgar Allan Poe Evermore." ("Edgar Allan Poe Evermore" is macabre and includes direct readings from Poe. It is recommended for older children, from thirteen up.) From Thanksgiving weekend until after Christmas, the estate is decked out quite differently for a festive "Dickens of a Christmas," recommended for all ages.

Lititz

Julius Sturgis Pretzel House (ages 6 and up)

219 East Main Street; (717) 626–4354; www.sturgispretzel.com. Open year-round Monday through Saturday 9:30 A.M. to 4:30 P.M. Closed Sunday. Admission is $.

You can actually twist your own pretzel here at the first pretzel bakery in the country.

Ephrata

Ephrata is an interesting town where you may wish to browse in the art galleries and craft shops. Stop by at Artworks at Doneckers, 100 North State Street (717–738–9503).

Ephrata Cloister (ages 10 and up)

632 West Main Street (Route 272 and U.S. Route 322); (717) 733–6600; www.ephrata cloister.org. Open Monday to Saturday 9:00 A.M. to 5:00 P.M. and Sunday noon to 5:00 P.M. On Monday through Saturday, tours leave at 10:00 and 11:00 A.M., and 1:00, 2:00, 3:00, and 4:00 P.M. Admission is $$ for adults and $ for ages 6 to 17. Children under 6 are free.

Older children may be interested in learning about a true alternative lifestyle at one time practiced in the eighteenth century at Ephrata Cloister. Here you can step into another reality in twelve restored buildings where hymns still seem to echo.

The guided tour starts with a film, *Anticipating Paradise,* and proceeds through three of the ten restored buildings. There are two cemeteries, a physician's house, a bakery, and more. Candlelight tours are offered in December. Most of the historic structures have some limits to wheelchair accessibility.

From March through October, on the second Sunday of the month, the Cloister features a special "themed" day, with extra demonstrations and sometimes hands-on activities, at the regular admission price. Check the Web site for each month's theme.

Intercourse

Plain & Fancy Farm 🔒

3121 Old Philadelphia Pike on Route 340 between Bird-in-Hand and Intercourse; (717) 768–4400; www.amishexperience.com. Open daily. Call ahead for hours.

Easily accessible to Mt. Hope on the opposite side of Route 340 between Bird-in-Hand and Intercourse, you'll find Plain & Fancy Farm with its buggy rides and Pennsylvania Dutch crafts and food. There are a lot of things to do at Plain & Fancy, including buggy rides, "The Amish Experience," and Amish dining. Also at Plain & Fancy, you can visit the Amish Country Homestead (717–768–3600, ext. 10).

You can also take a guided bus tour of Amish country starting at Plain & Fancy Farm. Admission to each attraction may be purchased separately, or you may choose a combination ticket to the theater and homestead, or even a super-saver ticket that includes the theater, homestead, and guided bus tour. While here, pick up a copy of *The Amish Country News.*

Amish Country Tours ($$$) depart from the Amish Experience Theater, stopping at roadside stands, bake shops, and craft shops along the scenic roads of the Amish farmlands. Children receive a worksheet and a small gift to make the tour more fun.

Amish Country Homestead (all ages) 🏛

Plain & Fancy Farm, 3121 Old Philadelphia Pike; (717) 768–8400; www.amishnews.com. Hours subject to change seasonally. Admission to the homestead is $$ for adults, $ for children ages 4 to 11. Combination tickets available for homestead, theater, and bus tours.

This is the only Amish house open for guided tours that has received designation as a Lancaster County Heritage Site. The family depicted in the homestead is the Fisher family, also featured in *Jacob's Choice,* seen at The Amish Experience/FX Theater.

Aaron and Jessica's Buggy Rides (all ages)

Plain & Fancy Farm; (717) 768–4400; www.buggyrides.com.

Lancaster County offers several opportunities to ride in a Pennsylvania Dutch buggy, but only one ride is owned and operated by an Amish family: Aaron and Jessica's Buggy Rides at Plain & Fancy Farm. The Web site offers a virtual tour and answers questions about the Amish and Mennonites.

Amish **Buggy Rides**

- **Abe's Buggy Rides;** (717) 392–1794; www.800padutch.com/abes.html.

- **Ed's Buggy Rides;** (717) 687–0360; www.edsbuggyrides.com.

- **Aaron and Jessica's Buggy Rides,** at Plain & Fancy Farm; (717) 768–4400; www.amishbuggyrides.com.

The Amish Experience/FX Theater (ages 7 and up) 🎵
Plain & Fancy Farm; (717) 768–8400 or (717) 768–3600; www.amishexperience.com.
Hours subject to change seasonally. Admission to theater only is $$ for adults, $ for
children 4 to 11. Combination tickets available to homestead, theater, and bus tour.

In a multimedia interactive "experiential theater" that defies labeling, a well-researched, forty-minute program immerses the audience in the world of the Amish. This program was remastered in 2003, with improved visuals and added sound design. The unique theater has five different image areas showing different pictures, and special effects. The show *Jacob's Choice* introduces a fictional Amish teenager and his family. Although younger kids will be entertained, children ages seven and up will get the point of what it means to be Amish.

Where to Eat Amish–Style with Kids

- **Amish Barn Restaurant,** Route 340 between Bird-In-Hand and Intercourse; (717) 768–8886; www.amishbarnpa.com. Children's menu, petting zoo, gift shop, open seven days a week. Kids eat **free.**

- **Bird-in-Hand Family Restaurant,** Old Philadelphia Pike, 5 miles east of Lancaster on Route 340; (717) 768–8266; www.bird-in-hand.com/restaurant. Menu-style.

- **Harvest Drive Family Restaurant,** Intercourse; (717) 768–7186 or (800) 233–0176; www.harvestdrive.com. Great view. Full menu or family-style.

- **Plain & Fancy Farm,** 3121 Old Philadelphia Pike; (717) 768–4400.

Manheim

Kreider Farms 🐄

Route 72 (ten minutes from Route 283) at 1461 Lancaster Road; (717) 665–5039; www.kreiderfarms.com. Farm tour hours: Monday, Wednesday, and Friday 9:30 and 11:30 A.M. by reservation only.

"Daddy, where does milk come from?" Here's a great way to answer this perennial question. At Kreider Farms, see cows milked on a carousel and learn how the milk gets from the farm to the supermarket shelf. Then top off your visit with lunch or dinner at Kreider Farms restaurant, adjacent to the farm tour. (Kreider Farms also has restaurants at three other locations in the area.)

Bird-in-Hand

Americana Museum of Bird-in-Hand (ages 6 and up) 🏛️

Route 340 East (2709 Old Philadelphia Pike); (717) 391–9780; www.bird-in-hand.com/americanamuseum. Open April through November, Tuesday through Saturday 10:00 A.M. to 5:00 P.M. (Last tour begins at 4:40 P.M.) Admission is $.

The Americana Museum focuses on American life from 1890 to 1930. Touring this indoor complex with a self-guided tour pamphlet, you can stroll through a re-created town of the period including a fully stocked country general store and eight shops common to the era. A children's activity sheet is available.

Weavertown One-Room Schoolhouse (all ages) 🏛️

Route 340, east of Bird-in-Hand; (717) 768–3976 or (717) 291–1888; www.800padutch .com/wvrtown.html. Open March to April 11, Saturday and Sunday 10:00 A.M. to 5:00 P.M. From April 12 to October 24, open daily 10:00 A.M. to 5:00 P.M. From October 25 to November 30, open Saturday and Sunday 10:00 A.M. to 4:00 P.M. Closed remainder of year. Admission is $.

Class is in session, with thirty animated figures of a teacher and pupils in the Weavertown One-Room Schoolhouse. The building, desks, and blackboard are original. The school was built in 1877 and held classes for close to one hundred years.

Abe's Buggy Rides (all ages) 🐴

2596 Old Philadelphia Pike; (717) 392–1794; www.800padutch.com/abes.html. Open year-round, but closed on Sunday. Admission is $$$ for adults and $$ for children ages 3 to 12; children under 3 are free.

This authentic Amish buggy ride passes by beautiful farmland and farmhouses. The driver tells about the area and answers questions. Check the Web site for a coupon.

Ronks

Amazing Maize Maze (all ages)

Cherry-Crest Farm; (717) 687–6843; www.amazingmaze.com. Open seasonally. Call ahead for current admission prices.

The Discovery Channel has named this "the World's Biggest Free-Standing Mind-Bender." In 2004 the annual Amazing Maize Maze featured a five-acre cornfield sculpted in the shape of an Amish horse and buggy. A visit here begins with a staff member who explains it all to get you started. Then, try to find your way out of the maze. As you work your way through, you'll come upon clues, tunnel slides, watering stations, all nine planets, rest areas, the "waters of Neptune," and more. There are two bridges that afford a complete view of the maze. Average time to complete the maze is about an hour but you could spend much longer exploring the farm. Watch for different designs in coming years. There are also four smaller mazes, a petting zoo, hayride, a "snack shack," and special events. Many people arrive to explore the maze by way of the Strasburg Rail Road.

The Outhouse (ages 4 and up) 🔒

The Village of Dutch Delights, Dienner's Restaurant Complex, 2853 Lincoln Highway East (U.S. Route 30), (717) 687–9580. In winter, open weekends only. During the rest of the year, open Monday through Saturday 9:00 A.M. to 6:00 P.M.

This combination store and funhouse features a "man-eating chicken" and "free foot of chocolate." A country store full of surprises and puns!

Strasburg

A reporter for the *New York Times* called the Strasburg area "command central for railroad buffs." Here in the town of Strasburg, transportation enthusiasts can learn about toy trains, real trains, classic cars, and more. It's the perfect place to take little boys who are "into" vehicles.

Railroad Museum of Pennsylvania (all ages) 🚂

300 Gap Road, on Route 741 East; (717) 687–8628; www.rrmuseumpa.org. Open Monday through Saturday 9:00 A.M. to 5:00 P.M., Sunday noon to 5:00 P.M. Closed Monday from November through April. Admission is $$ for adults and $ for children 6 to 12. A family rate is available.

The Railroad Museum of Pennsylvania will entrance your junior engineers. It's almost overwhelming to walk into the huge collection of locomotives and rolling stock at this museum, which specializes in railroad trains built or operated in Pennsylvania. Rolling Stock Hall is designed with a balcony and a pit so that you can see the forty-six locomotives and passenger cars from different angles. The new Stewart Junction Railway Education Center, located in a late-Victorian-era freight station, offers hands-on activities. Outdoors you can see some thirty-three more cars. The HO-scale layout and education center are open selected hours. There are changing tables in both the men's and women's restrooms. Wheelchair accessible.

Strasburg Rail Road (all ages) 🏛

Route 741 East; (717) 687–7522; www.strasburgrailroad.com. Hours vary seasonally. Coach fares are $$ for adults, $ for children 3 to 11. Fares for open-air cars and deluxe lounge cars are $$. Children under 3 ride free.

After you've seen the railroad museum, cross the street for a forty-five-minute ride on the Strasburg Rail Road. Food service is available. The East Strasburg Rail Road Station was built in 1882 and includes railroad gift shops and the Dining Car restaurant. The Strasburg Rail Road is the nation's oldest short-line railroad.

Choo Choo Barn—Traintown USA® (all ages) 🧺🍽

Route 741 East; (717) 687–7911; www.choochoobarn.com. From April through December, open 10:00 A.M. to 5:00 P.M. daily. Closed January 1 through March for annual renovations. Admission is $$ for adults, $ for children 5 to 12. Children under 5 enter free.

The Choo Choo Barn has twenty-two operating miniature trains that chug through 130 animated scenes. If your kids are like ours, you'll want to visit Thomas's Trackside Station, a shop devoted exclusively to Thomas the Tank Engine and his friends from the Island of Sodor. All displays and restrooms are wheelchair accessible, but not all the shops. If you get hungry, there's a picnic area, candy shop, and Isaac's Restaurant and Deli.

National Toy Train Museum (all ages) 🧺

300 Paradise Lane; (717) 687–8976; www.traincollectors.org. Open daily May through October 10:00 A.M. to 5:00 P.M. Open weekends only in April, November, and December. Admission is $.

This museum features metal electric trains and five operating layouts with buttons for the kids to push. And they let you blow the whistle! There is also a short video, plus display cases full of trains. The museum's theater shows cartoons and comedy films about trains. The gift shop offers a great selection of train-related toys.

Ed's Buggy Rides (all ages) 🐎

Route 896 directly across from Sight & Sound Theatre; (717) 687–0360; www.eds buggyrides.com. Fares: $$ for adults, $ for children 6 to 12.

Now that you've seen trains and cars, you can include horse-drawn vehicles by taking a 3-mile ride at Ed's Buggy Rides.

Amish Village (all ages) 🏛

Two miles north of Strasburg on Route 896; (717) 687–8511; www.800padutch.com/ avillage.html. Hours vary seasonally. Admission is $$ for adults, $ for children 6 to 12.

Tours of the Old Order farmhouse at the Amish Village, which dates back to 1840, emphasize the culture of the Plain People. There's also a one-room school, a windmill, and a blacksmith shop. The smokehouse sells specialty foods like apple butter, candies, and cider. There is a wheelchair-accessible restroom with a changing table, but the second floor of the house is not accessible. In December special house tours feature hot mulled cider.

Sight & Sound Theatre (ages 8 and up) 🎵

Route 896; reservations: (717) 687–7800; www.noahonstage.com. Tickets are $$$$ for adults and $$$ for children.

The specifically Christian shows at Sight & Sound's two huge theaters will remind you of something from the glory days of Radio City Music Hall. Recent spectacular productions have included *Noah, Behold the Lamb, The Miracle of Christmas* and starting in 2005, *Ruth. Noah,* for example, featured a four-story ark, 56 actors, 100 live animals, and 125 animatronics (animated figures).

Nottingham

Herr Foods, Inc. (preschool and up)

At intersection of Route 272 and Route 1 in Nottingham. For details and reservations call (800) 284–7488 or (800) 63–SNACK; www.herrs.com. Tours are free, but reservations are requested. Open weekdays 8:00 A.M. to 5:00 P.M. Tours are conducted Monday through Thursday 9:00 A.M. to 3:00 P.M. and Friday 9:00 to 11:00 A.M.

You can see how Herr's snacks are made, and then try some chips still warm from the fryer at Herr Foods, Inc. Cutting-edge tour technology uses DVD screens for close-up viewing in production areas. Chipper's Cafe offers hot dogs, chicken nuggets, PB&J, pizza, and cookies. Wheelchair accessible, with a changing table in the women's room.

Willow Street

Hans Herr House (ages 8 and up) 🏛

1849 Hans Herr Drive; (717) 464–4438; www.hansherr.org. Open April through November 31, Monday through Saturday 9:00 A.M. to 4:00 P.M. Closed Sundays, Thanksgiving, and December 1 to March 31. Admission is $.

The date 1719 appears on the door lintel of the Hans Herr House. The Mennonite home is the oldest surviving home of European settlers in what is now Lancaster County. Andrew Wyeth, himself a relative of Hans Herr, created a well-known painting of the house.

Lancaster

Many of the nonprofit museums in the Lancaster area have cooperated in a joint ticketing program. Save your ticket stub from one museum, and when you go to another, you'll get a reduced rate. These museums include the Railroad Museum, Heritage Center Museum of Lancaster County, Ephrata Cloister, Wright's Ferry Mansion, National Association of Watch and Clock Collectors Museum, and many more.

Dutch Wonderland (ages 12 and under) 🎡
2249 US 30 East; (717) 291–1888 or (866) FUNATDW, (866) 386–2829; www.dutch wonderland.com. Open weekends in spring and fall and daily from Memorial Day to Labor Day. Admission includes everything but food and select activities and is $$$–$$$$. Wheelchair accessible.

Dutch Wonderland is still the family-oriented park you remember, only now it's had a $1.2 million makeover, and it has a new motto: A Kingdom for Kids! The new VR Voyager is a three-axis, computer-controlled motion simulator. A SONY Super Bright digital video compression system and Bose Acoustimass Ten surround-sound system create a virtual-reality experience with more than fifteen different action videos to choose from.

A new zero-depth water play area called Duke's Lagoon delights with bubbling geysers, tipping buckets, slides, and designated areas designed for toddlers, preschoolers, kids between five and eight years old, and kids nine to twelve years of age. You can meet the new Princess of Dutch Wonderland, who loves to read stories to kids in the park, and her sidekick Duke the Dragon.

New kid-friendly rides include Duke's Dozers, Froghopper, Off-Road Rally, and The Wonder Whip, and there's a new interactive play for families presented by Middle-earth Theatre.

Your six-year-old can drive an old-fashioned motorcar, your twelve-year-old can brave the Sky Princess roller coaster, your family can take a walk in the botanical gardens, and everyone can grab a burlap sack and race down the Giant slide. There are changing tables in both men's and women's rooms, and food offerings include chicken, pizza, and sandwiches.

Dutch Wonderland is next door to the Discover Lancaster County History Museum and within minutes of the Amish Farm and House, the Weavertown One-Room School, the Old Mill Stream Camping Manor, and a great deal of outlet shopping.

Amazing Hershey–Pennsylvania Dutch Facts

For exactly one day in 1777, Lancaster served as the U.S. capital.

North Museum of Natural History and Science (all ages)

400 College Avenue; (717) 291–3941; www.northmuseum.org. Open Tuesday through Saturday 9:00 A.M. to 5:00 P.M., Sunday 1:30 to 5:00 P.M. Admission is $.

The North Museum, on the campus of Franklin and Marshall College, offers collections of Native American artifacts, birds, fossils, minerals, and a planetarium. Children especially enjoy the Discovery Room and hands-on science and nature exhibits, and the herpetarium with more than forty live reptiles.

Discover Lancaster County History Museum (all ages)

2249 US 30 East; (717) 393–3679; www.discoverlancaster.com. For 2005: January 2 through April 30, open daily 9:00 A.M. to 4:00 P.M., Easter noon to 4:00 P.M. May 1 through 23, Sunday through Friday 9:00 A.M. to 5:00 P.M., Saturday 9:00 A.M. to 7:00 P.M. Memorial Day through Labor Day open 9:00 A.M. to 6:00 P.M. daily. September 7 through November 18, open daily 9:00 A.M. to 5:00 P.M., Friday, Saturday, and Sunday, 9:00 A.M. to 7:00 P.M. Closed Thanksgiving, Christmas, and New Year's Day. Admission is $$ for adults, $ for children ages 5 to 11. Children under 5 enter **free.**

When you see the animated exhibit in which Daniel Boone grows up before your eyes, you can put on a Daniel Boone hat and, using one-way mirror imaging, observe yourself transforming into Daniel Boone, too. Interactive exhibits include touchscreen computers. You can learn to count tree rings and twist pretzels. Employees are now dressed in period costume, and more educational items are offered in the gift shop.

Discover Lancaster County History Museum now joins Dutch Wonderland and Wonderland Mini-Golf as part of Dutch Wonderland Family Entertainment complex.

Amish Farm and House (ages 6 and up) 🏛

2395 US 30 East, ½ mile east of Dutch Wonderland; (717) 394–6185. Open daily at 8:30 A.M., the site closes at 4:00 P.M. in winter, 5:00 P.M. in spring and fall, and 6:00 P.M. in summer. On selected dates in September and October, hours are extended for kerosene-lamp tours. Admission is $$ for adults and $ for children 5 to 11.

This is the only operating Amish farm open to the public. The farm itself dates from the 1700s, the house from 1805. Guided tours show the house and describe the history, culture, and clothing of Old Order Amish. You can take a guided tour of the farm, with its barns, carriage sheds, springhouse, and animals. Also on the grounds is an Early-Americana museum. A food pavilion is open seasonally, and there are changing tables in both men's and women's rooms. Sheep shearing days are in April, and there are kerosene-lamp tours in the fall.

Hands-On House, Children's Museum of Lancaster
(ages 2 through 10) 🔵

721 Landis Valley Road; (717) 569–KIDS; www.handsonhouse.org. Admission is $. Open Labor Day through Memorial Day, Monday through Thursday, 11:00 A.M. to 4:00 P.M., Friday 11:00 A.M. to 8:00 P.M., Saturday 10:00 A.M. to 5:00 P.M., Sunday noon to 5:00 P.M. Memorial Day through Labor Day, open Monday through Thursday 10:00 A.M. to 5:00 P.M., Friday 10:00 A.M. to 8:00 P.M., Saturday 10:00 A.M. to 5:00 P.M., Sunday noon to 5:00 P.M.

The museum has eight interactive areas for children ages two through ten, including the exhibit "E-I-E-I-KNOW," which teaches kids about farming in Lancaster County through computer touch-screens, interactive games, and hands-on exhibits. The Hands-On House is on the grounds of the Landis Valley Museum, all on one level, completely wheelchair and stroller accessible.

Landis Valley Museum (elementary-school age) 🔵

2451 Kissel Hill Road; (717) 569–0401; www.landisvalleymuseum.org. Open year-round, Monday through Saturday 9:00 A.M. to 5:00 P.M., Sunday noon to 5:00 P.M. Closed some major holidays. Admission is $$ for adults and children 6 to 12. Children under 6 enter free.

The Landis Valley Museum is a Pennsylvania German living-history museum with fifteen historic buildings, including a farmhouse, tavern, country store, and inn.

Downtown Lancaster

Downtown Lancaster is worth a visit, offering the Central Market, Lancaster Newspapers' "Newseum," Steinman Park, and more. A walking tour is available. For information contact the Pennsylvania Dutch Convention and Visitors Bureau at (717) 299–8901 or (800) PA–DUTCH, ext. 4255.

Living the Experience (ages 8 and up) 🎵

Lancaster Bethel African Methodist Church, 512 East Strawberry Street; (800) 510–5899 ext. 113 or (717) 538–0427; www.livingtheundergroundrailroad.com. Performances February through December, Saturday 1:00 P.M. Additional performances for groups of thirty-five or more. For these groups, a meal is served after the performance.

This living-history performance intertwines storytelling and spirituals to reenact experiences of participants in the Underground Railroad in a vibrant and moving way.

Heritage Center of Lancaster County (all ages) 🏛

Penn Square; (717) 299–6440; www.lancasterheritage.com. The museum and hands-on room are open free year-round, Tuesday through Saturday 10:00 A.M. to 5:00 P.M. and Sunday noon to 5:00 P.M. Open daily from the day after Thanksgiving through December. Donations accepted.

The Heritage Center comprises two museums: the Lancaster Cultural History Museum and the new Lancaster Quilt and Textile Museum. In the Cultural History Museum, kids can pick up a children's guide designed for families and linked to a series of ten different interactive stations around the museum. In the midst of all the furniture, silver, paintings, needlework, folk art, and rifles, kids can try their hands at puzzles and games, paper-cutting, and more. The Quilt and Textile Museum is a feast of color and pattern.

Central Market (all ages) 🍴 🔒

West King Street on Penn Square; (717) 291–4739. Open Tuesday and Friday 6:00 A.M. to 4:30 P.M. and Saturday 6:00 A.M. to 2:00 P.M.

Next to the Heritage Center, breathe in the delicious smells of Amish baked goods coming from the Central Market, the site of which has been operating as a farmers' market since the 1730s.

James Buchanan's Wheatland (ages 10 and up) 🏛

1120 Marietta Avenue; (717) 392–8721; www.wheatland.org. Open daily April through November 10:00 A.M. to 4:00 P.M. and Friday through Monday in November. Also open selected days in December. Admission is $$ for adults and $ for seniors, students (up through college with ID), and children 6 to 11.

In spite of the pivotal role that Pennsylvania played in our history, the Keystone State produced only one U.S. president, James Buchanan. Located on the outskirts of downtown Lancaster, James Buchanan's Wheatland, Buchanan's home, is an excellent example of a Victorian home.

Hands-on tours and educational programs are offered for school groups and Scout troops.

Landisville

1852 Herr Family Homestead (ages 6 and up) 🏛

1756 Nissley Road; (717) 898–8822; www.herrhomestead.org. Open April 1 through October 31, Saturdays and Sundays 1:00 to 4:00 P.M.

Although open only seasonally, the folks at the 1852 Herr Family Homestead do a nice job for children. There is a pleasant park nearby if you'd like to pack a picnic lunch.

Columbia

National Association of Watch and Clock Collectors Museum (ages 8 and up) 🏛

514 Poplar Street, just off US 30; (717) 684–8261; www.nawcc.org. Open April through December, Tuesday through Saturday 10:00 A.M. to 5:00 P.M., Sunday noon to 4:00 P.M. Closed Monday and major holidays. January through March, open Tuesday through Saturday 10:00 A.M. to 4:00 P.M. Closed Sunday, Monday, and major holidays. Admission is $.

Now containing more than 12,000 items, this is the largest and most comprehensive horological collection in North America. Water clocks, candle clocks, sundials, musical clocks, grandfather clocks, wristwatches, pocket watches. . . . You've never seen so many kinds of timepieces as you'll find at the National Association of Watch and Clock Collectors Museum. Parents of school-morning slugabeds will get inspiration from the alarm-clock collection. For example, there's one alarm clock that gives the sleepyhead's big toe a yank. One tall musical clock runs seven days and plays seven different tunes.

Wright's Ferry Mansion (ages 10 and up) 🏛

Second and Cherry Streets; (717) 684–4325; www.ohwy.com/pa/w/wryfryman.htm. Open May through October, Tuesday, Wednesday, Friday, and Saturday 10:00 A.M. to 3:00 P.M. Last tour begins at 3:00 P.M. Admission is $$ for adults, $ for children ages 6 to 18.

Susanna Wright was known as the "bluestocking of the Susquehanna," but she was really more of a "Renaissance woman." (*Bluestocking* was a derogatory term for an intelligent unmarried woman.) At Wright's Ferry Mansion, you can get acquainted with this colorful but little-known character in American history. Wright operated a ferry here, drew up legal documents, raised silkworms, practiced medicine, and corresponded with people like Benjamin Franklin. The house also served as a station on the Underground Railroad.

York

Harley-Davidson, Inc. Antique Motorcycle Museum (all ages) 🏍️

1425 Eden Road, just off US 30; (717) 848–1177; www.harley-davidson.com. Museum tours are offered at specified times Monday through Friday. Plant tours are offered Monday through Friday 10:00 A.M. to 2:00 P.M. and are open to people over 12. No cameras, no sandals allowed on factory tours. Visitors under 18 must be accompanied by an adult. Visitors over 18 must present 2 valid, government-issued photo IDs. Visitors will pass through a metal detector. Call ahead to check for times of museum-only tours or to make reservations for factory tours. Free.

Our seven-year-old was disappointed to learn that kids under twelve are not allowed on the factory tours at Harley-Davidson, Inc. All ages are welcome, however, at the adjacent Harley-Davidson Museum, where antique motorcycles on display include police bikes, army bikes, and bikes owned by celebrities. Wheelchair accessible.

Hershey

If ever there were a town made for family enjoyment, it's Hershey, Pennsylvania. What child could resist the city that chocolate built, with Hersheypark as its main attraction. Even the streetlights are shaped like Hershey kisses! If you park your car at the Hersheypark entrance, you can get around town on foot. After you've enjoyed Hersheypark, ZooAmerica, and the other big attractions, if you're in the mood for something more low-key, there's a great playground on Cocoa Avenue near Chocolate Avenue.

Hershey's Chocolate World Visitors Center (all ages) 🔒

Hersheypark Drive; (717) 534–4900. Open year-round, free, from 9:00 A.M. to 5:00 P.M. in the off-season daily. Summer hours coincide with Hersheypark, when park is open. Admission to the chocolate tour is free.

Hershey's Chocolate World, one of America's most popular attractions, hosts nearly three million visitors a year, and entrance is free. Learn about the chocolate production process "bean-to-bar" through a free chocolate-making tour ride. You can also view *Hershey's Really Big 3D Show.*

Chocolate World has just added the new Hershey's Factory Works, where visitors are invited to be part of an interactive, imaginative chocolate factory. Get your own employee ID and factory worker's hat. Stop by the Kiss Works machine and you can package Hershey Kisses as they stream by on a conveyor belt. Have lunch at the Kit Kat "Gimme a Break" Café or enjoy desserts from Hershey's Bake Shoppe.

York County: Factory Tour Capital of the World

York, Pennsylvania, is home to more than twenty of America's favorite products, including Harley-Davidson, Martin's Potato Chips, Pfaltzgraff, and Wolfgang Candy. These and many other companies invite visitors to get a behind-the-scenes look at how their products are made. To get a *York County Visitors Guide* or for more information, call (888) 858–YORK or visit www.yorkpa.org.

Hersheypark (all ages) 🎢 🍴

100 West Hersheypark Drive; (800) HERSHEY or (717) 534–3090; www.hersheypa.com. Hersheypark's season runs from mid-May through mid-September. The gates open at 10:00 A.M., and the rides open at 10:30 A.M. Closing times vary from 6:00 to 11:00 P.M. Admission plans range from regular (ages 9 to 54) at $$$$ to junior and senior, both at $$$. Children 2 and under are free, and the sunset savings plan (after 5:00 P.M.) is $$$. Admission includes all rides, all live performances, and a same-day visit to ZooAmerica (see page 98). There is a separate charge for paddleboats and miniature golf.

Hersheypark was built in 1907 by Milton S. Hershey, "the man behind the chocolate bar." Hershey planned the park as a picnic and pleasure grounds for his employees. Today, Hersheypark has grown into a 110-acre world-class theme park with more than sixty rides and attractions.

In 2005, Hersheypark plans to create a Founder's Circle, a gathering place with a sense of nostalgia. Founder's Circle will welcome the reintroduction of two classic Hershey family rides, Balloon Flite and Starship America. A new musical "The Milk-men" will salute one of the key ingredients in Hershey's chocolate: milk!

Hersheypark has ten other exhilarating coasters including Storm Runner, the world's first hydraulic launch coaster featuring inversions.

As you enter Hersheypark, have your kids stand next to the "measure-up" signs. Kids of a certain height are "Hershey Kisses" and can ride Hershey Kiss rides. Taller kids are "Reese's Peanut Butter Cups," "Hershey Milk Chocolate Bars," "Twizzlers," or "Nutrageous." If your kids would like to get a bracelet that shows what candy-height they are, you can stop by the rides office in the operations building, located inside the park beside Swing Thing. (If you don't choose to get a bracelet, there are signs next to every ride.)

This manageable theme park is divided into small sections, which are centered around a different theme—and there's something for everyone. This way, your family can stay together and everyone can stay happy. For example, little ones can ride the Swing Thing, which is a kid-size version of Wave Swinger. The antique carousel will delight many visitors, whereas others flock to the Comet with its 95-foot drop. And don't stand anywhere near Tidal Force unless you don't mind getting wet! If you get hot and tired, a visit to the air-conditioned Music Box Theater may be just the ticket. If you do decide to split up, the Kissing Tower makes a good meeting spot.

You may choose to ride the water rides in your clothes or bathing suits, but shoes are required, so we recommend wearing something waterproof like flip-flops or water shoes.

Traveling with an infant, we were delighted to find that Hersheypark offers facilities for nursing mothers and baby food at the first-aid station. Even some of the men's rooms have changing tables.

Besides its regular season, Hersheypark opens for two special family events: Creatures of the Night at Halloween, and Hersheypark Christmas Candylane. At each of these events the park is specially lighted and decorated, and most of the family-oriented rides are open.

Zooamerica North American Wildlife Park (all ages)

Hersheypark Drive; (717) 534–3860; www.hersheypa.com. Open year-round. Hours vary seasonally; the zoo is open 10:00 A.M. to 8:00 P.M. whenever Hersheypark is open and 10:00 A.M. to 5:00 P.M. the rest of the year. Admission is $$. Children under 2 enter free.

You can enter ZooAmerica North American Wildlife Park directly through Hersheypark, and admission to the zoo is included in your Hersheypark ticket. The zoo is open year-round, not just seasonally, and a separate admission is also available. ZooAmerica focuses on plants and animals from different regions in North America.

Many of Hershey's attractions grew out of Milton Hershey's special interests. The rose garden at the Hotel Hershey developed from his own passion for the flowers, ZooAmerica started out with the animals Hershey collected, and the Hershey Museum sprang from Hershey's original collection of artifacts.

The Hershey Museum (all ages)

170 Hersheypark Drive; (717) 534–3439; www.hersheymuseum.org. Open year-round. Admission to the museum is $$ for adults and $ for youth.

Administered by the Hershey Foundation, the Hershey Museum is located at the west end of Hersheypark Arena. Its permanent exhibits celebrate the history of Hershey—the town, its founder, and its industries. Younger children will enjoy the Discovery Room, which has hands-on activities on these themes.

What We Remember about Hersheypark

—by Judah (12½) and Seth (10)

Seth: At Hersheypark there was this booth with water guns and we had to shoot at a blue button. If you shot the blue button enough, a bell would go off and you could win a stuffed animal. Judah and I didn't win anything, but Judah's friend Gabbi won three times and she gave us each one of her prizes.

Judah: We went on a Ferris wheel. The cars on the Ferris wheel went around. When we got to the top, I said "AHHHH!" We all laughed.

ALSO IN THE AREA

You may want to check the schedule of events at **Hersheypark Stadium and Arena** (717–534–3911). Hershey also offers several golf courses, Milton Hershey School, and the Derry One-Room School.

Hummelstown

Indian Echo Caverns (ages 8 and up) 🍁
368 Middletown Road; (717) 566–8131; www.indianechocaverns.com. **From Memorial Day to Labor Day, open 9:00 A.M. to 6:00 P.M. Last tour enters cavern at 6:00 P.M. Labor Day to Memorial Day, open 10:00 A.M. to 4:00 P.M., last tour at 4:00 P.M. Closed Thanksgiving, Christmas, and New Year's Day. Call for current admission prices.**

Your young geologists can take a forty-five-minute tour of Indian Echo Caverns and hear the story of William Wilson, a hermit who lived in the caverns for nineteen years. You can also pan for gemstones at Gem Mill Junction (Memorial Day to early October). The cavern is open year-round, but the food cart is open only during the summer season. Strollers not permitted in cave.

Middletown

Middletown and Hummelstown Railroad (all ages) 🏛
136 Brown Street; (717) 944–4435; www.mhrailroad.com. **Operates seasonally. Call for fares and schedule.**

All ages seem to get a kick out of this folksy ride in a 1920 vintage railroad coach. You take a guided scenic ride 11 miles to Indian Echo Caverns. Your train will cross Swatara Creek on a 35-foot-high bridge. You can get off at the caverns, if you like, and take a forty-five-minute tour. On your return trip an accordionist leads a sing-along. The steam locomotive is used on Saturday and Sunday in summer only. Wheelchair accessible.

Harrisburg

Whitaker Center for Science and the Arts (ages 6 and up) 🖼

The Kunkel Building, 301 Market Street; (717) 221–8201; www.whitakercenter.org. Open Monday through Saturday 9:30 A.M. to 5:00 P.M., Sunday 11:30 A.M. to 5:00 P.M. IMAX theater shows begin at 5:30 P.M. A combination ticket to both the science center and the theater costs $$. Tickets to the theater only and to the science center only are $$. For tickets to the Sunoco Performance Theater, check the Web site or call (717) 214–ARTS. For all tickets, children under 3 enter free.

The Whitaker Center describes its theme as "science through the arts," making science fun through dance, film, music, and more. The center includes a state-of-the-art Select Medical IMAX 3-D movie theater, Hansco Science Center, and a Broadway-size Sunoco Performance theater, which hosts many concerts and performances. The Hansco Science Center includes nine permanent exhibits that explore physical science, natural science, life science, and technology. If you park at Strawberry Square, you can enter the Whitaker Center by way of an enclosed walkway.

Walking Tour of Downtown Harrisburg

It's convenient to park your car at the Walnut Street parking garage, located right at Strawberry Square (North Third and Market Streets), an urban shopping mall with a food court and many shops. The Whitaker Center is across the street in the Kunkel Building.

Look up and you'll see the dome of the State Capitol Building. The circular building to the right as you leave the capitol is the State Museum of Pennsylvania.

If your feet aren't sore yet, you can walk over to the riverfront and cross Walnut Street Bridge, now exclusively for pedestrians. The bridge spans the Susquehanna River from Riverfront Park to City Island. (At night this bridge is illuminated, adding to the nighttime view of the city.)

State Capitol Building (ages 10 and up) 🏛

Third and State Streets; (717) 787–6810; www.legis.state.pa.us. Open to the public daily. Tours are given Monday through Friday, every half hour 8:30 A.M. to 4:00 P.M. Weekends and most holidays, tours are offered at 9:00 A.M., 11:00 A.M., 1:00 P.M. and 3:00 P.M. All tours are **free.** Reservations are strongly suggested, and for groups of ten or more, they are required. Call (800) TOUR N PA for reservations. Wheelchair accessible.

Since 2001, new security procedures have been instituted for the State Capitol Building. On weekdays, access is through any entrance, at which you will be screened and provided with a visitor's pass. On weekends and holidays, access is only through the front of the building, on Third Street at State. In 2006, our beautiful State Capitol Building will celebrate its one hundredth birthday.

The dome of the State Capitol Building is said to be the most impressive one of any state capitol in the country. Inside, huge murals depict scenes such as Penn's treaty with the Native Americans, the signing of the Declaration of Independence, and Washington's troops at Valley Forge. The floors are made of tiles from the Moravian Pottery and Tile Works in Doylestown (see entry under Philadelphia Countryside). The main floor of the rotunda displays more than 350 flags formerly carried by regiments from Pennsylvania.

In the East Wing visit the eighteen interactive exhibits of the welcome center, including a kinetic sculpture that depicts how a bill becomes law.

State Museum of Pennsylvania (all ages) 🔖

Third and North Streets; (717) 787–4979; www.statemuseumpa.org. Open Tuesday through Saturday 9:00 A.M. to 5:00 P.M. and Sunday noon to 5:00 P.M. Closed holidays except for Memorial Day and Labor Day. Admission is **free,** but there is a small charge for Curiosity Connection and the planetarium show. Wheelchair accessible.

The State Museum is in the midst of a planned ninety-two million dollar renovation. In March 2005, the museum plans to introduce its new digital planetarium.

This museum strives to describe the entire history and prehistory of the state. You'll work your way down, starting at the third floor. There you'll begin with geology and the earth and go on through paleontology, archaeology, and the beginning of civilization. In Dino-Lab you can observe a real paleontologist at work, freeing a dinosaur skeleton from the rock. Using an intercom, you can ask questions about this painstaking process.

Going down to the second floor, you can see a series of life-size dioramas that depict the life cycle of a Native American in this area. There are also displays about the Revolution and the Civil War, including a huge mural of the Battle of Gettysburg. One gallery re-creates a typical early American Main Street.

Curiosity Connection, the State Museum's new kid-inspired exhibit for young children and families, opened in Spring 2004. This 2,300-square foot exhibit encourages children seven and under to explore, discover, and imagine through the power of play. The adventure begins in a Magical Child's Bedroom and continues through secret portals leading to an entire miniature world of *Curiosity*. Other areas include The Living Forest, Industry and Transportation Zone, Farm Land, Construction Zone, and Art Wall. There's even a special area for the very youngest visitors. Curiosity Connection is open Tuesday through Saturday, 10:00 A.M. to 4:00 P.M., Sunday noon to 4:00 P.M. Admission for adults and children is $. Children under age one are admitted **free.**

On the first floor the museum displays a facsimile of its treasure, the original charter from the British crown that gave Pennsylvania to William Penn in 1681. This charter granted William Penn "rights, privileges and obligations" to Pennsylvania, as a payment of debts owed to Penn's father by King Charles II.

City Island Attractions (all ages)

City Island sits in the middle of the Susquehanna, a spot of greenery amid the water. Its sixty-three acres of parkland now include Riverside Stadium, where Class AA minor league baseball is played. You'll also find a steam train for children, a paddlewheel riverboat, an arcade, miniature golf, jogging and skateboarding facilities, a free nautical-themed playground, Riverside Village Eatery, carriage rides, HarbourTown, and more.

Pride of the Susquehanna Riverboat (all ages) ⚠

City Island; (717) 234–6500; www.harrisburgriverboat.com. Boat sails on the hour in June, July and August, Tuesday through Sunday, and on a more limited schedule in May, September, and October. Call ahead to confirm because schedule is subject to change, especially in May, September, and October. Fares are $. Children under 12 ride free.

From City Island take a ride on the *Pride of the Susquehanna* (operated by Harrisburg Area Riverboat Society, P.O. Box 910, Harrisburg 17108).

The riverboat tour gives an excellent view of this riverside city. Kids love looking up at the underside of the six bridges under which you'll pass, including the Walnut Street Bridge. Take your choice: You may sit indoors in air-conditioned comfort, where there is the Pride Galley for snacks and souvenirs, or on the lower or upper decks, where the wind blows through your hair.

From the riverboat you can see the wrought-iron railing around the grave of the city's founder, John Harris. You can visit his home, the John Harris/Simon Cameron Mansion, at 219 South Front Street. This historic home was built in 1766 and now houses the collection of the Historical Society of Dauphin County.

Amazing
Hershey–Pennsylvania Dutch Facts

The State Museum of Pennsylvania in Harrisburg displays the original charter that gave Pennsylvania to William Penn. It's amusing to note that Penn was to pay the king two beaver furs and all the gold and silver found in the colony. Of course, there was no gold or silver found in Pennsylvania.

Fort Hunter Mansion (ages 8 and up) 🏛

5300 North Front Street; (717) 599–5751; www.forthunter.org. Open May through November, Tuesday through Saturday 10:00 A.M. to 4:30 P.M., Sunday noon to 4:30 P.M. Admission is $.

Just outside Center City, on a bluff overlooking the Susquehanna River, stands Fort Hunter Mansion, surrounded by its outbuildings and park. The Federal-style mansion, built in 1814 by Archibald McAllister, is in remarkably good condition. While touring the house, open the closet doors to discover surprises such as sets of china or collections of fashionable clothing left behind by Helen Reily, last owner of the house. In the guest-room closet, you can peek at Mrs. Reily's bonnets (she had some one hundred), fans, hat pins, and other accessories. She also left a collection of dolls, toy soldiers, and even paper dolls. The dollhouse features a tiny hobby horse, a little dog curled up in a minute dog bed, and postcards glued to the walls for paintings. And don't miss the garden with its spicebush, smokebush, and boxwood. The Web site offers a downloadable walking tour.

In December, when the mansion is decorated for Christmas, it is open Tuesday through Sunday from noon to 7:00 P.M. In September Fort Hunter Day brings the whole park alive with bagpipe music (in honor of the McAllisters), arts and crafts, children's activities, food, and more. Programs for children and families are offered periodically.

Carlisle

The town of Carlisle is known for country inns and antiques shops—not exactly what most kids want to see. Perhaps more kid-friendly are attractions such as the Carlisle fairgrounds (depending on what's going on), and, for older children interested in history, the Carlisle Barracks.

Farms of Lancaster County

There's a reason why towns in Lancaster County have names like Eden and Paradise. This idyllic landscape is not only lush and green, but fertile as well. In fact, Lancaster County has the most fertile, nonirrigated farmland east of the Mississippi. According to Penn State University Agricultural Extension Office, every second, the county produces ninety eggs, twenty-one pounds of corn, and thirteen pounds of hay.

Many Lancaster farms have been passed down from generation to generation. Since 1976, about 150 farms have been designated as Century Farms, or farms that have been in the same family for at least 150 years. For example, the sixty-acre Esbenshade Turkey Farm in Paradise is the oldest turkey farm in the United States.

You can experience this abundance at roadside produce stands and farmers' markets overflowing with whatever is in season: tomatoes, pumpkins, strawberries, cantaloupes, watermelons, and sweet corn.

Another way to get to experience Lancaster farmland is to plan a farm vacation. For a listing of farm vacations in Pennsylvania, go to www.pa farmstay.com. Milk a cow, feed the chickens, and experience farm living firsthand. You can get a list of working farms that offers lodging at www.padutchcountry.com/lodging. You can make reservations online or by calling (800) PA–DUTCH (723–8824). Here are a few suggestions:

- **Country Vistas Bed & Breakfast,** Manheim; (717) 664–2931.

- **Country Gardens Farm Bed & Breakfast,** Mount Joy; (717) 426–3316.

- **Cedar Hill Farm Bed & Breakfast,** Mount Joy; (717) 653–4655.

Carlisle Barracks (ages 10 and up) 🏛

Enter from Claremont Road vehicle access center. Drivers will need a valid driver's license, vehicle registration, and proof of insurance to enter. Adult passengers are required to present photo identification. The Military History Institute and Bradley Museum are open Monday through Friday, 9:00 a.m. to 4:45 p.m., closed weekends and federal holidays. The Hessian Powder Magazine is open daily, 8:00 a.m. to 5:00 p.m. For information, contact Patron Services at (717) 245–3971 or (717) 245–3949.

Carlisle Barracks was originally established by the British Army as a camp in 1757. During the War for Independence, the post served as an arsenal for the Continental

Army. The Hessian Powder Magazine, built to store munitions during the American Revolution, is located at the corner of Garrison and Guardhouse Lanes. Walking tour brochures of the grounds are available in the Museum. The Carlisle Indian Industrial School was established here in 1879. The school educated thousands of Native American children including famous athletes such as Jim Thorpe, Charles Bender, and Louis Tewanima.

The U.S. Army War College moved to Carlisle Barracks in 1951. It is a senior-service college for colonels and lieutenant colonels that prepares senior leaders "to pursue mastery of the art of strategy, and apply strategic leadership in a unified, joint, or multinational environment." Graduates include President Dwight D. Eisenhower, General Richard B. Myers, General Omar Bradley, and many others.

The U.S. Army Military History Institute (Ridgway Hall) is located off the grounds at 950 Soldiers Drive, off Army Heritage Drive, adjacent to Claremont Road. The Military History Institute is the primary research facility for the historical study of the U.S. Army and holds over 14 million items documenting military history.

Carlisle Fairgrounds (ages 8 and up) 🔒

1000 Bryn Mawr Road. For a schedule of events, contact Carlisle Productions at (717) 243–7855 or www.carsatcarlisle.com.

Maybe somebody in your family is nuts about cars or antiques. The eighty-two-acre Carlisle Fairgrounds hosts major collector events on many weekends throughout the year.

ALSO IN THE AREA

For hiking, cross-country skiing, hunting, and other outdoor activities, contact **King's Gap Environmental Center** on Route 174 West (500 Kings Gap Road) at (717) 486–5031; www.dcnr.state.pa.us/stateparks.

Boiling Springs

This lovely lakeside town is the home of the Allenberry Resort Inn and Playhouse. The Allenberry stretch of the Yellow Breeches River attracts many families to try their hands at fly fishing. Here, the rules are "catch and release" and "artificial lures only." It's a little different on the Letort Spring Run (pronounced lee-tort), which is considered more challenging, and attracts devotees of *A River Runs Through It*.

Allenberry Resort Inn 🎵 🎣

Route 174; (717) 258–3211; www.allenberry.com.

An eighteenth-century estate where you can enjoy professional theater, fishing, and special events. Call for a list of upcoming dinner theater productions.

Gettysburg

Every student in America should get a chance to visit Gettysburg. Before your visit, older kids and parents can prepare by watching either Ken Burns' PBS *Civil War* documentary or the 1993 movie *Gettysburg*. Placing the battle in context will enhance your visit.

Another great way to prepare for your trip is the award-winning *Gettysburg Expedition Guide* offered by TravelBrains or at the visitor center. It includes a CD-ROM, driving-tour tape or CD, and a guidebook. Check out the Web site at www.TravelBrains.com.

You can also plan ahead by choosing a battlefield tour. To find the tour that best suits your needs and to receive at booklet about Gettysburg, call the Gettysburg Travel Council at (717) 334–6274 or go to their Web site at www.gettysburg.com. You can also contact the Convention and Visitors Bureau at www.gettysburgcvb.org.

You may choose an individualized tour or a group tour. Group tours are available by bicycle, bus, or even on horseback.

- For a personalized tour with a licensed guide in your own vehicle, contact the Association of Licensed Battlefield Guides at (877) 438–8929. You can also sign up for one of these guides at the visitor center. This is one of the best ways to learn about the battlefield.

- Tours on tape or CD are available around town or through Gettysburg Battlefield Tape Tours (717–338–0631), CC Inc. Auto tape Tours (717–334–6245), or Battlefield Driving Tours (717–337–1217).

- Bus tours on air-conditioned buses are available through Gettysburg Bus Tours, 778 Baltimore Street, across from the National Cemetery (717–334–8000; www.gettysburgbattlefieldtours.com).

- Tours on horseback, called "Ride into History," are available through National Riding Stables (717–334–1288). Reservations six to eight weeks in advance are highly recommended. Tours are $$$$. Inexperienced riders welcome.

- Tours on mountain bike are offered by Battlefield Bicycle Tours (800–830–5775).

The Gettysburg Convention and Visitors Bureau asks that drivers be aware of all the other visitors crossing the streets at peak times, especially after dark when "ghost tours" are out. The speed limit in town is 25 miles per hour and state law requires you stop for pedestrians.

The battlefield presents the military picture of the battle. While in the town of Gettysburg, you can get a feel for the civilians' experience of the battle by visiting two new attractions: Schriver House Museum and Rupp House History Center. Please note that the Lincoln Room Museum closed in spring 2005 and is expected to reopen

Our Class Trip to Gettysburg

—by Judah Paulsen–Sacks, age 12½

When I was in the fifth grade, my classmates and I went to Gettysburg.
Our social studies teacher was telling us about the Civil War. Each of us
brought some lunch and money. I also brought my camera.

First we went to a museum of the Civil War. We came to see a special
room. The walls were electronic. They showed in pictures the story of
the Battle of Gettysburg.

We ate lunch in the van. (We were careful not to get the car messy.)
Then we went to a horse stable. My horse was named Cowgirl. Anthony's
horse was Bubblegum, and Mike's was Abbey. I've forgotten the other
horses' names. Abbey was always leaving the trail. Bubblegum kept eating off the trees. The owner of the stable had warned us not to let our
horses eat leaves or grass because once they'd started, they'd never stop.
Even though the horses didn't always behave right, it was fun. I mean,
who doesn't like horseback riding? It was that trip that inspired me to
someday get a horse.

My favorite part of the trip was Devil's Den. That's a place where
many people claimed to have seen ghosts and demons and things like
that. Me and Anthony went exploring there. We found a little cave-type
place that I was just thin enough to squeeze through. We all went inside.

I was the leader. In the dark, we thought we saw two green eyes!

None of us are quite sure whether what we saw was a demon or not.
It could have been a ghost. Or maybe a hoax.

The trip to Gettysburg was one of the
funnest, most memorable trips I've ever
taken and it really made me think, "Ain't
this a great planet?"

as the Lincoln and Gettysburg Address Museum, in an expanded and restored form in 2006.

Beginning in 2007, a shuttle service will link the battlefield with the town of Gettysburg.

The Gettysburg Travel Council recommends a minimum visit of three days to see all that Gettysburg has to offer. To prevent an overdose of history, plan for breaks and vary your activities. Here are some highlights.

Gettysburg National Military Park (ages 8 and up) 🏛 🔷 🚶

Steinwehr Avenue (Business U.S. Route 15 South); (717) 334–1124; www.nps.gov/gett. The visitor center is open daily 8:00 A.M. to 5:00 P.M. Although admission to the park and visitor center are free, there is a small charge for the Cyclorama and Electric Map attractions. Twenty-minute Cyclorama showings are offered every half hour from 9:00 A.M. to 4:30 P.M. The thirty-minute Electric Map showings are given every forty-five minutes from 8:15 A.M. to 4:15 P.M. For either show the fees are the same: $. Children under 6 are free.

A visit to this ghostly battlefield can be a truly moving experience. Gettysburg National Military Park brings to life the story of three days in July 1863. About 400 artillery guns stand along the Union and Confederate battle lines, and more than 1,300 monuments help visitors picture what happened here.

Plan to stop at the visitor center first thing. Don't miss the Cyclorama, a 356-by-26-foot circular painting by Paul Phillippoteaux. You'll feel as if you're standing on the battlefield just before Pickett's charge. (Just think what an effect this painting must have had when it was completed in the 1880s!) A sound-and-light program brings the painting to life and adds to the experience. The visitor center also has an Electric Map of the battlefield and the Museum of the Civil War, the largest collection of Civil War artifacts anywhere. Beginning in November 2005, the *Cyclorama* will undergo restoration. Once restored, the painting will go on display in a new visitor center, expected to open in 2007, about ⅔ of a mile away from its current site.

There is a self-guided driving tour that takes about two or three hours. The park roads are open 6:00 A.M. to 10:00 P.M. Hikers, bikers, and horses are welcome. Licensed battlefield guides are also available from the National Park Visitor Center. Tours begin at 8:00 A.M. and depart hourly. The fee is $$$$ per car for each two-hour tour.

Gettysburg National Military Park offers a Junior Ranger program. Go to the information desk to pick up a free Junior Ranger booklet.

From mid-June to mid-August, the park offers a new, free kids' program called "Join the Army." This hour-long program takes place daily at 11:00 A.M. (Just sign up at the Cyclorama Center.) You'll learn how to march and drill, get to try out the job of captain or drummer, and even get to charge.

We found that when children have prepared by studying the battle before their trip, many are able to imagine themselves as soldiers on the field. When "reenacting" Picketts' Charge with our kids, we heard them say, "That was really hard! Imagine how hard it would be if we were carrying rifles and surrounded by cannon smoke!"

For information about Living History Encampments by units of the Gettysburg National Military Pak and American Civil War Museum, call (717) 334–1124, ext. 446.

Eisenhower National Historic Park (ages 10 and up) Ⓜ
Located on Business US 15 South, adjacent to the battlefield; (717) 344–1124; www.nps.gov/eise. The farm is open daily from April through October. It is closed Monday and Tuesday from November through March. Admission: Adults $$, children ages 6 to 16 $, under 6 free.

Adjacent to the battlefield is the Eisenhower National Historic Site, the 189-acre retirement home and farm of President and Mrs. Dwight Eisenhower. If you wish to tour the home, pick up tickets at the Gettysburg National Park Visitor Center, and then take a shuttle bus to the Eisenhower farm.

To liven up the visit for children ages five to thirteen, there's a Junior Secret Service Agent program. Pick up a free booklet at the information desk. Kids get a chance to use a park radio, look through binoculars, learn how the President is protected, and earn a Junior Secret Service Agent badge at the end.

Pace yourself, because you've only just begun. You may wish to take a walking tour of downtown Gettysburg to get yourself oriented before visiting some of the many sites in town. The town's official information center is located at 35 Carlisle Street, across from Lincoln Square in the center of town.

Walking Tour of Downtown Gettysburg

After you've toured Gettysburg National Military Park and, optionally, Eisenhower National Historic Park, you may think you've "done" Gettysburg. Well, think again, because you've only just begun! Downtown Gettysburg offers an array of museums, shops, and attractions.

Start at the town's official information center, located at 35 Carlisle Street, across Lincoln Square from the center of town.

Cross Lincoln Square and turn left down Baltimore Street, where most of the museums and sights are.

Going down Baltimore Street away from Lincoln Square, you can stop at points of interest such as Schriver House Tour, Farnsworth House, and the free Rupp House History Center.

Baltimore Street then forks. The left fork is the continuation of Baltimore Street, where you'll find such sites as the Confederate States Armory Museum, Jennie Wade House and Olde Town, Soldiers National Museum, and Hall of Presidents and First Ladies.

The right fork is Steinwehr Avenue, where you'll find the National Civil War Museum, and the Lincoln Train Museum.

Schriver House Museum (ages 5 and up) 🏛 🖼

309 Baltimore Street; (717) 337–2800; www.schriverhouse.com. Guided tours every half hour April through November, Monday through Saturday 10:00 A.M. to 5:00 P.M., Sunday noon to 5:00 P.M. Closed January except for special appointments.

The Battle of Gettysburg didn't just take place on the battlefield; it also took place in the streets of the town. At the time of the battle, there were less than 3,000 permanent residents of the town of Gettysburg. When the battle was over, about 22,000 wounded were left behind for the residents to care for. This award-winning museum is dedicated to the civilian experience during and following the battle. Schriver House has been restored to its 1860s appearance. Guides in period costume lead tours through all four floors of the house, including the attic, where Confederate sharpshooters set up their nest.

Rupp House History Center (all ages) 🖼

451 Baltimore Street; (717) 334–7292; www.friendsofgettysburg.org. Open March through December, Friday noon to 8:00 P.M., Saturday 10:00 A.M. to 8:00 P.M., and Sunday noon to 5:00 P.M. Free.

In June of 2003, the Friends of the National Parks at Gettysburg opened the Rupp House History Center. The house currently on this site was built shortly after the battle, but there was a house that stood here earlier in July 1863. The History Center, right in the center of town and within walking distance of the park, offers visitors a hands-on, interactive experience of the sights, sounds, touch, and even the smell of nineteenth-century Gettysburg. And it's free!

Jennie Wade House (ages 8 and up) 🏛

758 Baltimore Street; (717) 334–4100. Admission is $$ for adults, $ for children. The Jennie Wade House and Olde Town are open daily. In summer hours are 9:00 A.M. to 9:00 P.M. and in the off-season 9:00 A.M. to 5:00 P.M.

In addition to the thousands of men who died at Gettysburg, there was one woman. Twenty-year-old Jennie Wade was baking bread for the Union soldiers when she was hit by a stray bullet. You can see the bullet hole. A clever holographic display tells Jennie's story. Jennie Wade's house is adjacent to Olde Town, where the streets of Gettysburg of 1863 are re-created.

Hall of Presidents and First Ladies (ages 8 and up) 🖼

789 Baltimore Street; (717) 334–5717. Open daily 9:00 A.M. to 5:00 P.M. Admission $$ adults, $ students.

You can hear U.S. presidents "speak" at the Hall of Presidents and First Ladies. A series of life-size wax figures and taped messages can help kids learn the difference between Andrew Jackson and Andrew Johnson. The first ladies appear in reproductions of their inaugural gowns.

American Civil War Museum (ages 8 and up) 🖼️

297 Steinwehr Avenue; (717) 334–6245; www.e-gettysburg.cc. Hours vary seasonally, but usually 9:00 A.M. to 5:00 P.M. daily. Admission: $; children 5 and under, free.

The American Civil War Museum has organized its more than 200 life-size figures into an audiovisual presentation including thirty different scenes. You can see animated figures reenact the Battle of Gettysburg and an animated Lincoln deliver the Gettysburg Address. On weekends from May until Labor Day, special events include living reenactments.

Lighter Attractions in Gettysburg

Okay, so your younger ones have had enough history. Now's the perfect time for some lighter fare. For something spookily different, hear stories by candlelight at **Farnsworth House Mourning Theater and Ghost Walks** at 401 Baltimore Street. In season, stories are given Tuesday through Friday at 9:30 P.M. and Saturday at 8:00 and 9:30 P.M. Hours vary seasonally. Call (717) 334–8838 for details and the current schedule. Tickets are $$ for adults; children under six are free. Not recommended for children who are afraid of the dark or for very young children.

In season you can enjoy these lighter attractions: **The Gettysburg Family Fun Center,** 1 mile from Town Square on Route 30 East (717–334–GOLF), has miniature golf, batting cages, an arcade, and a snack bar. **Mulligan McDuffer Adventure Golf,** adjacent to the battlefield, offers miniature golf and ice cream. Call (717) 337–1518.

Land of Little Horses is outside Gettysburg at 125 Glenwood Drive. The smallest Falabella horses may weigh seventy pounds and stand less than 20 inches high. Kids less than eighty pounds can climb up on their backs (for an additional fee). The horses perform tricks three times a day from Memorial Day through Labor Day. There's also a carousel, train tram, nature area, gift shop, and snack bar. The Land of Little Horses is open 10:00 A.M. to 5:00 P.M., daily, April through October. Call (717) 334–7259; www.landoflittlehorses.com. Admission is $$ for adults, $ for children two to twelve. "Herd" rates are available. Wheelchair accessible.

Another fun stop—but one that could get expensive—is **Boyd's Bear Country** (866–367–8338, www.BoydsBearCountry.com), off Business Route 15 (Steinwehr Avenue) at 75 Cunningham Road. Here you can see and, of course, purchase the popular collectible stuffed toys.

Lincoln Train Museum (ages 8 and up)

425 Steinwehr Avenue; (717) 334–5678. Open in summer 9:00 A.M. to 9:00 P.M. and in spring and fall 9:00 A.M. to 5:00 P.M. Closed during the winter months. Admission is $$ for adults, $ for children.

You can join Lincoln for the train ride to Gettysburg on a twelve-minute simulated trip at the Lincoln Train Museum. The museum also exhibits a toy train collection including a model-railroad layout that represents the Civil War.

Gettysburg Scenic Railway (all ages)

106 North Washington Street; for schedules and fares, plus information about theme trains, call (717) 334–6932; www.gettysburgrail.com. Open seasonally. Tickets cost $$ for adults, $ for children.

Board the Gettysburg Railroad Train about 2 blocks from Lincoln Square and choose between the 16-mile and 50-mile trips on trains that pass by the Gettysburg Battlefield.

Soldiers National Museum (ages 10 and up)

777 Baltimore Street; (717) 334–4890. Hours vary seasonally. Admission $$ adults, $ children.

Ten Civil War dioramas are housed in the building that was General Howard's headquarters during the battle and later the Soldiers' National Orphanage. The museum features artifacts and memorabilia from the Civil War as well as other major American conflicts.

General Lee's Headquarters (ages 10 and up)

Route 30 West, 8 blocks west of Lincoln Square; (717) 334–3141; www.civilwarhead quarters.com. Open daily 9:00 A.M. to 5:00 P.M. mid-March through November. Extended hours in summer. Admission is $.

In this house General Lee and his staff made plans for the battle. Now the building houses a collection of Civil War relics.

Where to Eat

IN READING/BERKS COUNTY

These non-fast food restaurants offer kid-friendly dining:

Antique Airplane Restaurant, Best Western Dutch Colony Inn, 4635 Perkiomen Avenue, US 422, East Reading; (610) 779–2345. An authentic 1927 airplane hangs from the ceiling, and aviation memorabilia hang from the walls.

Arner's Family Restaurants, three convenient locations throughout Berks County: 2101 Howard Boulevard, Reading; (610) 779–6555; 1714 State Hill Road, Wyomissing Hills; (610) 372–6101; and 4643 Pottsville Pike, Route 61, Reading; (610) 926–9002. Casual atmosphere.

Peanut Bar and Restaurant, 332 Penn Street, Reading; (610) 376–8500; www .peanutbar.com. Lunch through late night, it's one of the few places where parents can enjoy gourmet selections while youngsters eat more kid-friendly choices. Besides, where else can you tell the kids, "go ahead, throw the peanut shells on the floor"?

IN GETTYSBURG

These non-fast food restaurants in Gettysburg offer children's menus:

Dobbin House Tavern, 89 Steinwehr Avenue; (717) 334–2100; www.dobbinhouse.com. A historic building with country store, bakery, and underground slave hideout. Children's menu available.

Farnsworth House Inn, 401 Baltimore Street, (717) 334–8838; www.farnsworthhousedining.com. A historic building with one hundred bullet holes. Gettysburg's only Civil War dining. Inn has been named one of America's Ten Most Haunted Inns by the Travel Channel.

General Lee's Family Restaurant, US 30, (717) 334–2200. Casual, country dining rooms.

Where to Stay

IN LANCASTER AND PENNSYLVANIA DUTCH COUNTRY

Bird-in-Hand Family Inn, 2740 Old Philadelphia Pike, Bird-in-Hand; (717) 768–8271. Indoor/outdoor pools, free bus tour, restaurant, bakery.

Fairfield by Marriott—Lancaster, 150 Granite Run Drive, Lancaster; (717) 581–1800. Indoor pool.

Quality Inn & Suites, 2363 Oregon Pike, Lancaster; (717) 569–0477. Restaurant, outdoor pool.

Outdoor World: Pennsylvania Dutch Country, 185 Lebanon Road, Manheim; (717) 665–2500 or (800) 588–2222 (for reservations); www.campoutdoorworld.com. One of the Outdoor World camping resorts.

Red Caboose Motel, P.O. Box 303, Strasburg 17579; (717) 687–5000 or (888) 687–5005. Sleep in authentic cabooses and dine in authentic dining car. Seasonal buggy rides, petting zoo, flea market, country music.

IN THE HERSHEY AREA

Chocolatetown Motel, 1806 East Chocolate Avenue, Hershey; (717) 533–2330. Good location.

Cocoa Nights Motel, 1518 East Chocolate Avenue, Hershey; (717) 533–2384.

Hershey Highmeadow Campground, 1200 Matlack Road, Hummelstown; (717) 534–8999 or (800) 533–3131. Cabins, campsites, pool, playground equipment, showers, and **free** shuttle buses to Hersheypark.

The Hershey Lodge, West Chocolate Avenue and University Drive, Hershey; (717) 533–3311 or (800) 533–3131. Casual resort with indoor/outdoor pool, a playground, children's pool, and free shuttle buses to Hersheypark.

The Hotel Hershey, Hotel Road, Hershey; (717) 533–2171 or (800) 533–3131; www.hersheypa.com/accommodations. Luxurious resort hotel with indoor/outdoor pool, children's pool, and free shuttle buses to Hersheypark. Has two restaurants to suit different tastes. Choose the Fountain Cafe if you're traveling with young children.

Spinners Inn, 845 East Chocolate Avenue, Hershey; (717) 533–9157; www.spinnersinn.com.

IN HARRISBURG

Ramada Inn on Market Square, 23 South Second Street; (800) 2–RAMADA or (717) 234–5021. Restaurant, indoor pool. Minutes from Hershey, Lancaster, Gettysburg.

For More Information

While surfing the Web, you may wish to check out the Web site of the **Harrisburg-Hershey-Carlisle Tourist and Convention Bureau** at www.visithhc.com or any of the Web sites given in this chapter.

Laurel
Highlands
Region

The beauty of the Laurel Highlands area of Pennsylvania will take your breath away. One hundred miles of countryside, mountains, and valleys; two mountain ridges; and thirteen state parks and forests provide the setting for golfing, skiing, fishing, and hiking. The Youghiogheny River (the "Yock") means white-water rafting, and Raystown Lake offers calmer boating, swimming, and more.

In this area the Rails-to-Trails Conservancy is converting old railroad paths to hiking and biking trails. (For a $$ guidebook, call Rails-to-Trails of Pennsylvania at 717–238–1717 or go to www.railtrails.org/pa.)

Faith & Emily's
FavoriteAttractions
in the Laurel Highlands Region

1. Idlewild Park, Ligonier

2. Family float trip on Youghiogheny River, Ohiopyle

3. Laurel Canyons, Uniontown

4. Lincoln Caverns, Huntington

5. Raystown Lake, Hesston

6. Old Bedford Village, Bedford

7. Bat hike in Canoe Creek State Park, Hollidaysburg

8. Rockhill Trolley Museum, Rockhill

9. Horseshoe Curve Railroad, Altoona

10. Johnstown Incline, Johnstown

LAUREL HIGHLANDS REGION

Here you'll find a masterpiece of modern architecture, Frank Lloyd Wright's Fallingwater. Old Bedford Village re-creates our history, and Idlewild Park takes us to the Land of Make-Believe.

The year 2004 marked the 250th anniversary of the French and Indian War. The Laurel Highlands is rich in history, especially sites associated with this conflict that helped pave the way for the American Revolution—sites such as Fort Necessity and the authentically restored Fort Ligonier.

In 1806 the National Road was built to link the East with what was then the Western frontier. This road is now Route 40, where every May wagoners with teams of horses commemorate the opening of the nation's first turnpike (the National Road Festival; www.nationalroadpa.org). Two old tollhouses still exist along Route 40, which is also a great foliage route in October.

This area saw remarkable industrial development: coal mining, the steel industry, the growth of railroading, and the building of canals. Many families enjoy driving the 500-mile Path of Progress Heritage Route, which takes them past many of the sites described in this chapter. (For further information about the Path of Progress, call 800–898–3636 or check the Web site at www.allegheny.com.)

If you're looking for something completely different, a visit to Gravity Hill should give you something to talk about. In Bedford County, near the town of Schellsburg, is an area where gravity goes backwards. It may be an optical illusion, but in this area, cars seem to roll uphill and water flows the wrong way. For very clear directions go to www.gravityhill.com or call (800) 765–3331.

Faith & Emily's
FavoriteEvents
in the Laurel Highlands Region

- **Hidden Valley Resort Winter Carnival** (late January); (814) 443–2600 or (800) 443–SKII.

- **Seven Springs Resort Spring Festival** (March); (800) 452–2223.

- **National Road Festival** (May); (724) 329–1560.

- **Ligonier Scottish Highland Games,** Idlewild Park (September); (412) 238–3666.

- **Pioneer Days,** Old Bedford Village (September); (814) 623–1156.

- **Fort Ligonier Days** (October); (724) 238–4200.

Point Marion

Friendship Hill National Historic Site (ages 10 and up) (icons)

Off U.S. Route 119; (724) 725–9190; www.nps.gov/frhi. Open daily year-round 8:30 A.M. to 5:00 P.M. Closed major holidays. Free.

Friendship Hill is the home of Swiss-born patriot Albert Gallatin, who was elected to the U.S. Senate and the House of Representatives, played an important role in the Whiskey Rebellion, was Secretary of the Treasury, a member of the team that negotiated the end of the War of 1812, minister to France, and sometimes called the "father" of the National Road.

There are 8 miles of trails and a picnic area. You can take a pleasant walk to the grave of Gallatin's first wife, Sophia Allegre. The site overlooks the Monongahela River, but watch out for the steep banks. Also, be aware that there may be potential dangers in old buildings and mine works that have not yet been restored. Since the house is sometimes closed for restoration work, it's wise to call ahead: (412) 725–9190.

Uniontown

In the Uniontown area, you can visit Searight Toll House, Fort Necessity National Battlefield, and Laurel Caverns.

Searight Toll House (ages 8 and up) (icon)

U.S. Route 40 West; (724) 439–4422. Open Tuesday through Saturday 10:00 A.M. to 4:00 P.M. and, from mid-May to mid-October, Sunday 2:00 to 6:00 P.M. Admission is $ for adults; children enter free. Group tours arranged by appointment.

The U.S. government authorized construction of the National Road in 1806 to connect the East and the West. One of the National Road's tollhouses, Searight Toll House is open to the public and is administered by Fayette County Historical Society. Built in 1835 and recently restored, the octagonally shaped tollhouse includes the toll keeper's office, kitchen, living room, and living quarters.

Fort Necessity National Battlefield National Park
(ages 9 and up) (icon)

On US 40 (the National Road), 11 miles east of Uniontown; (724) 329– 5512; www.nps .gov. The fort building is open daily from dawn to dusk. The visitor center is open 9:00 A.M. to 5:00 P.M. Closed all federal holidays except Memorial Day, July 4th, Labor Day, and Columbus Day.

At Jumonville Glen, 5 miles from here, the 22-year-old George Washington met with his first experience of battle in 1754, during the French and Indian War. Washington's forces won the first encounter. The fort was built afterward in expectation that the

French would return, which they did, but this time Washington was forced into the only surrender of his career. Here you can also visit the grave of General Braddock.

Fort Necessity was reconstructed in 1952. At the visitor center here, you can view an audiovisual presentation about the fort, the battle, and the research behind the reconstruction effort. You'll probably be surprised when you see the size of the reconstructed fort. The circular stockade is 53 feet in diameter. The gate is only 3½ feet wide.

While you're in the neighborhood, you may wish to visit the Mount Washington Tavern, built in the 1820s on land once owned by George Washington himself. The tavern has been restored to look as it might have in the period when it was constructed to serve travelers along the new National Road, which was built in 1818.

Laurel Caverns (all ages) 🐾

Located 5 miles east of US 40, at the crest of Summit Mountain; (800) 515–4150; www.laurelcaverns.com. Open daily from May to October, 9:00 A.M. to 5:00 P.M., and weekends only in March, April, and November. Family guided tours leave every twenty minutes. Tours: $$; preschoolers are free. Group rates are available with advance notice. Indoor miniature golf course: $$ per person, $ group rate.

Located on a mountainside, Pennsylvania's largest cave offers not only the underground caves but a breathtaking view. Although the adventurous may choose the challenging Caving Adventure, the guided family tour is recommended for families with children under twelve and the physically challenged. Watch your step in the narrow passageways.

At the end of the tour, don't miss the sound-and-light show, sort of an underground *Fantasia*. There's even "Kavern Putt," a wheelchair accessible miniature golf course housed in a huge man-made cave.

Bring a jacket and a flashlight. Rappelling and climbing sessions are available to groups inside the caverns, as are fossil-hunting excursions. Bathrooms in the visitors center are handicapped accessible and include changing tables. There is a picnic shelter, or you can pick up Zeb's Pizza nearby.

Amazing
Laurel Highlands Facts

This region includes twenty-three state parks and forests.

Brownsville

Nemacolin Castle (ages 8 and up) 🏛
**Front Street in Brownsville; (724) 785–6882; www.nemacolincastle.org. Open week-
ends only 11:00 A.M. to 5:00 P.M. mid-March through mid-October. In June, July, and
August, it's also open Tuesday through Friday 11:00 A.M. to 5:00 P.M. Admission: adults
$$, children 12 and under $.**

Despite its name, Nemacolin Castle is not a castle but the home of Jacob Bowman,
who opened a trading post in Brownsville in 1786. Refurbished in 2001, it does look a
little like a castle, though, with its turreted tower and battlements. You can take a
guided tour of more than twenty furnished rooms. Around the holidays, Christmas
candlelight tours are offered.

Connellsville

Crawford Cabin (ages 6 and up) 🏛
**North Seventh Street at the Youghiogheny River; (724) 628–5640; www.fay-west.com.
Open by appointment only. Free.**

The Connellsville Area Historical Society (275 South Pittsburgh Street; 724–628–
5640) administers Crawford Cabin. George Washington visited his lifelong friend Col.
William Crawford in this humble log cabin, 14 by 16 feet, built in 1765. Colonel Craw-
ford and his men served Washington at the crossing of the Delaware and the battles
of Trenton, Princeton, Brandywine, and Germantown.

Ohiopyle

Ohiopyle State Park's Youghiogheny River (affectionately nicknamed the Yough, pro-
nounced "Yock") offers a wide range of river adventures. From March into October
thousands of vacationers challenge the Yough. Find the guided or unguided trip that
suits your family's taste and ages.

Rafting on the Youghiogheny (ages 4 and up for the Middle Yough only) ⚠

For novices or families with younger children, the **Middle Yough** is the best choice, with its gentler class I and II rapids and relaxing scenery. Laurel Highlands River Tours offers a guided trip on the Middle Yough, which they call their Family Float Trip, for families with children ages four and up. (Many seniors also enjoy this trip.) Both Wilderness Voyageurs and White Water Adventures offer similar relaxing float trips. For kids under twelve, Mountain Streams offers free rafting on Tuesday. Wilderness Voyageurs rents easily maneuverable rafts for unguided rafting. (See below for information on these establishments.)

The **Lower Yough's** class III and IV rapids are a little wilder. The minimum age for this 7½-mile stretch of the river is twelve. Mountain Streams offers a minitrip on the Lower Yough that lasts about two hours. Many of these organizations also provide bike rentals, kayaks, or "duckies." A duckie is sort of an inflatable kayak, used with a double-ended paddle, available with one or two seats. Most outfitters recommend duckies rather than canoes. A Thrillseeker, also used with a double-ended paddle, is made of a harder plastic.

Teenagers and adults with a taste for adventure can take on the **Upper Yough.** This 11-mile stretch of the river includes class IV and V rapids and is recommended for experienced paddlers only. The minimum age is sixteen.

Ohiopyle State Park (all ages) 🧍🚠🅰

Park office, located on Dinnerbell Road; (729) 329–8591. Open dawn to dusk.

Ohiopyle is also the starting point for the **Laurel Highlands Hiking Trail.** You can hike 70 miles here from Ohiopyle to an area near Johnstown. Eight overnight sites have been set up along the trail, which is designed for serious hikers.

There are flush toilets and shower facilities in Ohiopyle State Park, and Fox's Pizza is not far away. Nearby, the community center offers a licensed day-care center for children under the minimum rafting age of four.

Any of the following outfitters can help you select your trip:

- **Laurel Highlands River Tours,** P.O. Box 107, Ohiopyle 15470, (800) 4–RAFTIN or (724) 329–8531; www.laurelhighlands.com

- **Mountain Streams and Trails Outfitters,** P.O. Box 106, Route 381, Ohiopyle 15470, (800) RAFT NOW (723–8669); www.mtstreams.com

- **White Water Adventurers, Inc.,** P.O. Box 31, Ohiopyle 15470, (800) WWA–RAFT; www.wwaraft.com

- **Wilderness Voyageurs, Inc.,** P.O. Box 97 Department PA, Ohiopyle 15470, (800) 272–4141 or (724) 329–5517; www.wildernessvoyageurs.com

Kentuck Knob (ages 9 and up) 🏛
Kentuck Road, Chalk Hill; (724) 329–1901; www.kentuckknob.com. **Open Tuesday through Sunday and Monday holidays. Regular tours depart from 10:00 A.M. to 4:00 P.M. Reservations are recommended. Tours are $$$. Longer, in-depth tours are $$$$ and depart at 8:30 A.M. or by reservation.**

If you are a Franklin Lloyd Wright fan, you won't want to miss this example of one of Wright's late designs, built in 1953. Children nine and up are welcome to join the regular tour. There are no day-care facilities for younger ones.

Mill Run

Fallingwater (ages 9 and up except for children's tours for ages 5 to 9) 🏛
Route 381; (724) 329–8501; www.wpconline.org/fallingwaterhome.htm. **Open for guided tours April to mid-November, Tuesday through Sunday and Monday holidays 10:00 A.M. to 4:00 P.M. In December tours are offered weekends only 11:00 A.M. to 3:00 P.M. Closed January and February. On weekends, tours are $$$; on weekdays, tours are $$. Children under 9 are not permitted on the regular tour. Special tours for children ages 5 to 9; call for schedules and admission prices.**

The story goes that Frank Lloyd Wright told Edgar Kaufmann, "I want you to live with the waterfall, not just look at it." Because of the technology of cantilevers, Wright was able to do just that.

In a beautiful wooded setting, Wright placed Fallingwater, one of his most significant architectural achievements. It seems as if it has always been here, with the waterfall cascading from it. Inside the house, walls of windows look out into the woods. The American Institute of Architects has called Fallingwater "the best all-time work of American architecture."

The regular tour takes about forty-five minutes to an hour, but if you like, you may make a reservation for a longer tour, which is very detailed and can take up to two hours. (These in-depth tours are available at 8:30 A.M. and carry a fee of at least $$$$ per person.) Tours do require a fair amount of walking. Only the first floor is wheelchair accessible.

Please note that children under six are not permitted to take the regular one-hour tour of the house. If you wish to see it yourself, however, you may take advantage of child care provided here ($ per child per hour). There's also an in-depth two-hour tour. Children must be nine to attend this tour. Reservations are strongly recommended for both regular and in-depth tours. Lunch is available in Fallingwater's restaurant.

If you would like to see more of Wright's work, try Kentuck Knob described earlier in the Ohiopyle section.

ALSO IN THE AREA

Fallingwater is operated by the Western Pennsylvania Conservancy, which also runs **Bear Run Nature Preserve,** ½ mile away. It is very convenient to Ohiopyle.

The family can camp at **Yogi Bear's Jellystone Park,** but even if you're not camping here, you can take advantage of the waterslides, playground, and other recreational activities. For information and pricing schedule, call (800) 439–4644 or go to www.jellystonemillrun.com.

Champion

Seven Springs Mountain Resort (all ages) ⊗⊖

Located between exits 9 and 10 on the PA Turnpike; (800) 452–2223; www.7springs.com.

Ski magazine has rated Seven Springs Mountain Resort number-one ski resort in the mid-Atlantic. New features include two new chairlifts and a "magic carpet" conveyor lift. This large facility offers lodging for more than 5,000 people in hotel rooms, condos, and chalets. Besides ski and snowboard rentals and ski lessons, the resort offers snowtubing (eight chutes), swimming, bowling, concerts, snowmobile tours, snowcat rides, indoor miniature golf, and game rooms. The sleigh rides are picture-perfect. And in summer, there's an alpine slide, chairlift rides, hayrides, horseback rides, fly fishing, and more.

Donegal

Caddie Shak Family Fun Park (all ages) ⊛

Located 1½ miles east on Route 31 off exit 9 of the PA Turnpike; (724) 593–7400 or (877) 416–7400; www.caddieshak.com. Open daily March through October. Admission and parking are free.

You can't drive past Caddie Shak Family Fun Park without a reaction from your kids. ("Their tongues hang out," says one parent.) Convenient to the turnpike, Caddie Shak has three go-kart tracks, miniature golf, batting cages, games, and food. Other attractions include bumper cars with water cannons, a petting zoo, paintball, and horseback riding. A nice way to break up the trip. The rides and attractions are moderately priced, and family discounts are available. Wheelchair accessible.

Living Treasures Animal Park (all ages)

Route 711, south of Route 31; (724) 593–8300; www.ltanimalpark.com. Open Memorial Day through Labor Day 10:00 A.M. to 8:00 P.M. In April, May, September, and October, open daily 10:00 A.M. to 6:00 P.M. Admission is $$ for adults and $ for children 3 to 11; children 2 and under are **free.** Please note that there are two "Living Treasures" locations. The other, also listed in this guide, is in Moraine.

Get up close to more than one hundred species of friendly animals from all over the world at Living Treasures Animal Park.

Hidden Valley

Hidden Valley Four Seasons Resort (all ages)

4 Craighead Drive; (814) 443–2600 or (800) 443–SKII; www.hiddenvalleyresort.com.

The instructors at Hidden Valley Ski want you to learn to ski with them. One of the mid-Atlantic's most popular family ski resorts, Hidden Valley has twenty-five ski slopes and trails, more than 30 miles of cross-country ski trails, and a half-pipe for snowboarders. There's also a kids' camp, indoor and outdoor pools, boating, fishing, tennis, ecotouring, and more.

In spring and summer, there's still a lot to do, such as golfing, mountain biking, and swimming. The many restaurants cater to a variety of tastes, and all are kid-friendly with the possible exception of the Snow Shoe Lounge (kids may be served with parents, but it is a lounge). Mountain Munchkins Child Care offers babysitting for children eighteen months to eight years. There are changing tables in both men's and women's restrooms.

Greensburg

Hanna's Town (ages 8 and up)

951 Old Salem Road; (724) 836–1800. Open Memorial Day through Labor Day, Wednesday through Saturday 10:00 A.M. to 5:00 P.M.; Sunday 1:00 to 4:00 P.M. Open weekends only in May, September, and October 1:00 to 4:00 P.M.

Archaeological research in Greensburg has unearthed nearly one million artifacts at Hanna's Town, which was founded in 1773.

A stockade fort, the home of Robert Hanna, the town jail, and a wagon shed are reconstructed. Klingensmith House has been moved here. You can visit the field museum and see archaeological artifacts unearthed here.

ALSO IN THE AREA

You may want to check out the cozy Kid Space at the **Westmoreland Museum of American Art** (221 North Main Street, 412–837–1500, www.wmuseumaa.org) or the **Westmoreland Symphony Orchestra** (412–837–1850).

Jeannette

Depending on how you look at it, Bushy Run Battlefield is in either Jeannette or Harrison City. Either way, it's about 11 miles northwest of Greensburg, and it's an interesting place to visit.

Bushy Run Battlefield (ages 8 and up) 🏛 🚻 🏕

Route 993; (724) 527–5584; www.bushyrunbattlefield.com. Visitor center: April through October, Wednesday to Saturday 9:00 A.M. to 5:00 P.M. and Sunday noon to 5:00 P.M. Battlefield: Wednesday to Sunday 9:00 A.M. to 5:00 P.M. year-round. From November to March the museum is closed. Admission is $.

Here's an opportunity to acquaint your family with a lesser-known conflict: Pontiac's War. In 1763 Native American forces, under the command of war chief Pontiac, struggled against the British, eventually laying seige to Fort Pitt. At the Bushy Run Battlefield, the British turned the tide against this rebellion and saved Fort Pitt.

At the visitor center a fiber-optic map helps you get your bearings. Take some time to observe the interactive exhibits, maps, flags, and weapons and learn about this episode in our history. In the Kids' Corner you can try on a reproduction uniform. Then you can take a guided tour of the battlefield. There are 3 miles of historic hiking trails, education programs, and special events. On the Edge Hill Trail, each stop represents one aspect of the Battle of Bushy Run, including the Flour Bag Entrenchment in which flour bags were used to protect the British wounded. There is also a gift shop. Wheelchair accessible.

Another trail, the Flour Sak Discovery Trail, focuses on how humans have used things from the forest. For example, the black walnut tree provided food, dye, insect repellent, gunstocks, and furniture.

The Iroquois Nature Trail was designed by the Boy Scouts to demonstrate the changes in the environment between the nineteenth and twenty-first centuries. There are thirteen stations, such as Beauty in Nature Through Adaptation, where you can see how nature has healed itself in what was once a stone quarry.

Ligonier

Idlewild and Soakzone (all ages)

U.S. Route 30 West; (724) 238–3666; www.idlewild.com. Operating season runs from late May through Labor Day. Open daily from mid-June through late August. The gates and Story Book Forest open at 10:00 A.M., rides and attractions at 11:00 A.M. Closing times vary. Fun-Day passes include all rides and attractions. Season passes also available. Children 2 and under enter free.

Idlewild and SoakZone, once named "America's Most Beautiful Theme Park," is the home of Mister Rogers' Neighborhood of Make-Believe, complete with the Neighborhood Trolley your preschoolers have always wanted to see. Fred Rogers himself served as creative consultant for this charming replica with the castle, King Friday, Queen Sarah Saturday, and all the details you'll recognize right away. In July, characters such as Mr. McFeeley may appear in person.

Located about 50 miles east of Pittsburgh and a sister park to Kennywood and Sandcastle, Idlewild and SoakZone began as a picnic area in 1878. This relaxing and manageable park, nestled in the woods, is perfect for children twelve and under, but it also has rides for older kids such as the Wild Mouse steel coaster and Rollo Coaster, a classic wooden coaster built in 1938. At present the three-row carousel, built by the Philadelphia Toboggan Company in the 1930s, still entrances children of all ages. The entire family can cool off on Paul Bunyan's Loggin Toboggan—a wet and wild water ride.

The beloved Story Book Forest was added in 1956, with its more than forty scenes and characters from fairy tales and nursery rhymes. You'll literally step through the pages of a storybook to visit the homes of The Old Woman Who Lived in a Shoe, Snow White and the Seven Dwarfs, and The Three Little Pigs, among others. It takes about an hour to explore Story Book Forest.

Jumpin' Jungle gets families climbing, crawling, and, well, jumping! Climb up the netting or jump in a ball pit. SoakZone is a giant water attraction for all ages. It has Hydro Racers, Pipeline Plunge, Tipping Bucket, and a huge swimming pool, plus Little Squirts—wet fun for younger ones. Bring your bathing suit if you plan to go on any of the waterslides or swim in the pool.

Amazing
Laurel Highlands Facts

Mt. Davis in Somerset County is the highest peak in Pennsylvania.

Fort Ligonier (ages 8 and up) 🏛

Intersection of Routes 30 and 711; (724) 238–9701; www.fortligonier.org. The fort is open daily April to October, Monday through Saturday 10:00 A.M. to 4:30 P.M., and Sunday noon to 4:30 P.M. Admission is $$ for adults, $ for children 6 to 14 years old.

Fort Ligonier was built by the British during the French and Indian War. The entire fort, except for its foundation, was destroyed by 1800, but it has been carefully reconstructed. It has gun batteries and a retrenchment. The visitor center offers exhibits and a film. You can visit several restored buildings such as a quartermaster's storehouse, magazine, hospital, and commissary.

Every October, on the anniversary of its most famous battle, the fort celebrates Fort Ligonier Days.

Laughlintown

Compass Inn Museum (ages 8 and up) 🏛

Three miles east of Ligonier, on US 30 East; (724) 238–4983; www.compassinn.com. Open May through October, Tuesday through Saturday 11:00 A.M. to 4:00 P.M. and Sunday noon to 4:00 P.M. Admission is $$ for adults, $ for students, free for children under 5.

If you want to get a picture of what it was like in a typical roadside inn of the eighteenth and nineteenth centuries, visit the Compass Inn Museum. The log part was built in 1799, and the stone addition in 1820. The Ligonier Valley Historical Society has restored the building, and the kitchen, blacksmith's shop, and barn have been reconstructed on their original sites.

You can find out where terms like "upper crust" and "toasting" came from. You can see how travelers spent the night crammed into beds with other guests. You can visit the family's quarters, as well as the barn, where old horse- and ox-drawn vehicles still remain, and sometimes a blacksmith is on duty, demonstrating the craft. You can also see tools of the period.

During summer, living-history days are held on the third weekend of each month. In November and December candlelight tours are offered on weekends only.

Johnstown

The town of Johnstown will always be remembered as the site of the tragic flood that occurred on May 31, 1889. The stress of a storm proved too much for the town's neglected dam, which broke, sending a wall of water down the mountain and through the town, killing more than 2,000 people.

But Johnstown is not just a place of tragedy; it is a town full of life. In late June, Johnstown hosts "Thunder in the Valley," an unusually family-oriented motorcycle rally. In August, the Cambria County Ag-Tour offers a day in the country with **free** refreshments at several area farms. The Log House Arts Festival, during Labor Day weekend, has many activities for children. Also, the Pasquerilla Performing Arts Center has "Sydney's Series" of plays for children. Besides these annual events, Johnstown has the BOTTLE WORKS Ethnic Arts Center.

Johnstown Flood National Memorial (ages 8 and up) 🏛

Located in Saint Michael, 10 miles northeast of Johnstown; (814) 495–4643; www.nps .gov/jofl. Open Memorial Day to Labor Day 9:00 A.M. to 5:00 P.M. Closed on Veterans Day, Martin Luther King Jr. Day, Presidents' Day, Thanksgiving, Christmas, and New Year's Day. Admission $; children 16 and under enter free. Call for details. Take U.S. Route 219 to the Saint Michael/Sidman exit. Head east on Route 869, and turn left onto Lake Road at the sign.

The Johnstown Flood began on the site in Saint Michael where you can see the Johnstown Flood National Memorial, administered by the National Park Service. In fact, you can see what little is left of the South Fork Dam from here. A weakness in this dam is suspected of having made the flood so disastrous.

An award-winning documentary, *Black Friday,* brings the events to life. The thirty-five-minute film puts you inside the terror of the flood. In fact, it is so effective parents are warned that it may be too frightening for young children.

In summer you can see reenactments of some of the events surrounding the flood. You can also take a tour around the dam. The flood happened on Memorial Day, so every year during that holiday weekend, the abutments of the dam glow with the light of thousands of luminaries. Special presentations are offered, including *Tales of the Great Flood,* a theater event in which costumed interpreters read from eyewitness accounts of the flood.

Johnstown Incline (all ages)

711 Edgehill Drive; easily accessible to Routes 56 and 403, and Route 271; (814) 536–1816; www.inclinedplane.com. Seasonal hours. Call ahead or check the Web site. Free parking is available at both the top and the bottom.

After visiting the memorial, you'll want to complete the story with a tour of the Johnstown Flood Museum. But first you might want to break up the seriousness with an exhilarating ride on the Johnstown Inclined Plane. You'll travel up on an amazing 71.9 percent grade, the steepest vehicular inclined plane in the world. Your car can ride the incline with you, if you desire, so that you can drive around the borough of Westmont.

In Westmont, you can see Luzerne Street, noted in the *Guiness Book of World Records* as the longest street with elm trees. Historic Grandview Cemetery is just a ten-minute walk from the Incline.

After the Johnstown Flood, the frightened residents of the area wanted to live at the top of the hill, but they needed a way to commute to and from the city, so this incline was built. An "incline" is an unusual kind of cable railway found in Johnstown and Pittsburgh. During Johnstown's two subsequent floods (1936 and 1977), the incline became the people's escape route. At night, when both the tracks and the cars are lit up, the incline is a spectacular sight.

At the top of the incline, 634 feet above the city, there is an observation deck, visitor center, and the City View Bar and Grill Restaurant, due to open in Spring 2005. The view of the Conemaugh Valley is spectacular, as seen from the glass-walled Plane Visitor Center. From this vantage point you can see the largest free-flying American flags in the country.

The Johnstown Flood Museum (ages 6 and up)

304 Washington Street (P.O. Box 1889, Johnstown 15907); (814) 539–1889; www.jaha .org. Open seven days a week, year-round, 10:00 A.M. to 5:00 P.M. From Memorial Day through Labor Day, hours are extended to 10:00 A.M. to 7:00 P.M. on Friday and Saturday. Tickets are $ and are good for admission to both the Johnstown Flood Museum and the Heritage Discovery Center.

The museum, located in a former Carnegie Library, tells the story of the Johnstown flood disaster. Photos show how the town looked before the waters came, and after. An animated map with light and sound effects shows how the water swept through Johnstown, destroying thousands of homes and businesses.

First, see the documentary film *The Johnstown Flood,* which won the Academy Award for Best Documentary Short Subject in 1989. This twenty-five-minute movie is shown hourly and was made using black-and-white still photos taken after the flood. A longer version of this movie has been shown on PBS's *The American Experience.* Then visit the two floors of permanent exhibits, artifacts, and a 3-D multimedia presentation. The museum store offers a large selection of books and gifts.

Johnstown Heritage Discovery Center (ages 8 and up)

Route 56, Broad Street and Seventh Avenue; (814) 539–1889. www.jaha.org. Open daily 10:00 A.M. to 5:00 P.M., with extended hours in the summer months. Admission is $$ for adults, $ for seniors and students, and tickets are good for both the Heritage Discovery Center and the Johnstown Flood Museum.

The Heritage Discovery Center is housed in the former Germania Brewery Company building, built in 1907. Opened in 2001, the Frank and Sylvia Pasquerilla Heritage Discovery Center immerses the visitor in turn-of-the-century Johnstown as experienced by immigrants from Eastern and Southern Europe who came to Johnstown from 1870 to 1914 to work in the mills and mines.

As you enter the museum, you'll receive a card with a photo of one of eight immigrant characters. As you move through the exhibits, you can plug in your card into different interactive stations that demonstrate the immigrant's experience. The permanent exhibit, *America Through Immigrant Eyes,* allows you to experience the sights, sounds, and even the smells of immigrants' daily lives.

BOTTLE WORKS Ethnic Arts Center (ages 6 and up)

411 Third Avenue; (814) 536–5399; www.bottleworks.org. Open Tuesday through Friday 10:00 A.M. to 4:00 P.M. and Saturday 11:00 A.M. to 3:00 P.M. Admission is free. Some special events have additional fees.

In 1994 the old Tulip Bottling Company building was converted into the BOTTLE WORKS, whose mission is "to educate, preserve, and celebrate the ethnic heritage of the people of the Johnstown region." The Tulip Bottling Company was founded by a family of Russian and Hungarian Jews. In just a few years, the BOTTLE WORKS has become well known in the area for its Celebrations of Heritages through visual, performing, and folk arts. Summertime offers ethnic camps for children and ethnic arts and crafts at the FolkFest.

ALSO IN THE AREA

Every September, the Johnstown Area Heritage Association hosts **Johnstown Folk-Fest,** a three-day outdoor music festival with four stages providing more than seventy hours of entertainment. For information call (888) 222–1889, or check the Web sites www.jaha.org and www.johnstownfolkfest.org.

The Johnstown Area Heritage Association also administers the **Wagner–Ritter House,** which will open its doors in 2005 to re-create the domestic lives of the thousands who toiled "in the shadow of the mills." For information check the Web site www.jaha.org.

Stackhouse Park offers many special programs for children in its 277 acres of wooded land.

The **Windber Coal Heritage Center,** in the nearby mining town of Windber, offers an interesting interactive view of the everyday life of a coal mining family. Open 10:00 A.M. to 5:00 P.M. Tuesday through Saturday May 1 to October 31. Adjacent to outdoor Miner's Park and within walking distance of the shops and restaurants of Windber. Call (814) 467–6680 for admission fees and information, or check the Web site www.allegheny.org/windber.

Claysburg

Blue Knob All Seasons Resort (all ages)

U.S. Route 20 North (from PA Turnpike, exit 11). For details call in-state (814) 239–5111; out-of-state, call (800) 458–3403; www.blueknob.com.

One of the top ski resorts in the area, Blue Knob offers a KinderSki program, a ski school, an outdoor ice rink, tubing park, and cross-country skiing. In the warmer months, there's golf, hiking, biking, tennis, and swimming.

Amazing
Laurel Highlands Facts

The Laurel Highlands get more than 100 inches of real snow per year, plus another 60 to 80 inches from man-made snow machines.

Cresson

Allegheny Portage Railroad National Historic Site
(ages 8 and up) (m)

Twelve miles west of Altoona and 10 miles east of Ebensburg on US 22, off the Gallitzin exit; (814) 886–6150; www.nps.gov/alpo. Open daily 9:00 A.M. to 5:00 P.M. Closed some holidays. Admission is $; children under 17 enter free.

In the middle of the nineteenth century, when Philadelphia was being linked to Pittsburgh by rail and canal, this portion of the Allegheny Mountains between Hollidaysburg and Johnstown seemed impassable. So someone came up with a "portage railroad." A series of inclines carried the freight and passengers up the hills.

The visitor center has exhibits, a twenty-minute movie, and well-informed rangers. The Engine House Interpretive Building features full-scale models, and hands-on exhibits. The railroad no longer exists, but you can walk along a portion of its route and see one section of restored track. As you enjoy the view from the overlook, be sure to note Skew Arch Bridge, which is actually twisted so that a wagon road could pass over the track. Rangers can direct you to the newly-opened Staple Bend Tunnel, located 25 miles from Allegheny Portage Railroad in another section of the park. Costumed presentations and ranger-led hikes are available during the summer months.

Hollidaysburg

Trough Creek State Park (all ages) (m) (m) (A)
Route 994. For information and pricing schedule, call (814) 658–3847; www.dcnr.state .pa.us. Twenty-four-hour access. Free.

The 554-acre Trough Creek State Park is a scenic gorge created by Trough Creek as it cuts through Terrace Mountain and empties into Raystown Lake. If you want to stay in comfort in a beautiful forested setting, Trough Creek Lodge, at Trough Creek State Park, is available for rental year-round. It is a two-story home built in the 1800s as an ironmaster's house. Now completely renovated, it offers a modern eat-in kitchen, four bedrooms, a bathroom, and central heat. The lodge is fully accessible for people with disabilities.

Canoe Creek State Park (all ages)

On US 22, about 13 miles east of Altoona, and about 7 miles east of Hollidaysburg or 11 miles west of Water Street; (814) 695–6807; www.dcnr.state.pa.us. The "day use" side is open 8:00 A.M. to sunset. The cabin area and east side have twenty-four-hour access. Admission is free.

You can reserve either a rustic or modern cabin and enjoy a wide variety of nature education programs at Canoe Creek State Park, one of a few parks that offer bat hikes, a favorite with our boys. At Canoe Creek you can join in on a bat hike to look in on Pennsylvania's largest bat nursery colony (females and young) in the attic of an old church. As night falls, they emerge from their home—about 10,000 of them! Children under twelve must be accompanied by an adult. Bring a flashlight. Other programs teach about bluebirds, birds' nests, frogs and toads, and wildflowers. Persons with disabilities may call (814) 695–6807 if assistance will be needed to participate in the program.

Patton

Seldom Seen Tourist Coal Mine (ages 8 and up)

Located on Route 36, 4 miles north of Patton, 7 miles from Prince Gallitzin State Park; (800) 237–8590 or mine phone, in season only, (814) 247–6305; www.seldomseenmine .com. Open Memorial Day, July 4th, and Labor Day, plus weekends throughout June, as well as Thursday and Friday in July and August. Haunted Mine Tours offered during the last three weekends in October. Hour-long tours are conducted daily from noon to 6:00 P.M. Admission: adults, $$; children under 12, $. Group rates available.

Many of the coal mines in southwestern Pennsylvania were small, family-run mines like this one. This nonprofit educational attraction is one of the region's most popular sites. Many of the tour guides are former miners and descendants of immigrant miners. Somehow once your kids have imagined themselves hand digging and hand loading coal for 25 cents a ton, taking out the garbage doesn't seem so bad.

Altoona

Altoona has a lot to offer, including its new minor-league baseball team, the Altoona Curve.

Railroaders Memorial Museum (all ages)

1300 Ninth Avenue; (888) 4–ALTOONA; www.railroadcity.com. From April to the end of October, open Monday through Saturday 9:00 A.M. to 5:00 P.M. and Sunday 11:00 A.M. to 5:00 P.M. In November and December, open Saturday and Sunday noon to 5:00 P.M. Closed January through March, except for group tours (by appointment), and special events. Admission is $$; children under 5 are free.

There are many museums devoted to the technology of railroading, but the Railroaders Memorial Museum tells the story of the men and women of the Pennsylvania Railroad (PRR). Here, you'll experience Altoona at the height of industrial America. Located in the former Pennsylvania Railroad Master Mechanics building, this high-tech interpretive facility guides visitors through a firsthand experience of life in a booming railroad town. A film about the men and women of the PRR is also featured and included in the admission price. The Railroaders Memorial Museum celebrates its twenty-fifth anniversary in 2005, and plans to celebrate in style with the full-steam return of the state's official steam locomotive, the K–4 1361, the last of its kind.

The museum is across from the Amtrak station, so real fanatics can come by train, see the trains, and go home by train. After your visit, stop by the adjacent Boyer Candy and browse through the specialty shops in the historic downtown business district.

Horseshoe Curve National Historic Landmark (all ages) 🏛

Located 6 miles west of Altoona; (814) 946–0834 or (888) 4–ALTOONA; www.railroad city.com. Open April through the end of October, Monday through Saturday 10:00 A.M. to 6:00 P.M., Sunday noon to 6:00 P.M. During November and December the visitor center and funicular incline are closed weekdays, but open Saturday and Sunday, noon to 6:00 P.M. Admission is $; a yearly pass is $$. Children under 5 are free.

At the Railroaders Memorial Museum, you can see a film that describes how the **Horseshoe Curve Railroad** was built by some 450 immigrants with picks and shovels, and opened in 1854. Then you can drive about 5 miles to watch the trains at Horseshoe Curve National Historic Landmark. Administered by the Railroaders Memorial Museum, this incredible engineering feat revolutionized rail travel, cleared the way for the westward expansion of the railroad, and made the Allegheny Portage Railroad obsolete (see previous entry under Cresson).

The story of Horseshoe Curve is told at a modern interpretive center. Visitors can ride to track elevation onboard the single-track funicular or walk the 194 evenly spaced stairs. At track elevation, more than fifty trains can be viewed every day along the Norfolk Southern mainline. One round-trip funicular ride is included in the admission.

There is a food concession open seasonally, and all bathrooms have changing tables. In 2005, Horseshoe Curve will host its first-ever Horseshoe Tournament.

Quaint Corner Children's Museum (ages 3 to 10) 🧒

On Route 36, at 2000 Union Avenue, only a few blocks from the Railroaders Memorial Museum; (814) 944–6830. Open Thursday, Friday, and Saturday from 1:00 to 5:00 P.M. Admission is $.

Kids love exploring closets and attics, and they're welcome to snoop around in the fourteen rooms of the Quaint Corner Children's Museum. Peek in the International Closet or the Amish Closet, the Medical Room, or Pirate Treasure Closet.

The Quaint Corner Children's Museum was designed as a place for families to explore together, promoting creative hands-on learning and an appreciation for art, history, and science. The house itself is charming with its stained-glass windows and fine woodwork. Children love the craft room, dress-up clothes, and the sandbox in the basement. There's even a player piano in the gift shop. The bathroom, like the house, is old, with no changing or wheelchair facilities. The annual Quaint Corner Children's Fair comes in mid-August with puppet shows, games, and food.

Benzel's Pretzel Bakery (all ages)

5200 Sixth Avenue (Route 764); (814) 942–5062; www.benzels.com. Open Monday through Friday 9:00 A.M. to 5:00 P.M. and Saturday 9:00 A.M. to 1:00 P.M. Tours are free.

You can walk to Benzel's from the Quaint Corner Children's Museum. Operated by a third generation of the Benzel family, Benzel's Pretzel Bakery makes about five million pretzels every day. At one time the pretzels were shaped by hand, but at present the dough goes through an extruder. There is a changing table in the wheelchair-accessible restroom.

Lakemont Park (all ages) 🎠

700 Park Avenue; (814) 949–PARK; www.lakemontparkfun.com. Open early May through mid-September, plus selected weekends in October, November, and December. Several different passes are available, with the most expensive All Day Ride & Slide Pass costing $$ per person.

In 2000, Lakemont Park reopened its treasured historic Leap the Dips roller coaster, the world's oldest roller coaster and the last remaining example of the side friction figure-eight design. In 2001 the Tin Lizzy Antique Auto ride opened. In all, there are more than thirty rides and attractions, including the Island Waterpark, two roller coasters, two go-kart tracks, an arcade, food, and more.

Every year from Thanksgiving through the Sunday after New Year's, Lakemont hosts its "Holiday Lights on the Lake."

Sinking Valley

Fort Roberdeau Historic Site and Natural Area (ages 8 and up) 🏛 🚌

Off Route 433 north of the Bellwood exit of Interstate 99; (814) 946–0048; www.fort roberdeau.org. Fort and visitor center open May 15 through September 30, Tuesday to Saturday 11:00 A.M. to 5:00 P.M. and Sunday 1:00 to 5:00 P.M. Closed on Monday. Trails open year-round daily 8:00 A.M. to sunset.

Sinking Valley, which is between Altoona and Tyrone, is the site of Fort Roberdeau. This 1778 stockade has been reconstructed, and it now offers living-history reenactments, forty-five acres of field and forest, nature trails, tours, and a picnic area.

Going **Batty**

For Judah's tenth birthday, we took about twelve of his friends on a bat hike. We also brought Seth, who was seven and a half, and Gideon, a newborn in a baby sling. Judah was very interested in bats.

The guide told us that July was a good time for a bat hike because the bats would recently have had young, and the colony would be at its largest.

As the sun set we waited outside the dilapidated barn that was the bats' home. The kids were all impatient to see the bats fly out to feed on the millions of insects that congregated over the nearby field.

Our guide had brought a device that amplified the bats' sonar sounds. He explained how to distinguish the sounds the bats made as they located and devoured their prey.

As darkness fell, first one bat emerged from a crack in the roof of the barn. Then another. Then another, then more and more until we counted more than 200, then lost count. The sky over the field was dark with bats.

Tipton

Del Grosso's Park (all ages)

Twelve miles north of Altoona on old US 220, off I–99 exit 41 or 46 ; (814) 684–3538; www.delgrossos.com. Open seasonally. All-day Waterworks and rides: $$. All-day Waterworks, rapids, and rides: $$$.

Three new rides highlighted the 2004 season at Del Grosso's Park, which features more than thirty rides, an extensive water park, an interactive children's park, an eighteen-hole minigolf course with five waterfalls and two lakes, go-karts, and miniature train rides.

Tyrone

Gardners Candies (all ages)

30 West Tenth Street; (800) 24–CANDY for information or to schedule a tour; www .gardnerscandies.com. Open Monday through Saturday 9:30 A.M. to 9:00 P.M. and Sunday 1:00 to 9:00 P.M. Admission is free.

A sweet taste of nostalgia for children of all ages, Gardners Candies has been making candies for more than a century. Here you can see first-hand how chocolates are made; this is not a simulated tour. Inside its History of Candyland Museum, you can see antique candy-making equipment, a 10-cent Coke machine, and other nostalgic artifacts.

Spruce Creek

Indian Caverns (all ages) 🕸 🏛

Eleven miles east of Tyrone on Route 45, between Water Street and State College in Huntington County; (814) 632–7578; www.indiancaverns.com. Open daily Memorial Day through Labor Day 9:00 A.M. to 6:00 P.M. In May, September, and October, open 9:00 A.M. to 4:00 P.M. daily. Closed November through March. Call for admission prices.

Indian Caverns celebrates its seventy-fifth anniversary season in 2004. One reason for its popularity is the real cave paintings on the walls of Indian Caverns. Here, you can see ancient paintings of a turtle, a tepee, and a Mohawk chief.

More than 400 years ago, Native Americans used these caverns as a winter shelter, council chamber, and burial ground. Adjacent to Indian Caverns is a second cavern, Giant's Hall, where you can view the Grotto of the Wah Wah Taysee, a cave that glows, and the Frozen Niagara, which is more than two stories tall. Kids enjoy the sounds made by a musical rock.

The wide concrete walkways and Native American artifacts make this an excellent cavern if your family includes a wide range of ages, attention spans, and energy levels.

Huntingdon

Greenwood Furnace State Park (all ages) 🏛 👫 ⛺

On Route 305; 5 miles west of Belleville; park office (814) 667–1800; visitor center: (814) 667–1805; www.dcnr.state.pa.us. The visitor center is open 9:00 A.M. to 5:00 P.M. Wednesday through Sunday during the summer and 9:00 A.M. to 5:00 P.M. on weekends only in spring and fall.

Less than thirty minutes from Huntingdon, Lewistown, or State College is a green park area on the site of the Greenwood iron furnaces and the "village built around an inferno." You can take a one-hour, self-guided walking tour of a portion of the historic district and see parts of the town such as the tramway, historic roads, charcoal hearths, a stone mansion, stone church, and stables. History and nature programs are presented every weekend during the summer. The park's most popular event is Old Home Days, during the first full weekend of August, when living-history interpreters offer historical demonstrations such as soap making, brew making, and bonnet making. Campsites are available.

Lincoln Caverns and Whisper Rocks (all ages)

On US 22, 3 miles west of Huntingdon; (814) 643–0268; www.lincolncaverns.com. Tour hours vary seasonally. Admission is $$ and free for children 3 and under. A single admission fee gets you into Lincoln Caverns and Whisper Rocks.

These two caverns are a bit more challenging than some other nearby caverns. The walkways are often damp, but the minerals in the water droplets keep this a living cave. The rock formations are spectacular: flowstones, stalactites, calcite, and crystals.

Many educational programs are available, including geology and speleology workshops, as well as programs focused on debunking common misconceptions about bats. Bring a sweater. Special offerings include a kids cave camp in June and Ghosts and Goblins tours in October.

The Swigart Museum (all ages)

US 22 East, 4 miles east of Huntingdon; (814) 643–0885; www.swigartmuseum.com. Open daily Memorial Day through October, 9:00 A.M. to 5:00 P.M. Admission is $; children under 6 enter free.

This museum is the oldest automobile museum in America, established by the late W. Emmert Swigart in 1920. William E. Swigart Jr. continued the collection upon his father's death in 1949. The Swigart collection emphasizes the era when America was first becoming a mobile society. Featured cars include its newest acquisition, a 1909 Overland; a 1900 Winton; 1904 Rambler; and the only remaining Carroll. Other highlights include two Tuckers and Herbie, the "Love Bug." About thirty-five cars from the collection of 200 are on display at any given time. Supporting these is an outstanding collection of license plates and name plates. Children will enjoy seeing the exhibits of antique toys, trains, and bicycles. In August the museum and the local chapter of the Antique Automobile Club of America sponsor the Swigart Museum Meet.

Hesston

Area residents believe that **Raystown Lake** doesn't get the attention it deserves. This huge man-made lake is located in Huntington County, surrounded by two state forests, trout-stocked streams, museums, historic sites, campgrounds, and lots of family recreation. Call (800) RAYSTOWN.

Amazing
Laurel Highlands Facts

This region includes more than twenty golf courses (including the Latrobe Country Club owned by Arnold Palmer); 700,000 acres of game land; 120 lakes and streams, plus white-water rafting on the Youghiogheny River; and Raystown Lake, Pennsylvania's largest man-made lake.

Seven Points Marina (all ages) ⚠

Raystown Lake, off Route 26; (814) 658–3074 for departure times and details; www .7pointsmarina.com. The boats operate for both private charter and for the public, April through October. Public cruises depart up to three times a day at the height of the summer season and cost $$ for adults, and $ for children under 12.

Seven Points Marina, Pennsylvania's largest marina, offers a variety of ways to enjoy the lake and its countryside, including houseboat rentals and daily boat rentals. The 75-foot lake cruiser *Princess* is available for public cruises, dinner cruises, and private charters. Seven Points Restaurant, with both indoor and outdoor tables, overlooks the inner harbor. Kids enjoy feeding the hundreds of carp at the Fish Feeding Station.

Entriken

Lake Raystown Resort and Lodge 🏨

100 Chipmunk Crossing, Raystown Lake; (814) 658–3500; www.raystownresort.com.

Raystown Resort is a great spot for recreation. The resort includes twenty-five lakeside vacation cabins new in 2004, 122 campsites, several different kinds of cabins (some with hot tubs), luxury houseboats for rent, and a lodge. The list of activities for families goes on and on: the WildRiver Water Park (with a brand-new totally dark waterslide called the Atomic Blaster), Caddy's Revenge miniature golf, bank-shot basketball court, and a full-service marina featuring boat rentals, Jet Skis, etc. From Memorial Day to Labor Day, there are daily organized activities for children.

Rockhill

East Broad Top Railroad and the Rockhill Trolley Museum jointly host a Fall Spectacular during Columbus Day weekend. On the first Saturday in December, Santa's Trolley runs with decorations, an outdoor train display, and hot cocoa.

East Broad Top Railroad (all ages)

Route 994, 1 mile west of Orbisonia in Rockhill; (814) 447–3011; www.spikesys.com/ EBT. Open from June through October, Saturday and Sunday, with three train trips daily. Trains depart at 11:00 A.M., 1:00 P.M., and 3:00 P.M. Fares are $$; children under 2 ride free. Group rates available for groups of twenty or more.

Now a National Historic Landmark, East Broad Top Railroad once carried coal and other raw materials. At present it is the most complete and authentic rail site in North America.

Board the train at Orbisonia Station for a ride on the only narrow-gauge railroad in the East still running at its original site. The narrated train ride takes about fifty minutes and carries you past countryside that is virtually unchanged since the days when East Broad Top Railroad transported coal along these tracks. If you like, bring along a picnic lunch. You can get off at Colgate Grove, picnic, and go back on a later train. There are no restrooms or concessions on the train. Riders using wheelchairs are encouraged to call ahead so arrangements can be made.

Every year during Columbus Day weekend, railroad buffs come from all over the United States to East Broad Top's Fall Spectacular. For this event all four locomotives operate at once, and scheduled shop tours are available.

Rockhill Trolley Museum (all ages)

Meadow Street (Route 994); on weekends call (814) 447–9576; other days call (610) 965–9028; www.rockhilltrolley.org. Open weekends only Memorial Day through October, 11:00 A.M. to 4:00 P.M., plus some holidays. Fares are $; children under 2 ride free. For more information write to Railways to Yesterday, Inc., P.O. Box 1601, Allentown 18105.

Adjacent to East Broad Top Railroad, the Rockhill Trolley Museum has twenty-six trolleys and streetcars, including cars from Philadelphia, Johnstown, Harrisburg, Scranton, and York. Nine trolleys are currently operational, including open cars, closed cars, an interurban car, a snowplow, a sweeper, and a Philadelphia PCC. You can take a more-than-3-mile ride on a restored trolley, passing the Rockhill Iron Furnace.

Like the National Trolley Museum near Pittsburgh, the Rockhill Trolley Museum is staffed by volunteers who love what they're doing. Volunteers here are members of Railways to Yesterday, Inc. Your trolley ticket is good for unlimited rides on the date purchased. Most days, you can try out two or three different cars. If you time it right, you can meet the returning East Broad Top Railroad train, passing just a few feet away.

Robertsdale

Broad Top Area Coal Miners Museum and Entertainment Center
(ages 8 and up)
Reality Theater, Main Street; (814) 635–3807, (814) 635–3220, or (814) 635–2013. Open year-round Friday and Saturday 10:00 A.M. to 5:00 P.M. and Sunday noon to 5:00 P.M. Admission is $. On show nights, tickets are $$ for adults, $ for children.

This museum offers exhibits about coal mining and railroading in the area.

Bedford

If you like the tradition of stealing a kiss on a kissing bridge, you'll love Bedford County. It has fourteen covered bridges, and you can cuddle your toddlers and embarrass your older kids on every one of them. You can take a pleasant walking tour of Historic Downtown Bedford and stop at several historic houses and the Fort Bedford Museum. For information, call the Visitors Bureau at (800) 765–3331 or go to www.bedfordcounty.net. You can also find a driving tour on this Web site.

Old Bedford Village (all ages) 🏛
Business US 220, ½ mile south of PA Turnpike exit 11, also reachable from US 30; (814) 623–1156; www.oldbedfordvillage.com. Spring and summer hours: Memorial Day weekend through Labor Day weekend, open 9:00 A.M. to 5:00 P.M. daily except Wednesday. Fall hours: Thursday through Saturday 9:00 A.M. to 5:00 P.M., Sunday 10:00 A.M. to 4:00 P.M. Admission is $$ for adults and $ for students and children 6 and over.

Drive over the Claycomb Covered Bridge to Old Bedford Village. This village of more than forty reproduction and authentic log, stone, and frame structures is beautifully laid out to re-create a typical village of about 1750 to 1900, with homes, schools, a church, and shops. Interpreters in period costumes bake cookies and make brooms, and much more. About fourteen indigenous crafts are represented. The kids will love stopping for ice cream or doughnuts as you tour the town.

Meals are available at Pendergrass Tavern in the village. Dress comfortably and wear walking shoes. Wheelchair accessible. The Village Craft and Gift Shop offers many unusual crafts made in the village, as well as souvenirs.

Annual special events include a crafts festival in June, gospel music and a story-telling festival in August, Civil War reenactments in September, pumpkin festivals in October, and a holiday celebration in December.

Fort Bedford Museum (ages 8 and up)
Fort Bedford Drive; (814) 623–8891 or (800) 259–4284; www.bedfordcounty.net. Open daily May through October, except Tuesday in May, September, and October, 10:00 A.M. to 5:00 P.M. Admission is $; children under 6 are free. Family rate $$.

Old Fort Bedford was a British stockade built in 1758 during the French and Indian War. Later it was used as a British outpost on the frontier until the early 1770s. Fort Bedford is gone, but you can learn about its past by touring the Fort Bedford Museum. The museum includes a large scale model of the fort, Native American artifacts, weapons, uniforms, a Conestoga wagon, and children's toys of the period. Wheelchair accessible.

Where to Eat

IN THE JOHNSTOWN AREA

Applebee's Neighborhood Grill & Bar, 425 Galleria Drive, Johnstown; (814) 269–4500. This popular chain is consistent and family-friendly. Children's menu.

Coney Island Lunch, 127 Clinton Street, Johnstown; (814) 535–2885. This casual place serves hot dogs, hamburgers, etc. Children always welcome.

Grubb's Diner, US 22 at Fourth and Moore, Huntingdon; (814) 643–3934. Casual dinners. Children welcome.

Johnnie's Restaurant and Lounge, 415 Main Street, Johnstown; (814) 536–9309. Greek-style food including Greek salads and gyros, but also spaghetti and rigatoni. Children always welcome.

The Train Station, Philadelphia Street, Indiana; (724) 349–9005. Subs, steaks, seafood. Children's menu.

Where to Stay

IN OHIOPYLE

Ohiopyle State Park Kentuck Campground, (729) 329–8591; call (888) PA–PARKS to reserve.

Scarlett Knob Campground, Inc., Route 381 North; (412) 329–5200. Adjoining Ohiopyle State Park. Both campsites and cabins available.

Yough Plaza Motel, (800) 992–7238; www.wwaraft.com/lodgeing. Within walking distance of the river.

IN THE JOHNSTOWN AREA

Comfort Inn Ebensburg, US 22 West, Ebensburg; (814) 472–6100 or (800) 221–2222. Suites available, indoor pool, free continental breakfast.

Comfort Inn Johnstown, 455 Theatre Drive, Johnstown; (814) 266–3678 or (800) 228–5150. Centrally located near all major attractions.

Days Inn Johnstown, 1540 Scalp Avenue; (814) 269–3366.

Holiday Inn, downtown, 250 Market Street, Johnstown; (814) 535–7777. Indoor pool, Harrigan's restaurant, sidewalk cafe.

Sleep Inn Johnstown, 453 Theatre Drive, Johnstown; (814) 262–9292.

IN THE RAYSTOWN LAKE AREA

Lake Raystown Resort & Lodge, 100 Chipmunk Crossing, Route 994, Entriken;

(814) 658–3500. Wild River Waterpark, miniature golf, hiking, fishing, picnic areas, camping, and restaurants all nearby.

Seven Points Marina/Houseboat Rental, Seven Points Marina, off Route 26; (814) 658–3074. Fully equipped houseboats for rent. Cruises aboard the *Raystown Bell* and *Queen.*

For More Information

Allegheny Mountains Convention and Visitors Bureau, Logan Valley Mall, US 220 and Goods Lane, Altoona 16602; (800) 84–ALTOONA or (814) 943–4183; www.alleghenymountains.org.

Bedford County Visitors Bureau, 141 South Juliana Street, Bedford 15522; (800) 765–3331 or (814) 623–1771; www.bedfordcounty.net.

Fulton County Tourist Promotion Agency, 112 North Third Street, P.O. Box 141, McConnellsburg 17233; (717) 485–4064; www.fultoncountypa.com.

Greater Johnstown/Cambria County Convention and Visitors Bureau, 111 Market Street, Johnstown 15901–1608; (800) 237–8590 or (814) 536–7993; www.visitjohnstownpa.com.

Greene County Tourist Promotion Agency, 17 South Washington Street, Waynesburg 15370; (412) 627–TOUR; www.county.greene.pa.net.

Huntington Country Visitors Bureau, RD 1, Box 222A, Seven Points Road, Hesston 16647; (888) RAYSTOWN; www.raystown.org.

Indiana County Tourist Bureau, Indiana Mall/2090 Route 286 South, Indiana 15701; (724) 463–7505; www.visitindianacountypa.org.

Laurel Highlands Visitors Bureau, 120 East Main Street, Ligonier 15658; (800) 925–7669 or (724) 238–5661; www.laurelhighlands.org.

Pittsburgh and Environs

W hether you see it spread out below you from the dizzying height of one of its inclines, or from the *Gateway Clipper*, rising from the merging waters of the Monongahela, Allegheny, and Ohio Rivers, Pittsburgh is a sight filled with surprises!

In November 2004, the Children's Museum of Pittsburgh opened its newly expanded headquarters. Filled with delightful interactive sculptures and new exhibits, the treasure of the museum is still its re-created set of the television show, *Mister Rogers' Neighborhood*.

Faith & Emily's
FavoriteAttractions
in Pittsburgh and Environs

1. Kennywood, West Mifflin

2. Sandcastle Action Park, West Homestead

3. Carnegie Science Center, Pittsburgh

4. Children's Museum of Pittsburgh

5. Carnegie Museums of Art and Natural History, East Pittsburgh

6. Duquesne or Monongahela Incline, Pittsburgh

7. Pittsburgh Zoo and Aquarium, East Pittsburgh

8. The Gateway Clipper Fleet, Pittsburgh

9. The Pennsylvania Trolley Museum, Washington

10. Drop-In Studio at Society for Comtemporary Craft, Pittsburgh

PITTSBURGH AND ENVIRONS

Also in 2004, the Senator John Heinz Regional History Center opened its new five-story wing, solidifying its affiliation with Washington, D.C.'s Smithsonian Institution. This exciting new wing hosts Smithsonian exhibitions, as well as the new Western Pennsylvania Sports Museum, where you can see such classic artifacts as Satchel Paige's baseball glove and the shoes Franco Harris was wearing when he caught the "Immaculate Reception."

The Phipps Conservatory plans to open its $36.6 million expansion in 2005, offering a tropical forest conservatory, new state-of-the-art greenhouses, and a new welcome center.

The Carnegie Museum of Natural History, named by the *Discovery* Channel and Forbes as one of the best places in the world to see dinosaurs, will become even better when it opens its expanded Dinosaur Hall in 2007. Thanks to Andrew Carnegie and the museums he helped to create, your trip to Pittsburgh can include not only dinosaur bones but paintings, sculpture, history, and more.

In fall 2007, the African American Cultural Center of Greater Pittsburgh expects to open its new museum at Liberty Avenue in downtown Pittsburgh, featuring galleries, classrooms, a theater with 400-plus seats, a gift shop, a cafe, and, many multipurpose spaces to be used for visual and performing art and expression. Also coming soon is SouthSide Works, an entertainment complex on the banks of the Monongahela.

Faith & Emily's
FavoriteEvents
in Pittsburgh and Environs

- **Pittsburgh International Children's Theater Festival,** (Pittsburgh's North Side (april or May); (412) 321–5520.

- **Three Rivers Arts Festival** (first two weeks of June); (412) 281–8723; www.artsfestival.net.

- **"Fireworks Capital of the World" July Fourth Celebration** in New Castle; (724) 654–5593.

- **Greater Pittsburgh Renaissance Festival** (last three weeks of August through September on Saturday, Sunday, and Labor Day; (724) 872–1670; www.pgh-renfest.com.

- **"Pumpkin Patch Trolley,"** Pennsylvania Trolley Museum (October); (412) 228–9256.

- **Holidays at the Carnegie** (November through December); (412) 622–3131.

Pittsburgh is also home to Kennywood, America's favorite traditional amusement park, and Sandcastle, an outstanding waterpark. If you're looking for a decidedly different way to tour Pittsburgh, check out Just Ducky Tours, Inc, which offers tours aboard a World War II military amphibious vehicle. Call (412) 928–2489 for information.

When planning your visit, you may want to check out the Greater Pittsburgh Convention and Visitors Bureau Web site, www.visitpittsburgh.com, or any of the Web sites of the museums and attractions listed in this chapter.

Pittsburgh's North Side

Start your adventure in downtown Pittsburgh's North Side with a stop at the visitor center on Liberty Avenue near Stanwix Street, a handy place to pick up maps, brochures, and advice. Also in this area is the Children's Museum of Pittsburgh.

Children's Museum of Pittsburgh (ages 14 and under) 🖼

10 Children's Way, Allegheny Square–North Side; (412) 322–5058; www.pittsburgh kids.org. Open Monday through Saturday, 10:00 A.M. to 5:00 P.M., Sunday noon to 5:00 P.M. Admission $$ for adults, seniors, and children. Children under 2 are free.

In November 2004, the Children's Museum of Pittsburgh opened its newly expanded headquarters. The spectacular world-class children's center links the Children's Museum housed in the old Allegheny Post Office to the neighboring Buhl building, with a new three-story structure whose entire façade is "screened" by a shimmering wind sculpture. With four times more space, the museum presents programs, exhibits, and performances to nurture children's innate joy, creativity, and curiosity.

Kids interact with Real Stuff exhibits, where they can explore a MINI Cooper to learn about mechanics in the Garage; create and sail a boat down a 53-foot waterway in Waterplay; climb into the Attic, where gravity and common sense take a holiday; create a silkscreen, make paper, emboss and sculpt in the Studio, visit King Friday's palace, drive the trolley and sing familiar songs in a life-size re-creation of the original *Mister Rogers' Neighborhood* television set, and much, much more.

Point State Park (all ages) 🖼

Point State Park is at the tip of Pittsburgh's "Golden Triangle." The thirty-six-acre park is accessible from the east and west by Interstate 376 and 279, from the north by Route 8, and from the south by Route 51, www.dchr.state.pa.us.

You can stroll the park's paved promenade along the riverfront, enjoying the view. At the tip of the park, you can see the fountain also known as "The Point." The sites of both Fort Duquesne and Fort Pitt are located in Point State Park.

Fort Duquesne was built by the French and destroyed by the British in 1758. Today only a bronze marker shows where that fort once stood.

Fort Pitt Museum (ages 8 and up)

Point State Park; (412) 281–9284. Open in winter Wednesday to Sunday 9:00 A.M. to 5:00 P.M.; www.fortpittmuseum.com.

The British occupied Fort Pitt until 1772, when the Americans took over. You can see the Fort Pitt Blockhouse and the Fort Pitt Museum. Here you can view exhibits that describe Pittsburgh's early years.

Carnegie Science Center (all ages)

One Allegheny Avenue; (412) 237–3400; www.CarnegieScienceCenter.org. Open Sunday through Friday, 10:00 A.M. to 5:00 P.M., Saturday 10:00 A.M. to 7:00 P.M.

Carnegie Science Center connects science and technology to everyday life in a fun way. With a four-story Omnimax Theater, an interactive Planetarium, the largest sports science exhibit in the country, a real World War II submarine, the world's best model railroad display, three live demonstration theaters, and a building full of 400 hands-on exhibits, the Science Center brings the world of science alive for visitors of all ages.

National Aviary (all ages)

Allegheny Commons West; (412) 323–7235; www.aviary.org. Open daily 9:00 A.M. to 5:00 P.M. Closed Christmas. Admission: $$ for adults, $ for seniors and for children 2 to 12. Children under 2 enter free.

Visit over 600 exotic and endangered birds rain or shine at the National Aviary, an indoor facility that's pleasant no matter what the weather. Get up-close and personal with beautiful flamingos, talk with colorful parrots, and take photos of majestic bald eagles. Stroll through a free-flight indoor rainforest, a 210,000-cubic foot atrium featuring over 100 amazing birds. Guided tours require reservations. Limited free parking. ADA accessible.

The Andy Warhol Museum (all ages)

117 Sandusky Street, on Pittsburgh's North Side near the cultural district, and across the Seventh Street Bridge from downtown; (412) 237–8300; www.warhol.org. Open Tuesday, Wednesday, Thursday, Saturday, and Sunday 10:00 A.M. to 5:00 P.M. and Friday 10:00 A.M. to 10:00 P.M. Closed Monday and legal holidays. Admission is $$ for adults, $ for children (3 and over) and students.

Artist and pop icon Andy Warhol was born in Pittsburgh. Celebrating its tenth anniversary year in 2005, the Andy Warhol Museum is the most comprehensive single-artist museum in the United States. Housed in a funky historic industrial warehouse are 3,000 original works of art, including paintings, drawings, prints, films, and a lot more. Public parking lots with attendants are located under the North Shore Expressway, 1 block north of the museum off Sandusky Street. There is additional parking across the street from the museum.

At the Warhol museum children are especially drawn to the Silver Clouds gallery on the fifth floor, where silver, pillow-shaped balloons float around you. Hands-on activities are offered in the Weekend Factory on Saturday and Sunday noon to 4:00 P.M.

Mattress Factory (all ages)

500 Sampsonia Way; (412) 231–3169; www.mattress.org. Open Tuesday to Saturday 10:00 A.M. to 7:00 P.M., Sunday 1:00 to 5:00 P.M. Admission: Adults $$, students and seniors $. Children under 12 enter free. Free parking is available at 505 Jacksonia Street. Wheelchair accessible.

The Mattress Factory is a museum of contemporary installation art that presents "art you can get into" created by in-residence artists. Located on Pittsburgh's North Side since 1977, the Mattress Factory is one of few museums of its kind anywhere. Visitors of all ages examine the unique nature of site-specific art and explore a range of nontraditional media and environments—from recorded sound and running water to mirrored rooms and projected light. The museum's multisensory permanent collection includes works by Yayoi Kusama, Rolf Julius, Winifred Lutz, and more.

The Mattress Factory offers a variety of Family Fun Activities. During ARTLab, families can participate in thematic art-making projects that illuminate the creative process. ARTlab activities are offered on the first and third Saturdays of every month, 11:00 A.M. to 4:00 P.M., free with suggested admission. Children must be accompanied by an adult. Check the Web site for listings of exhibitions and events including youth art classes, family days, and public forums.

The "Strip District"

Pittsburgh's "Strip District" has nothing to do with exotic dancing. This is the nickname given to Pittsburgh's open-air marketplace. It's fun to take in the atmosphere on this ½-mile strip along Penn Avenue and Smallman Street, starting at Eleventh Street. Enjoy the colorful produce, the smells of ethnic food, bakeries, restaurants, and other shops.

Near the Strip District give your children a really extraordinary experience by participating in a children's workshop at the Society for Contemporary Craft.

Amazing
Pittsburgh Facts

With seven floors and more than 3,000 original works of art, The Andy Warhol Museum is the most comprehensive single-artist museum in the United States.

Society for Contemporary Craft (ages 4 to 12) 🔲

2100 Smallman Street; (412) 261–7003; www.contemporarycraft.org. Open Tuesday through Friday 10:00 A.M. to 5:00 P.M. and Saturday 9:00 A.M. to 5:00 P.M. The Exhibition Gallery and Drop-In Studio are **free** and open during public hours. Guided group tours of exhibitions are $ per person. Tour with artist-led craft activity is $$ per person. Please schedule group tours in advance.

The Society for Contemporary Craft (SCC) provides an unusual chance to make art a part of your life. SCC includes an exhibition gallery, an education center, The Studio, and The Store, featuring one-of-a-kind handmade works for all ages.

The gallery stages four craft exhibitions per year. Each exhibition is accompanied by a related artist-designed project that invites families to create art together in the Drop-In Studio. Past visitors have made object jewelry and cereal-box-cardboard quilts. Come as you are and stay until your masterpiece is complete.

More in-depth art experiences are available through studio classes in book arts, fiber, metal, and wood for adults, children, and families. SCC also hosts special family events throughout the year. Both the building and the restrooms are accessible to all visitors.

The Senator John Heinz Pittsburgh Regional History Center (all ages) 🔲

1212 Smallman Street; (412) 454–6000; www.pghhistory.org. Open daily 10:00 A.M. to 5:00 P.M. Admission: $$ for adults, $ for children ages 6 to 18, seniors (ages 65 and older), and students with ID.

In 2004, the Senator John Heinz Pittsburgh Regional History Center opened its new five-story Smithsonian wing, making it Pennsylvania's largest museum dedicated to history and one of the nation's finest historical and educational facilities. This History Center is now one of just a few history museums in the country to be affiliates of the Smithsonian Institution.

The first floor of the new wing serves as the Smithsonian's "home in Pennsylvania," hosting world-class traveling exhibitions from the Smithsonian.

The second and third floors house the Western Pennsylvania Sports Museum. The Sports Museum contains over 300 artifacts, seventy hands-on interactive exhibits and twenty audio-visual programs. Here you can see Satchel Paige's baseball glove, Billy Conn's gloves and light-heavyweight championship belt, Arnold Palmer's golf bag and trademark sweater, and the shoes Franco Harris was wearing when he caught the "Immaculate Reception."

The fourth floor showcases special collections, including an ethnic heritage exhibit and *Made in Pennsylvania*. The fifth floor houses an educational center and theater.

The center also features permanent exhibits spotlighting life in western Pennsylvania from 1750 to the present. In the Great Hall children immediately notice a 1949 restored trolley, a Conestoga wagon, and the Pittsburgh city fire bell, cast after the great fire of 1845.

The Children's Discovery Place tells the story of eight real children from the region whose lives exemplify different aspects of history.

The building is wheelchair accessible, and there are baby-care facilities on the first and third floors. There is also a cafe and a museum shop.

South Side

On the South Side of Pittsburgh, you'll have an excellent opportunity to see the city from the water or from one of two inclines.

Board the *Gateway Clipper* at Station Square, a five-minute stroll across the Smithfield Street Bridge from downtown Pittsburgh. Two contiguous railroad buildings have been beautifully restored to create Station Square, currently undergoing an expansion to include a Hard Rock Cafe, Joe's Crab Shack, and an observation tower.

Just Ducky Tours, Inc. (all ages)

Station Square Dock; call (412) 928–2489 for information and reservations; www.just duckytours.com.

There's a unique way to tour the city of Pittsburgh—by DUCK! Not the kind of duck with feathers, but a World War II military amphibious vehicle, a bright green bus-boat that carries passengers on a tour of Pittsburgh, on land and water. The only requirement for passengers is that they quack. Hour-long tours depart from the newly expanded Station Square on Pittsburgh's South Side.

Inclined Planes of Pittsburgh

Two of Pittsburgh's famous inclines are located near Station Square: the Monongahela Incline and the Duquesne Incline.

So what is an "incline" anyway? It's a cable railway designed to carry passengers or freight up Pittsburgh's steep hills. Inclines were invented before electric streetcars and before automobiles. At one time the city had seventeen of these steam-driven engineering marvels. At present two survive, although now they are driven by electricity. Thousands of commuters use the inclines every day. (Both stations and inclines are now wheelchair accessible.)

What's the difference between the two? Well, the Duquesne has red cars, and the tracks are lit with red lights. The Monongahela has green and yellow lights on the tracks, and the cars are ivory with black trim. Both have overlooks from Mount Washington, with a great view of the city. Both have historical information in their upper stations.

The Gateway Clipper Fleet (all ages) ⚠

9 Station Square Dock; call (412) 355–7980 for information and a schedule of cruises; www.gatewayclipper.com.

The Gateway Clipper Fleet has a schedule of day and night cruises year-round, ranging from narrated sightseeing trips to elegant dinner cruises with entertainment. Family Fun cruises are aimed at children twelve and under; these include the Goodship Lollipop Ride and seasonal cruises like Santa Family Fun, Halloween Monster Fun, and Bunny Fun. All the riverboats are climate controlled. The different vessels vary in facilities, but all have plenty of restrooms, some with changing tables, others with wide counters. Some also have snack bars, and certain cruises include boxed lunches or pizza. Goodship Lollipop cruises feature Lolli the clown.

Monongahela Incline (all ages)

Across the street from Station Square; (412) 442–2000; www.chwy.com/pa/m/monoincl .htm. It runs Monday through Saturday 5:30 A.M. to 12:45 A.M. On Sunday and holidays it is open 8:45 A.M. to midnight. The fare is $ each way.

The "Mon," the first passenger incline in the United States, is 635 feet long and rises to an elevation of about 368 feet at a thirty-five-degree angle. It is operated by the Port Authority.

Duquesne Incline (all ages)

Located on Carson Street, directly across the river from Three Rivers Stadium. Call (412) 381–1665 for information; http://incline.pghfree.net. The Duquesne operates Monday through Saturday 5:30 A.M. to 12:45 A.M., Sunday 7:00 A.M. to 12:45 A.M. The fare is $ each way. Free parking is available at the lower station.

Currently operated by the Society for the Preservation of the Duquesne Heights Incline, this incline has been in operation since 1877. The interiors are made of hand-carved cherry panels, with oak and bird's-eye maple trim and amber glass transoms. You can rise up 400 feet at a thirty-degree angle to the New Observation Deck at the upper station and take in the spectacular vista.

East Pittsburgh

Three miles east of downtown, you'll discover Pittsburgh's Oakland cultural district, where you can see the University of Pittsburgh, Carnegie-Mellon University, the Carnegie Museums of Art and Natural History, Schenley Park, and the Phipps Conservatory. Also in this area you can visit Kennywood, Sandcastle Waterpark, and the Pittsburgh Zoo and Aquarium. (Technically, Kennywood is in West Mifflin and Sandcastle is in West Homestead, both of which are east of the city, so it gets a little confusing. In this guide we have listed them under West Mifflin and West Homestead respectively.)

Big **Dinobones!**

I'll never forget the first time we took Judah to an exhibit of dinosaur bones. He was about three-and-a-half years old, and he looked up at the huge skeletons with his enormously wide eyes and shouted, "B-I-I-I-G dino-bones!"

Carnegie Museums of Art and Natural History (all ages)

Located side by side on Forbes Avenue; (412) 622–3131; www.carnegiemuseums. org. Both museums open at 10:00 A.M. Tuesday through Saturday and close at 5:00 P.M., except on Thursday, when they are open until 9:00 P.M. Open Sunday noon to 5:00 P.M.; closed on Monday, except in July and August. A combination admission to both museums is $$. Wheelchair accessible.

The Carnegie Museum of Natural History has one of the world's finest dinosaur collections, a hall of gems and minerals, Egyptian artifacts (including mummies), and Polar World.

Dinosaur Hall is currently closed during a $37 million expansion project, and is expected to reopen in 2007. The Hillman Hall of Minerals and Gems includes some of the finest specimens of their kinds, plus a dazzling display of fluorescent minerals. Polar World explores the culture of the Inuit, including their keenly observed carvings. There are also Egyptian artifacts; African and North American wildlife; colorful displays of insects, butterflies, birds; and so much more.

The Discovery Room, for all ages, is open selected hours. There are also special programs for children, including Camp Earth, a summer-camp program.

Founded in 1895 by Andrew Carnegie, the Carnegie Museum of Art was planned as a collection of "the old masters of tomorrow." At that time, that meant artists like Winslow Homer, James McNeill Whistler, and Camille Pisarro. Today the museum is known for its collections of American, French Impressionist, and post-Impressionist works. It also includes European and American decorative arts, Asian and African art, and the Hall of Architecture, housing a collection of plaster casts of architectural monuments, considered one of the world's three finest collections of this type.

Schoolchildren will get a kick out of the Hall of Sculpture, patterned after a real Greek temple. Family, youth, and children's programs are available. In fact, there's a free audio tour, including a kid-friendly version hosted by Art Cat, the museum's mascot for children's programs.

Since the museum of natural history and the museum of art are attached, one admission gets you into both, and there are often joint programs such as tours of both facilities. Also adjacent you'll find the Carnegie Music Hall and the Carnegie Library of Pittsburgh. There are two restaurants and a brown-bag lunchroom at the facility, as well as a six-level parking garage.

Nationality Rooms (ages 6 and up) 🖼️

Fifth Avenue entrance, Cathedral of Learning; (412) 624–6000; www.pitt.edu/~nat rooms. Reservations are recommended. Tour fees are $.

At the University of Pittsburgh's Cathedral of Learning you can compare New England Colonial architectural style with French Empire, Japanese, Indian, Austrian, Russian, Byzantine, Chinese Empire, first-century Israeli, or Irish Romanesque. Twenty-six different nations are represented in the Nationality Rooms Tours. Funded by gifts from Pittsburgh's ethnic communities, the Nationality Rooms are functioning classrooms in which your family can tour "around the world" with a university student guide who has been trained to adapt the tour to different ages and interests.

Younger children enjoy patting the laughing lion in the Chinese Room or identifying the fairy tales depicted in the German Room. The gift shop carries many unusual publications and an array of international gifts.

Also at the Cathedral of Learning:

Heinz Memorial Chapel (ages 8 and up)

Cathedral of Learning; (412) 624–4157; www.pitt.edu. Open 9:00 A.M. to 4:00 P.M. on weekdays. Mass is celebrated at noon every day. Services are also offered on Sunday, when the chapel is open 1:30 to 5:30 P.M.

Stained-glass windows set a tone of Gothic other-worldliness.

Phipps Conservatory (all ages) 🖼️ 🖼️

Schenley Park; (412) 622–6914; www.phipps.conservatory.org. Open year-round Tuesday through Sunday 9:00 A.M. to 5:00 P.M. Admission: $$ for adults, $ for students and children 2 to 12. Outdoor gardens are open dawn to dusk, free.

Inside the Victorian glass structure of the Phipps Conservatory, you can see hundreds of orchids, palms, ferns, and other plants. The Japanese Courtyard Garden has an excellent collection of bonsai. In winter the indoor gardens soothe your cabin fever, and in warm weather you can enjoy both indoor and outdoor gardens and fountains. Kids will especially enjoy the stegosaurus topiary in the Fern Room, the bizarre Bomarzo statue in the Stove Room, and the Discovery Garden. During the winter holiday season, the Conservatory hosts a Garden Railway and winter flower show.

In 2005, the Conservatory expects to complete an expansion to include a tropical-forest conservatory, new greenhouses, and a new welcome center.

The Frick Art and Historical Center (ages 8 and up) 🖼️

7227 Reynolds Street; (412) 371–0600; www.frickart.org. Open year-round Tuesday through Saturday 10:00 A.M. to 5:00 P.M., Sunday noon to 6:00 P.M. Closed Monday. Admission to the museum is free. Admission to Clayton is $$. Free, secure parking at the Reynolds Street entrance.

Another one of Pittsburgh's leading citizens was Henry Clay Frick, who lived at Clayton until 1905, when he moved to New York City (where his next house also became a favorite museum). The Frick Art and Historical Center is a six-acre site that includes Clayton, the Frick Art Museum, historic Car and Carriage Museum, visitor center, and cafe. The Victorian home has been meticulously restored, and about 95 percent of the furnishings are original. The Car and Carriage Museum displays old-fashioned automobiles, sleighs, and carriages. Little ones will be interested in the visitor center, which was once the playhouse of Helen, the Fricks' daughter. (Please note that neither backpacks nor strollers are permitted in Clayton.)

Pittsburgh Zoo and PPG Aquarium (all ages)

One Hill Road, in Highland Park (ten minutes from downtown Pittsburgh); (412) 665–3640; www.pittsburghzoo.com. Open daily except December 25. In winter the gates are open 9:00 A.M. to 4:00 P.M. If you're already inside the gate, you can stay until 5:00 P.M. In summer the gates open at 10:00 A.M. and close at 5:00 P.M., and you can stay inside until 6:00 P.M. Parking is $ per vehicle. Admission is $$.

In June 2000 the Pittsburgh Zoo became the Pittsburgh Zoo and PPG Aquarium. It is the only public aquarium in Pennsylvania, a 45,000-square-foot, state-of-the-art facility featuring more than 4,000 aquatic animals: penguins, barracuda, piranha, stingrays, jellyfish, sharks, a rare Amazon River dolphin, and much more. Innovative tank designs include a crawl-through stingray tunnel, two-story shark tank, and the first revolving tanks ever publicly displayed.

Kids Kingdom, the Children's Zoo at the Pittsburgh Zoo, has been ranked one of the top three children's zoos in the country. Kids Kingdom includes exciting interactive exhibits. Parents enjoy the fact that they can sit on the patio in Kids Kingdom while the kids learn to swing like spiders, slide like penguins, and enjoy the playground and live animals.

The animals here have natural enclosures. Highlights include the Siberian tigers in the Asian Forest; lions, leopards, rhinos, elephants, and gazelles of the African Savannah; and family groups of lowland gorillas, plus monkeys, gibbons, and orangutans of the Tropical Forest.

Out of the Mouths **of Babes**

We were looking at the photos we'd taken at the zoo. Seth was three and fascinated with all the animals.

I told him, "A gorilla is very strong."

He said, "So is a boy-rilla."

Amazing
Pittsburgh Facts

Pittsburgh has more than 275 public parks and playgrounds.

ALSO IN THE AREA

Pittsburgh offers plenty of action for sports enthusiasts. The Pirates and Steelers both moved to brand-new stadiums in 2001, the Pirates to the award-winning **PNC Stadium** and the Steelers to **Heinz Stadium.** For information and tickets for the Pirates, call (800) BUY–BUCS, or check the Web site at www.pittsburgh.pirates.mlb.com. For the Steelers, call (412) 323–1200 or visit www.pittsburghsteelers.com. The Pittsburgh Penguins (NHL hockey) still play in the same arena, but it's now called the **Mellon Arena** (formerly the Civic Arena). Call (800) 642–PENS, or visit www.pittsburgh penquins.com.

Pittsburgh visitors may also wish to take in a performance at one of the many cultural venues: **Heinz Hall for the Performing Arts** (600 Penn Avenue, 412–392–4900); **Civic Light Opera** (Benedum Center, 719 Liberty Avenue, 412–281–2022); **The Playhouse** (222 Craft Avenue, 412–621–6695); **Pittsburgh Center for the Arts** (6300 Fifth Avenue, 412–361–0873); **Pittsburgh Opera** (711 Penn Avenue, 412–281–0912); or call TicketMaster at (412) 323–1919.

West Mifflin

Memories of a childhood in Pittsburgh usually include scrambling around a rocking Noah's Ark in Kennywood. Voted "Favorite Amusement Park" for eleven years in a row by the National Amusement Park Historical Association (NAPHA), Kennywood has also been called the "Roller Coaster Capital of the World."

Amazing
Pittsburgh Facts

Kennywood, now more than one hundred years young, is one of only two amusement parks that are National Historic Landmarks. DAFE (Darkride and Funhouse Enthusiasts) voted Kennywood the "best darkride park" in the country.

Kennywood (all ages) 🎠 🎪

4800 Kennywood Boulevard; (412) 461–0500; www.kennywood.com. Open daily mid-May through Labor Day 11:00 A.M. to 10:00 P.M. Tickets are \$\$\$\$\$, Junior (under 46″) admission is \$\$\$\$. Senior general admission is \$.

Now more than a century young, Kennywood is only minutes away from downtown Pittsburgh, off the Swissdale exit (exit 9) of I–376 (Penn–Lincoln Parkway). Although some rides will get you wet, none require bathing suits.

A Pittsburgh landmark since 1898, Kennywood is now also a National Historic Landmark. The carousel pavilion and a restaurant are the original structures. Others were added over the years. One roller coaster, for example, the Jack Rabbit, with its "camel back" (double dip), looks just the way it did in 1921. "Pittsburgh's Lost Kenny-wood" re-creates Luna parks of the past. But Kennywood has continued to evolve, with rides like Phantom's Revenge, and the Pitt Fall, the world's tallest and fastest free-fall ride. Kennywood's Exterminator combines a roller coaster with virtual reality to give you the ride of your life, in the dark, through underground tunnels and sewers where you'll encounter who knows what.

Phantom Fright Nights takes place every Friday and Saturday evening in Octo-ber—but beware! It is *not* suggested for children under 13.

There are changing tables in all the bathrooms. In Kiddieland, there are kid-size bathrooms and an area for nursing mothers. Parking is free.

West Homestead

Sandcastle Water Park (all ages) 🌊 🎠

1000 Sandcastle Drive, on Route 837 between the Homestead High Level Bridge and Glenwood Bridge; (412) 462–6666; www.sandcastlewaterpark.com. Open daily in sea-son, usually June through Labor Day weekend, 11:00 A.M. to 6:00 P.M. The park stays open until 7:00 P.M. in July and August. Admission: Whitewater Pass (includes all water activities—hot tubs, pools, Lazy River, and fifteen water slides) is \$\$\$ for adults and children three and older.

Sandcastle Water Park, Kennywood's sister park in West Homestead, began life as an abandoned steel mill and was opened as a water park in July 1990. Sandcastle is a major riverside water park with a boardwalk, fifteen water slides, three pools, and a Lazy River. It also has two race-car tracks, video games, and miniature golf. Mon-Tsunami is a 20,000-square-foot wave pool with huge roller waves as well as diamond waves.

Only the bravest watersliders should attempt the Light-ning Express twin body slides, 60 feet high and 250 feet long, each with a double dip, followed by a monster free fall. (AAAH!)

Another slide, Cliffhangers, uses a new concept in waterslide design: sky ponds. Each pond is at a different level above the ground. You and your inner tube can float in one pond before sliding down to the next.

If that doesn't sound like your speed, relax on the Lazy River, with its whirlpools, fountains, and gentle current. Wet Willie's Waterworks is recommended for younger children, and The World's Largest Hot Tub is perfect for stressed-out parents.

Parking and boat docking are **free.** Special events and picnics are held in Sand-castle's Riverplex entertainment complex. Parking is $.

Springdale

Rachel Carson said, "Those who contemplate the beauty of the earth find reserves of strength that will endure as long as life lasts." The famous author of *Silent Spring* was born in 1907 in the farmhouse now known as the Rachel Carson Homestead, in Springdale, within minutes of Pittsburgh. As your family travels this region that is so much a part of our industrial development, a visit to Carson's home is a healthy reminder of the downside of "progress."

Rachel Carson Homestead (ages 8 and up) 🔖 🍁
613 Marion Avenue, approximately 30 minutes from downtown Pittsburgh; (724) 274–5459; www.rachelcarsonhomestead.org. Open Saturday and Sunday noon to 4:00 P.M. At other times you may call (724) 274–5459 for an appointment. Admission is $.

Tour this nineteenth-century house and find out about one woman who made a difference. This is the birthplace and childhood home of Rachel Carson, author of *Silent Spring,* published in 1962. Carson's books pointed out for the first time the dangers of DDT and other pesticides. Her special interest in exposing children to nature was illustrated by her 1956 article "Help Your Child to Wonder." You'll also enjoy the nature trail that Rachel Carson walked and the gardens, especially the Butterfly Garden.

Special children's programs are offered. In May Rachel Carson's birthday is celebrated.

Tarentum

In Tarentum, only a few miles northeast of the Rachel Carson Homestead, you can find out what life was like for miners in this area.

Tour-Ed Mine and Museum (ages 8 and up) 🏛
748 Bull Creek Road at exit 14 of Route 28 North, located on the Allegheny Valley Expressway, opposite Woodlawn Golf Course; (724) 224–4720; www.Tour-Edmine.com. Open Wednesday to Monday, Memorial Day to Labor Day, 1:00 to 4:00 P.M. Admission is $$ for adults, $ for children 12 and under. Group rates available.

You'll have to wear a miner's hard hat and mind your head as you board a mining car, modernized for comfort and electrically powered, to travel a ½-mile underground at Tour-Ed Mine and Museum into a genuine coal mine. Your tour guide, a real miner, will help you learn about the history of coal mining. It's chilly down here, so bring your sweater. This is not for the claustrophobic.

Kids will enjoy a tour in a locomotive on the surface to see a demonstration strip mine and auger mine. You can also see the company store, 1785 log home, and sawmill. You can even see a bedroom set up like the ones where the miners slept. There are covered picnic areas and snacks available.

Butler

The Butler County Historical Society administers several historic sites in the county, which are open seasonally. For information on any of these sites or to arrange a group or off-season tour, call the Historical Society at (724) 283–8116, or check the Web site www.butlercountyhistoricalsociety-pa.org.

Butler County Heritage Center (ages 8 and up) 🏛

119 West New Castle Street; (724) 283–2505; www.butlercountyhistoricalsociety-pa .org. Hours vary seasonally.

This center presents temporary exhibits on the history of this area. On permanent display are artifacts from Butler County's many industries, including a tin shop, a Bantam jeep, Spang oil tools, Franklin glasswork, and farm tools.

Cooper Cabin (ages 8 and up) 🏛

Off Route 356 on Cooper Road; (724) 283–8116; www.butlercountyhistoricalsociety-pa.org. Hours vary seasonally.

Built around 1810, Cooper Cabin was an original county homestead. On Halloween families gather around a bonfire at the cabin to hear ghost stories. On weekends from April to October the cabin offers demonstrations of horseshoeing, basket weaving, quilting, spinning, and weaving, as well as an herb garden and outbuildings such as a spinning house, springhouse, and tool shed.

Little Red School House Museum (ages 6 and up) 🏛

200 East Jefferson Street; (724) 283–8116; www.butlercountyhistoricalsociety-pa.org. Hours vary seasonally.

At the Little Red School House, built in 1838, you sit down in a real old-fashioned desk as your tour guide transforms into a teacher.

How Do You **Spell Pittsburgh?**

In 1768, the descendants of William Penn purchased land from the Native American tribes known as the Six Nations, calling it the "Manor of Pittsburgh"—with an "h." Officially, Pittsburgh has always been spelled with an "h," except for the period from 1890 to 1911, when the U.S. Post Department dropped the "h" in accordance with the U.S. Board of Geographic Names.

And yet people all over the country persist in misspelling Pittsburgh.

In 1921, *Pittsburgh First*, "the official organ of the Chamber of Commerce of Pittsburgh," urged all Patriotic Pittsburghers to assist the general public in the spelling of the name of their city. The "h" was important, they maintained, because it distinguished Pittsburgh, Pennsylvania, from all the other cities of the same name across the country.

Harmony

The village of Harmony was founded in 1804 by members of a religious communal group, the Harmony Society. This group eventually built about 130 buildings including two outlying villages. At present, Harmony is known for its antiques shops, museums, restaurants, and parks.

The Harmony Museum (ages 8 and up) 📷

218 Mercer Street; (724) 452–7341 or (888) 821–4822; www.harmonymuseum.org. Open year-round 1:00 to 4:00 P.M. daily except Monday. Appointments strongly recommended for weekends. Closed holidays. Admission is $; children under 6 enter free.

The Harmony Museum displays Native American artifacts, as well as artifacts of the Harmonists and Mennonites. The museum also offers walking tours of the historic district of Harmony, as well as the Ziegler Log House and the Wagner House. Limited wheelchair accessibility.

Amazing Pittsburgh Facts 🔍

The Pittsburgh Crawfords are considered the greatest Negro League baseball team of all time.

Portersville

Moraine State Park (all ages) 🚶‍♂️🚲

225 Pleasant Valley Road, off U.S. Route 422; (724) 368–8811; www.dcnr.state.pa/
stateparks/parks/moraine.aspx. Open year-round 8:00 A.M. to sundown. Free, but
there are rental fees for boats, cabins, etc. The beach is free.

Moraine State Park offers 17,000 acres of family-oriented nature programs. There are
nature walks and canoe trips. Having recently reintroduced ospreys to Lake Arthur,
the park offers educational programs about these and other waterfowl. You can rent
motorboats, pontoons, or sailboats. A ⁷⁄₁₀-mile paved bike trail winds around the north
shore of the lake.

McConnell's Mill State Park (all ages) 🚶‍♂️👫🚐

Five miles west of Moraine State Park, off US 422; (724) 368–8091 or (724) 368–8811;
www.dcnr.state.pa.us. The gristmill is open for free guided tours Memorial Day to
Labor Day, 10:00 A.M. to 6:00 P.M. This scenic park features a covered bridge and a
waterfall. For more information and park hours, call (724) 368–8091.

Also administered by Moraine State Park is McConnell's Mill State Park. It's definitely
worth the walk to see the 400-foot Slippery Rock Creek Gorge, formed by the glaciers
thousands of years ago. The huge boulders literally "slipped" down the walls of the
gorge, creating a strange and wonderful landscape. You can also explore the 2,500
acres of park land, have a picnic, hike one of the trails, or take a free guided tour. If
you have your own boat, you can go kayaking or rafting.

Jennings Environmental Center (all ages) 🚶‍♂️👫

2951 Prospect Road; (724) 794–6011; www.dcnr.state.pa.us. The education center is
open Monday through Friday, 8:00 A.M. to 4:00 P.M. or whenever educational programs
are offered. Free admission. Some programs have fees. Call for information.

Jennings Environmental Center is the only state park environmental
education center in western Pennsylvania, and one of only four in
the state. This site is a true relict prairie ecosystem.

A what? A relict prairie ecosystem is a prairie formed by pre-
historic glacial activity. Here, the glacier left only 4 to 6 inches of
topsoil, with clay underneath. As a result, trees don't grow here,
but grasses and wildflowers do. If you visit in late July or August,
you can see spectacular wildflowers in bloom, such as the spiky
purple blazing star. The prairie also supports unusual wildlife,
such as the eastern massasauga rattlesnake, one of Pennsylvania's three species of poisonous snakes and an endangered
species in the state.

You can hike or picnic here from dawn to dusk, seven days a week. Public interpretive programs are offered on weekends. Please call for program schedules. In spring and summer special programs highlight the wildflowers in bloom. In March you can learn about maple sugaring, and in April Earth Day programs teach about biodiversity and related topics. Many other programs are also available.

Volant

Main Street in the quaint rural town of Volant offers more than fifty shops and restaurants featuring Victorian collectibles, arts and crafts, Christmas specialties, housewares, pottery, and special events such as a Quilt Show and Sale in July, an Autumn Pumpkin Festival, Old Fashioned Christmas, and more. Volant is located north of New Castle, on Route 208, ten minutes from Interstates 79 and 80. It is just minutes away from McConnell's Mill State Park and Living Treasures Animal Park. There's also a thriving Amish community in this area.

The shops are open daily except for New Year's Day, Easter, Thanksgiving, and Christmas. Hours are 10:00 A.M. to 5:00 P.M. Monday through Saturday and noon to 5:00 P.M. on Sunday. For more information contact the Volant Merchants Association at (724) 533–2591.

New Castle

The Riverplex Partnership, in a joint venture with the state of Pennsylvania and the city of New Castle, has recently announced a three-phase regional project that will eventually include a restaurant and entertainment complex. Already the architectural feel of Main Street, New Castle, has been restored. In the coming years, Warner Brothers' first silent-film theater, which opened in 1907, will be restored to form the Cascade Center.

Bet you didn't know that New Castle, Pennsylvania, is the "Fireworks Capital of America." Two of the largest fireworks manufacturers, Pyrotecnico and Zambelli Internationale, are based in this city northwest of Pittsburgh.

So, if you happen to be in the area around Independence Day, check out the **"Fireworks Capital of America Fireworks Festival"** here on the Saturday after July 4th. Besides the fireworks festival, there's also "Back to the Fifties Weekend" at Cascade Park and the Ellwood City Arts, Crafts, and Food Festival at Ewing Park. All of these events feature fireworks, all are in June or July, and all are within a few miles of each other.

For details contact Lawrence County Tourism at (888) 284–7599 or (724) 654–8408. Or, check the Web site www.visitlawrencecounty.com.

Harlansburg Station's Museum of Transportation (all ages)

U.S. Routes 19 and 108; (724) 652–9002; www.harlansburgstation.com. Open season-ally, so call for current hours. Generally, the museum is open weekends only in fall and winter, Saturday 10:00 A.M. to 5:00 P.M. and Sunday noon to 5:00 P.M. In summer and fall, it is open Tuesday through Saturday 10:00 A.M. to 5:00 P.M. and Sunday noon to 5:00 P.M. Closed Monday, and January through February. Admission is $. Group tours available by appointment.

Family-owned, family-operated, and family-friendly, Harlansburg Station's Museum of Transportation looks just like an old railroad station, with four Pennsylvania Railroad cars in front. Inside one of the cars, you can see displays of railroad memorabilia such as uniforms, silver, linens, and more. As you enter the museum, a model conductor greets you. Inside the museum you're surrounded by planes, trains, trolleys, cars, and trucks—all kinds of transportation. In 2002 the museum opened an exhibit focus-ing on aviation in the 1920s. The highlight is a 1928 Franklin aircraft.

Hoyt Institute of Fine Arts (ages 8 and up)

124 East Leasure Avenue; (724) 652–2882. Open Tuesday and Thursday 10:00 A.M. to 8:00 P.M., Wednesday, Friday, and Saturday 10:00 A.M. to 5:00 P.M. Closed Sunday and Monday. General admission is **free.** Period House Tours $ by appointment only.

This regional arts center is housed in two neighboring 1917 mansions on five mani-cured acres of New Castle's historic North Hill. Collections include significant regional artwork, decorative arts, and Shenango china. Adult and youth art classes are offered year-round. Every year the Hoyt hosts a Summer Art Camp and a **free** Chil-dren's Summer Arts Festival.

Living Treasures Animal Park (all ages)

US 422, 4 miles west of I-79 in Moraine; (412) 924–9571; www. ltanimalpark.com. Open weekends 10:00 A.M. to 6:00 P.M. in May, September, and October, and daily 10:00 A.M. to 8:00 P.M. Memorial Day through Labor Day. Admission is $$ for adults, $ for children 2 to 12, and children under 2 are **free.** Please note that there are two "Living Treasures Animal Park" locations: this one, in Moraine; and the other in Done-gal on Route 711 south of Route 31. For the Donegal location, please call (724) 593–8300.

Get up close to more than one hundred species of friendly animals from all over the world at Living Treasures Animal Park.

Amazing
Pittsburgh Facts

The City of Pittsburgh contains more than 70 miles of riverfront land, one of the highest totals in the United States.

New Brighton

Merrick Art Gallery (ages 8 and up) 🔵

Fifth Avenue at Eleventh Street; (724) 846–1130; www.themerrick.org. Open Tuesday through Saturday 10:00 A.M. to 4:30 P.M. and Sunday 1:00 to 4:00 P.M. **Free** admission.

The Merrick Art Gallery houses the collection of French, German, English, and American paintings of the eighteenth and nineteenth centuries that belonged to Edward Dempster Merrick. It has a display of artifacts belonging to the New Brighton Historical Society as well. The gallery also mounts many special exhibits, such as its annual Victorian Christmas Toy Show.

Ambridge

Old Economy Village (ages 8 and up) 🏛

Fourteenth and Church Streets, 18 miles northwest of Pittsburgh on Route 65; (724) 266-4500; www.oldeconomyvillage.org. Open Tuesday through Saturday 9:00 A.M. to 5:00 P.M., Sunday noon to 5:00 P.M. Closed Monday and winter holidays and January through February. Admission: ages 6 to 12 and 60 and over, $; ages 12 to 59, $$; family rate, $$$; children ages 5 and under enter **free.**

Old Economy Village was built by the same Christian communal society that built Harmony (see previous entry in this section). Here you can visit seventeen restored buildings and gardens and learn about how this unusual community lived. Your whole visit takes about an hour and a half, including the orientation film *Economy: A Place of Promise* and a tour of the exhibits, gardens, and buildings. The society had its own textile mill, as well as a tailor, printer, shoemaker, cabinetmaker, locksmith, and more, and the village store still posts the 1827 price list. Kids will enjoy using the hand pump to pour themselves a drink. The Harmony Society's Natural History Museum opened in fall 2001, and a new visitor center that opened in 2003.

Many special events and tours are available, including events such as the Family Festival in June, Erntefest (food festival) in September, and Candlelight Christmas at the village in December. Wheelchair-accessible restrooms, diaper-changing areas.

Raccoon Creek State Park and Wilderness Reserve (all ages) 🚶 👨‍👩‍👧 🏕

Located in southern Beaver County, 25 miles west of Pittsburgh (take U.S. Route 22 or US Route 30; access to the park is via Route 18); (412) 899–3611; www.dcnr.state.pa .us. Trails are open year-round from 8:00 A.M. to sunset. **Free** admission.

One of the largest and most beautiful state parks in Pennsylvania, Raccoon Creek State Park has about 7,000 acres and Raccoon Creek Lake, which itself is more than one hundred acres.

Located within Raccoon Creek State Park, only steps east of the park entrance, is the 315-acre Wildflower Reserve, where you can choose between easy walking trails and trails with gentle grades. Your best bet to see the most blooms is April or May, but something is blooming from late March through summer. If you're lucky, you might see deer, raccoons, wild turkeys, mink, birds, and other wildlife. Comfortable shoes are a must. On Soldier Days you can view historic reenactments, military displays, and more.

Recreational facilities include boating, hiking, camping, swimming, and picnicking. Modern family cabins are available year-round, with electric heat, kitchens, and toilets.

While you're in Raccoon Creek State Park, you may wish to visit **Frankfort Mineral Springs,** about ½-mile south of the park entrance. From the 1790s to 1932, this was the site of a popular spa where many people were attracted to the purported medicinal properties of the spring water. Call (724) 899–2200.

Avella

Meadowcroft Museum of Rural Life (ages 6 and up) 🏛

401 Meadowcroft Road; (724) 587–3412; www.meadowcroftmuseum.org. Open weekends in June, July, and August; Saturday noon to 5:00 P.M., Sunday 1:00 to 5:00 P.M., otherwise open by appointment. Admission: $$ for adults, $ for children 6 to 16; children under 6 enter free. The last complete tour starts at 3:00 P.M. Call for information about group reservations and many special workshops and events.

Sixteen thousand years of history and prehistory in western Pennsylvania are brought to life at the Meadowcroft Museum of Rural Life, which has been operated by the Senator John Heinz Pittsburgh Regional History Center, in association with the Smithsonian Institution, since 2004. The grounds here include the archaeological site that contains the earliest evidence of human life in eastern North America. (This part of the site is not open to the public at this time, but displays explain about the work in progress.)

Tours are designed to engage the entire family. Everyone can sit down in a one-room schoolhouse and take part in a real school lesson, reading from *McGuffey's Reader.* Then try some of the playground games children played 150 years ago. Explore log houses, a covered bridge, a blacksmith's shop, and other exhibits.

Located off Route 50, less than an hour from Pittsburgh, the museum offers many hands-on educational programs for groups. Wear good walking shoes, because the paths between the buildings are natural. There is a snack bar and gift shop.

Washington

The Pennsylvania Trolley Museum (all ages) 🚋🚌

One Museum Road; (724) 228–9256 or (877) PA–TROLLEY; www.pa-trolley.org. Open 11:00 A.M. to 5:00 P.M. daily from Memorial Day to Labor Day; weekends 11:00 A.M. to 5:00 P.M. April 1 through December 30. Admission is $$ for adults, and $ for children 2 to 15.

Faith's kids could never resist a trolley. And here in Washington, you'll find the only museum where you can see, learn about, and actually ride historic electric-rail vehicles from Pittsburgh, Philadelphia, Johnstown, and other cities. Take several generations along for an opportunity for reminiscing and intergenerational storytelling.

First, go to the visitor education center to buy your tickets and view an exhibit. Stop and browse through the exhibits or take in a film. During the winter holidays you can even find yourself at the controls of a model-train layout.

Rides leave from the Richfor Shelter across the picnic area and next to the car barn. You just won't believe how beautifully these streetcars have been restored. Your motorman and most of the staff are volunteers. You'll clatter on a 3-mile journey past a scenic section that was once an old coal-mining railroad. After you climb off the trolley, you may view about twenty-five trolley cars from the museum's collection, including the real "Streetcar Named Desire" from New Orleans. You can even peek in on the car shop where volunteers restore the cars. Bring along a picnic lunch if you like.

Just 25 miles southwest of Pittsburgh, off I–79, exit 41 southbound or exit 40 northbound, the trolley museum is convenient to Meadowcroft Village in Avella. Special events include: the Anything on Wheels Fair in June, with a trolley parade, antique vehicle display, and motorcar and caboose rides; the Pumpkin Patch Trolley in October; and Santa Trolley in December.

Washington County Historical Society's Lemoyne House
(ages 8 and up) 🏛️

49 East Maiden Street; call (724) 225–6740 for admission prices; www.wchspa.org. Open February to mid-December, Tuesday to Friday 11:00 A.M. to 4:00 P.M. Saturday group tours available by appointment. Admission is $.

Dr. Francis Julius LeMoyne, a successful nineteenth-century physician, took the courageous step of opening his home and properties as stops along the Underground Railroad. LeMoyne House is now the headquarters of the Washington County Historical Society, including its military museum, collection of Civil War weapons, and a time capsule prepared by President Ulysses S. Grant. The beautiful stone home, which also served as Dr. LeMoyne's medical office, still contains some of his old medical instruments and books. In September the Historical Society hosts its annual African-American Cultural Festival.

Where to Eat

IN PITTSBURGH

Bobby Rubina's Place for Ribs, 10 Commerce Court Station Square; (412) 642–7427.

Crewser's Restaurant, 1501 Smallman Street, Strip District; (412) 281–1099. Nautical theme, located on the boardwalk in the strip.

Houlihan's Restaurant, #15 Freight House Shops, South Side; (412) 232–0302.

Spaghetti Warehouse, 2601 Smallman Street; (412) 261–6511. Italian food, casual atmosphere, located on the Strip.

Riverview Cafe, Carnegie Science Center, One Allegheny Avenue, North Side; (412) 237–3417. Casual atmosphere, city view on the Ohio River. Kid-friendly foods, booster seats.

Where to Stay

IN PITTSBURGH

Best Western University Center Hotel, 3401 Boulevard of the Allies; (412) 683–6100 or (800) 245–4444. Nearby: Oakland, downtown, stadiums, museums, university, Station Square, zoo, Kennywood.

Courtyard by Marriott Downtown, 945 Penn Avenue; (412) 434–5551.

Marriott Pittsburgh City Center, 112 Washington Place; (888) 456–6600 or (412) 471–4000, www.marriott.com/pitdt.

Pittsburgh Hilton & Towers, 600 Commonwealth Place, Gateway Center; (412) 391–4600; www.pittsburgh.hilton.com. Adjacent to Point State Park. Walking distance to sports games and Carnegie Museum.

For More Information

Greater Pittsburgh Convention & Visitors Bureau, (800) 359–0758; www.visitpittsburgh.com.

VisitPittsburgh Help Center, (877) LOVE–PGH.

Northeastern
Pennsylvania

With the Delaware and Susquehanna Rivers, the Pocono Mountains, wilderness areas, numerous lakes, and crystal-clear rivers, northeastern Pennsylvania has attracted vacationers since the 1800s. But northeastern Pennsylvania is more than just a resort area. The discovery of one of the world's largest deposits of anthracite coal made the region a center for industry. Entrepreneurs, immigrant workers, and others came to the area to make money or find work. The country's first railroads were built to transport the coal to the cities. Other industries moved their operations here to take advantage of the cheap fuel.

Thanks to its history—both natural and industrial—northeastern Pennsylvania offers a special mix to family vacationers today. Those looking for hiking, skiing,

Faith & Emily's
FavoriteAttractions
in Northeastern Pennsylvania

1. Float trip on the Delaware River

2. Mountain biking in the Lehigh Gorge

3. Skytop Lodge, Skytop

4. World's End State Park, Forksville

5. Pocono Environmental Education Center (PEEC), Dingmans Ferry

6. Steamtown National Historic Site, Scranton

7. Lackawanna Trolley Museum, Scranton

8. Lackawanna Coal Mine tour, Scranton

9. Woodloch Pines Resort, Hawley

10. Inn at Starlight Lake, Starlight

NORTHEASTERN PENNSYLVANIA

boating, and relaxing resorts will not be disappointed. But the region's industrial history adds some more unusual attractions, such as factories, railroad excursions, and coal-mine tours.

The Poconos are the classic vacation destination—and there's good reason, especially where families are concerned. With so many resorts to choose from, every family can find one that fits its needs.

Despite overdevelopment in some areas, the unspoiled areas of the Poconos are absolutely beautiful—and very accessible. We're not talking huge snowcapped mountains; we're talking gentle hills, lovely trails, and babbling brooks that are easy for all members of the family to enjoy.

For example, the Poconos ski resorts are perfect for families. The vertical drops are steep enough to keep it interesting for Mom and Dad while gentle enough for kids to learn easily. Most of the resorts have great learn-to-ski programs for kids, starting as young as three years old.

One of the hottest things on the slopes in recent years is snowtubing. This is also very good news for families. Though parents may worry a bit the first time the kids take to the slopes on skis or snowboards, snowtubing—with its cushy, fit-the-whole-family inflatable rafts—is something everyone can do together.

Faith & Emily's
FavoriteEvents
in Northeastern Pennsylvania

- **Delaware River Sojourn** at sites along the Delaware (mid-June).

- **Patch Town Day** at Eckley Miner's Village in Weatherly (mid-June); (570) 636–2070.

- **Central Pennsylvania Festival of the Arts** in State College (July); (814) 237–3682; www.arts-festival.com.

- **Wildflower Music Festival** in Hawley–Lake Wallenpaupack (July and August); (570) 253–5500.

- **Moscow Country Fair** (mid-August); (570) 842–9804.

- **Rail Expo** at Steamtown National Historic Site in Scranton (early September); (570) 340–5200 or (888) 693–9391.

- **Shawnee Mountain Lumberjack Festival** in Shawnee-on-Delaware (early October); (570) 421–7231; www.shawneemt.com.

Delaware Water Gap and the Stroudsburg Area

For vacationers arriving in Pennsylvania from New Jersey, the Delaware Water Gap serves as a gateway to the Poconos. This natural land formation along the Kittatinny Ridge is a dramatic backdrop for a host of outdoor activities. The town of Delaware Water Gap is a good place to start exploring.

Stroudsburg and East Stroudsburg are the commerce centers of this part of the Poconos. You'll find restaurants and some lodgings in these towns, but most of the tourist attractions and resorts are located in the surrounding smaller towns. For information on this area, check the Delaware Water Gap home page, www.microserve.net/~magicusa/delawarewatergap.html.

The Delaware Water Gap National Recreation Area (all ages)

Bushkill; (570) 588–2435; www.nps.gov/dewa. **Grounds are open year-round. Visitor centers, open seasonally, and hiking are free; day-use fee at beaches and some picnic areas.**

The 37-mile portion of the Delaware River extending from the Delaware Water Gap north to Milford was designated a National Recreation Area in the 1960s. The river offers great family canoeing, fishing, and rafting opportunities, and the hills on either side offer some fun trails and historic sites to explore on foot, skis, or snowmobile. There's excellent hiking in the area—the Appalachian Trail cuts through at the Water Gap—with some shorter trails that even little legs can handle without problems.

Other attractions that kids enjoy are visiting Millbrook Village (actually, it's about 16 miles from the Gap on the New Jersey side), gazing at dramatic waterfalls located around the area, and swimming in the cool, clear river at Milford and Smithfield beaches. Best of all, the park is less than two hours from New York or Philadelphia.

The best places to view the Gap itself are three overlooks along Route 611 just south of Interstate 80. U.S. Route 209 going north offers a nice family drive along the river valley, with the Pocono Plateau rising to the west. (The Poconos are not a typical mountain range but rather a plateau.)

There's a visitor center at Kittatinny Point, just off I-80 on the New Jersey side of the river. It's open daily May through October and on weekends year-round. Another visitor center, located at Dingmans Falls, about 30 miles north of I-80 on US 209, is open during the summer. To find out what's happening in the park during your visit and to get a ranger's recommendation on what to do and see, stop by one of the visitor centers. While you're there, pick up a Junior Naturalist Discovery Pack, a self-guiding booklet that helps children six to twelve explore the park. Kids who complete the pack are eligible to become Junior Rangers.

Delaware River
Canoe and Rafting Trips

The Delaware is a wonderful, calm river for family rafting and canoeing. Although children eight to twelve get the most out of this kind of trip, most liveries will accommodate younger children—even toddlers. Rafting is recommended over canoeing for children under twelve, says David Jacobi of Adventure Sports in Marshalls Creek. His organization is one of several that offer Delaware River rafting and canoe trips. Typical excursions range from a couple of hours to all day. Be sure to specify your family members' ages and abilities when talking with the liveries; they'll help you decide which excursion is best for you.

- **Adventure Sports in Marshalls Creek,** US 209, Marshalls Creek; (800) 487–2628 or (570) 223–0505; www.adventuresport.com. Trips run seven days a week in summer. Fees: $$$$ for adults, $$$ for children ages 13 through 17, and $$ for children ages 2 to 12.

- **Chamberlain's Canoes, Inc.,** River Road, Minisink Hills; (800) 422–6631 or (570) 421–0180; www.chamberlaincanoes.com.

- **Kittatinny Canoes, Inc.,** 102 Kittatinny Court, Dingmans Ferry; (800) FLOATKC; www.kittatinny.com. Rafting, canoeing, kayaking, tubing, and paintball.

- **Shawnee River Adventures** (offered by Shawnee Inn and Golf Resort), River Road, Shawnee-on-Delaware 18356; (800) SHAWNEE or (570) 424–4000, ext. 1120; www.shawneeinn.com. Midweek specials. Open daily April through October.

Water Gap Trolley (ages 2 and up)

Main Street, Delaware Water Gap; (570) 476–9766. Open April through October (weather permitting), 10:00 A.M. to 4:00 P.M. Admission: $$ for adults, $ for children ages 2 to 12, children under 2 free.

The Water Gap Trolley takes vacationers from the depot on Route 611 near the town's center (actually, it's right across from the town's only stoplight) into the National Recreation Area. The one-hour narrated tour covers the geological and cultural history of the region.

Shawnee Place Play and Water Park (ages 2 and up)

Hollow Road, Shawnee-on-Delaware; (570) 421–7231; www.shawneemt.com. Open weekends from Memorial Day to June 15 and daily from June 16 to Labor Day, 10:00 A.M. to 5:00 P.M. Admission is $$$ for adults and children, $$ spectators; children under 40 inches free.

Kids will enjoy swimming and sliding at Shawnee Place Play and Water Park, located just north of I–80 (take exit 52 to US 209 and follow signs). Especially geared for children under age twelve, the park has two slides and two pools, both about 3 feet deep. There are three magic shows daily as well as fifteen unique play elements.

Shawnee Mountain (ages 4 and up)

Hollow Road, Shawnee-on-Delaware; (570) 421–7231; www.shawneemt.com. Open mid-December to mid-March, 9:00 A.M. to 10:00 P.M. weekdays, 8:00 A.M. to 10:00 P.M. weekends. Varying prices for lift tickets, rentals, and learn-to-ski programs.

Shawnee Mountain has twenty-three trails, a snowboarding area, snowtubing, and a vertical drop of 700 feet. It also has an extensive ski program for kids. There's a Ski Wee program for six- to twelve-year-olds. Little ones (four to five years) can join the Pre-Ski Wee group. More adventurous kids ages ten to fifteen will want to hook up with the Mountain Cruisers. Beginning-to early-intermediate snowboarders can join the Young Riders for eight- to fifteen-year-olds. Programs are $$$$. Three- and five-day packages are available (reservations required). For nonskiing children eighteen months and up, the Little Wigwam Children's Center is open daily for babysitting 9:00 A.M. to 5:00 P.M. on weekdays and 8:00 A.M. to 5:00 P.M. on weekends.

Shannon Inn and Pub (all ages)

Exit 52 off I–80, East Stroudsburg; (800) 424–8052 or (570) 424–1951. A wide variety of ski and golf packages are available, custom-tailored to your needs, at reasonable prices.

Several of the attractions nearby recommend the Shannon Inn for families. With an indoor pool, on-site informal restaurant, and a kids-stay-free policy, this 120-room hotel has everything a family needs for a quality, budget-priced vacation. Through cooperative agreements with Shawnee and Camelback ski areas and other nearby sites, the Shannon Inn offers two-day ski and golf packages.

Quiet Valley Living Historical Farm (ages 3 and up)

US 209, 3½ miles south of Stroudsburg; (570) 992–6161; www.quietvalley.org. Open June 20 through Labor Day, Tuesday through Saturday 10:00 A.M. to 5:30 P.M.; Sunday 1:00 to 5:30 P.M. Admission: $$ for adults, $ for children ages 3 to 12.

Take a trip back in time at the Quiet Valley Living Historical Farm. Here your family will spend time with the Zeppers, a German immigrant family that settled this land back in 1765.

After a brief welcoming presentation, leave the present day and step back into the 1800s. In the 1763 cellar kitchen you will learn how food was prepared and how nothing was wasted on the farm. The farmhand will introduce you to the animals, demonstrate the farm equipment, and let your kids jump in the hayloft. Special demonstrations of various crafts and skills necessary to early life are held throughout the summer.

In addition to regular tours during the summer months, the museum also has a summer program for children, and special presentations, such as a Farm Animal Frolic in May, a Harvest Festival in October, and an Old Time Christmas celebration in December. Call for more information and specific dates. The Farm Animal Frolic is especially recommended for small children, with baby bunnies, hatching chicks, piglets, lambs, and more for children to touch and learn about.

Mount Pocono and Eastern Poconos
(Tannersville, Scotrun, Skytop)

Mount Pocono is in the heart of Pocono resort country. There are lots of resorts and attractions—everything from petting zoos to cheesecake factories—to choose from within a few miles of Mount Pocono, but here are some of our top picks.

Great Wolf Lodge (all ages)
Scotrun, www.greatwolflodge.com.

The Great Wolf Lodge chain of family indoor waterpark resorts plans to open its latest lodge in Scotrun in fall 2005. There will be 300 suites available for overnight stays, with a variety of themed bedrooms for children. There are many activities to keep families busy, but the centerpiece will be its 78,000-square-foot indoor waterpark, kept at 84 degrees year-round, with ten waterslides for all different ages and speeds. Watch for the 12-level tree house, with sixty geysers and water effects, and the 1,000-gallon tipping bucket that will douse you every fifteen minutes.

Camelback Ski Area and Camelbeach Waterpark (ages 4 and up)
Camelback Road, off I–80 (exit 45), Tannersville; (570) 629–1661; www.skicamelback .com (winter), www.camelbeach.com (summer). Open for skiing late November through late March, weather permitting. Water park open late May through Labor Day. Call for specific dates. Lift tickets: $$$$. Children's ski instruction: $$$$ per lesson (includes lift ticket, lesson, and rental). Check the Web site for "Value Days." $$$$ for adults (12 to 64), $$$ for children (3 to 11) and seniors. Children 2 and under enter free.

The Camelback Ski Area is worth a stop in any season. In winter Camelback is one of the Pocono's largest ski resorts, with thirty-three trails, thirteen lifts, and a vertical drop of 800 feet. One of the newer additions is snowtubing, a great family activity. There's a full-scale ski program where children ages four to twelve can spend the day learning to ski or snowboard.

From May until the end of fall, Camelback transforms from a ski resort to Camelbeach Waterpark, with eight waterslides, an action river, swimming pool, kids' play area, miniature golf, an alpine slide, and more. Ride the chairlift to the top of the mountain, enjoy the view of the Pocono Mountains, and take the alpine slide down. Buy a full ticket and enjoy the waterpark attractions all day. There's also a summer day-camp program at the facility, and kids ages five to twelve can sign up for a day, a week, or the whole summer.

Caesar's Brookdale-on-the-Lake Resort (all ages)

Route 611, Scotrun; (800) 233–4141; www.caesarspoconoresorts.com. Open year-round. Call for package rates.

Okay, I have to admit it: There's something a little comical about visiting a renowned couples resort with your toddler, but Caesar's really has something here. Though families don't have full use of all the couples-oriented facilities here (we were disappointed to know we weren't eligible for breakfast in bed), it is a great way to combine some time for yourselves *and* still have a family vacation. (After the kids are asleep, you can sneak into the bath and enjoy the Jacuzzi for two.) Kids five and older can join the Brookdale Kids Kamp and participate in a wide range of special activities just for kids, from face painting to special meals and magic shows.

We visited with our two youngest children, two and one-half and one and one-half at the time. The staff couldn't have been more accommodating, spreading out a tablecloth under the high chair at each meal, filling our sippy cups and bottles each day, and making us bagels for the road. At each meal we sat with a different family, which was fun for adults and children alike. While we ate, a clown, magician, or other entertainer made the rounds of the tables, creating animals from balloons or cracking jokes with the kids.

Many rooms sleep up to eight people, and some have 36-inch TVs or Bose Wave radios.

During the summer and winter seasons, there are lots of activities at the nearby ski resorts, National Recreation Area, petting zoos, and other Poconos attractions.

Skytop Lodge (all ages)

Route 390, Skytop; (800) 345–7759; www.skytop.com. Open year-round.

When we were children, our parents took us to several resorts within a couple hours of our home in New York. Although some resorts were by the ocean, others in the mountains, all had a few elements in common: a stately lodge, a rocking-chair porch, great trails for hiking and walking, and a casual but classy approach to everything.

Skytop Lodge was one of those places—and it has only gotten better in the intervening years. A spa has been added, guest rooms renovated, and twenty executive-style bedrooms added.

Rather than a resort that caters to kids, Skytop accommodates families the same way it accommodates all its guests: with individual attention and concern for detail. Families can check into Skytop for a weekend or a week and find plenty to do for everyone: There are hiking and cross-country ski trails from 1 mile to 10; guided nature walks and self-guided fitness trails; downhill skiing, mountain bikes, rowboats, canoes, and sporting clays available on site; a swimming lake and indoor and outdoor pools; a game room; and a gorgeous golf course.

Skytop offers Camp in the Clouds for children ages four to ten every day in summer and weekends year-round. The program, which runs from 9:00 A.M. to 4:30 P.M., includes arts and crafts, nature walks, swimming, and other supervised activities. The cost is $$$ per full or half day.

Winter Camp in the Clouds is offered every Saturday January through March, 6:00 to 9:00 P.M. **free** of charge. Parents can dine alone while kids ice skate, watch movies, and more, after a kid's dinner.

Skytop is a splurge; however, if you can swing it, it's an excellent family vacation. Accommodations are on the American plan, which means all meals are included. The menu includes some excellent entrees for adults and some favorites for kids. There is a per-day charge ($$$$) for children under sixteen who stay in their parents' room.

ALSO IN THE AREA

Pocono Cheesecake Factory, Route 611, Swiftwater; (570) 839–6844. Open daily 10:00 A.M. to 6:00 P.M. See cheesecakes made fresh daily.

Callie's Candy Kitchen and Pretzel Factory, Route 390, Mountainhome; (570) 595–2280 or (800) 252–7750; www.calliescandy.com. The Pretzel Factory is open daily April through December, weekends only January, February, and March. The candy factory is open year-round except January.

Located about 5 miles apart on Route 390, Callie's factories let you watch while candy and pretzels are made. Of course, then you'll want to buy some in the gift shop.

Bushkill

US 209 from I–80 up to Milford is a lovely drive along the Pennsylvania side of the Delaware River. Here are some suggested stops on the way.

Mary Stolz Doll Museum (ages 3 and up)

Route 209 North and McCole Road; (570) 588–7566. Open daily 11:00 A.M. to 5:00 P.M. Admission is $.

The Mary Stolz Doll Museum is definitely a don't-touch place, but if you have a doll lover in the family, the collection of more than 125 dolls from around the world makes it well worth resisting the temptation. Kids especially like the impressive array of Barbie and Jem dolls. There's also a fine display of miniature rooms, bears, and old toys.

Pocono Indian Museum (ages 6 and up)

Route 209 North; (570) 588–9338; www.pocoindianmuseum.com. Open daily (call ahead for hours and admission prices).

The Pocono Indian Museum is the only museum in Pennsylvania dedicated to portraying the life and times of the Delaware Indian. Its six rooms display artifacts, weapons, and tools, most of which were unearthed within a 20-mile radius of the museum. There's a reconstructed bark house you can actually walk through. Your admission includes a thirty-minute taped, self-guided tour.

Bushkill Falls (all ages)

Route 209; (570) 588–6682; www.visitbushkillfalls.com. Open April through October, 9:00 A.M. to dusk. Admission: $$ adults, $ for children ages 4 through 10; under 4 enter free. Free parking.

The Peters family started charging admission to see these eight magnificent falls, sometimes called the "Niagara of Pennsylvania," on their 300 acres one hundred years ago. The tourists haven't stopped coming since. Take a short nature walk back to the falls. Small children can usually manage the easy forty-five-minute to one-hour stroll. For the more energetic, there's a 2-mile hike that affords an even better view. A gift shop, food facilities, picnic area, and bathroom facilities are available to visitors. There are also paddleboat rides, fishing, miniature golf, an ice-cream parlor, a Pennsylvania wildlife exhibit, and a Native American exhibit.

Fernwood Hotel and Resort (all ages)

US 209, Box 447 Bushkill 18324; (570) 588–9500 or (888) FERNWOOD; www.fernwood hotel.com.

Fernwood Hotel and Resort offers year-round vacation possibilities, including an eighteen-hole golf course, snowtubing, ice skating, two lakes, themed restaurants, live entertainment, indoor and outdoor pools, and a planned schedule of daily activities for children and adults. There's also "The Zone," a 10,000-square-foot game center. Fernwood is convenient to many popular ski resorts.

Dingmans Ferry

Pocono Environmental Education Center (PEEC) (ages 3 and up)

RR2 Box 1010, Dingmans Ferry 18328; (570) 828–2319; www.peec.org.

For families interested in learning about the environment in a national park, there's no better deal than a weekend at the Pocono Environmental Education Center (PEEC). PEEC offers Family, Nature Study, and Recreational Weekends that help children and adults learn about the natural world around them. Enjoy activities such as hiking, canoeing, cross-country skiing, nature study, orienteering, natural history investigation, crafts, and field trips such as the Waterfall Hunt. PEEC's thirty-eight-acre campus is located within the borders of the Delaware Water Gap National Recreation Area and includes classrooms, an indoor pool, craft center, darkroom, library, bookstore, and overnight cabins.

Accommodations are in one-room cabins with private bathrooms that sleep between two and fourteen people. Group tenting is also available in the tent platform area. Meals are served at the dining hall. Weekends include lodging in a PEEC cabin, all meals, and programmed activities (everything from square dancing to live-animal presentations). Children under two are **free**, four and under are half price, and ages five to eight are 25 percent off. PEEC provides linens and towels for an additional cost. For more information, call, visit the Web site, or email peec@ptd.net. PEEC is close to home, where learning comes naturally!

ALSO IN THE AREA

Grey Towers, Milford; (570) 296–9630; www.fs.fed.us/na/gt. Grey Towers, a national historic landmark, was once the home of Gifford Pinchot, the first chief of the U.S. Forest Service and twice governor of Pennsylvania. It is managed and maintained by the USDA Forest Service in cooperation with the Pinchot Institute for Conservation. Public tours of the house are conducted daily, on the hour, 10:00 A.M. to 4:00 P.M. Many conservation programs are also offered.

Promised Land State Park, Route 390, 5 miles south of Interstate 84; (570) 676–3428; www.dcnr.state.pa.us. Promised Land State Park is a 3,000-acre park surrounded by state forest land—creating a total of 11,000 acres of preserved wilderness. The area is home to a wide variety of wildlife, including one of eastern Pennsylvania's bigger populations of black bear. There are numerous housekeeping cabin resorts along Route 390, and camping is available in the park. There are environmental programs for children during summer. One primitive campground stays open year-round for cross-country skiers who can't bear to go home at the end of the day.

Hawley–Lake Wallenpaupack

Lake Wallenpaupack, the state's third largest man-made lake, is 15 miles long with 52 miles of shoreline. It was created in the 1920s by Pennsylvania Power & Light (PPL) as part of a major hydroelectric project. The PPL Wallenpaupack Environmental Learning Center offers exhibits exploring the environment as well as cultural and historical resources of the lake region. For information call (570) 226–3702 or go to www.ppl projectearth.com. PPL also maintains Shuman Point, Ledgedale natural areas, and Beech House Creek Wildlife Refuge for public use. They are great places for short nature hikes and spotting wildlife such as beavers, herons, hawks, and more.

Just north of the lake is the town of Hawley, a great town for antiquing. Kids will be more interested in the following area attractions.

Tanglwood Ski Area & Winter Park (ages 3 and up)

Route 507, Lake Wallenpaupack; (570) 226–SNOW; www.tanglwood.com. Open daily December through March.

If you're in the area during winter, check out nearby Tanglwood Ski Resort, which offers nine trails of downhill skiing, a snowboarding area, a snowtubing park, and several cross-country ski trails. There's also a Ski Wee children's program and a nursery available for small children. The ski shop is one of the only ones in the area to rent cross-country as well as downhill equipment.

Claws 'N' Paws Wild Animal Park (ages 2 and up)

Off Route 590, near Hamlin; (570) 698–6154; www.clawsnpaws.com. Open daily May 1 through late October 10:00 A.M. to 6:00 P.M. Admission: $$$ adults, $$ ages 2 through 11 and seniors; children under 2 are free.

Claws 'n' Paws Wild Animal Park is a unique private zoo with 120 species of animals. Kids may feed the giraffes and lory parrots at scheduled feeding times. There are two different live animal shows through Labor Day. During the reptile show kids can pet an alligator and a python. Other exhibits include bears, otters, primates of several types, many species of birds, and rare white tigers. The new Dinosaur Outpost area lets kids dig for buried dinos, discover fossils at three dig sites, sit on a triceratops, and mine for gemstones. The easy-to-follow trails through the woods and the size of the facility help keep younger children from getting overwhelmed and overtired by the experience.

Triple "W" Riding Stables (ages 6 and up) 🐴😐

Follow blue and white state signs. Beechnut Drive, off Owego Turnpike near Lake Wallenpaupack; (570) 226–2620; www.triplewstable.com or www.doublewranchbnb.com. Stable (800) 450–2620. Open year-round (except hunting season).

Take a step beyond "follow-the-leader" riding at this 200-acre horse ranch in a secluded area on the top of the mountain, featuring western riding experiences tailored to the individual. The staff at Triple W ensure a fun and rewarding ride for all members of the family by taking into consideration level of expertise and ambition. Overnight camping on horseback, hayrides, and pony rides for children under seven are also available.

Triple W offers Wild West shows, complete with a beautiful stagecoach, at many local events, fairs, and rodeos. There are also Murder Mystery weekends, day trips, school trips, reunions, weddings, and company outings.

In the winter, there's enough snow at the top of the mountain to get a lot of use out of the horse-drawn sleigh with jingle bells.

If you're looking for overnight accommodations, stay at the Double "W" Ranch Bed and Breakfast, located on the same property. The B&B boasts a large dining room, ski lounge with fireplace, a game room, and a three-level outdoor deck with a hot tub and a great view. The grounds include flower gardens, gazebos, and hiking paths. For the bed-and-breakfast, call (877) 540–RANCH.

Lake **Cruises**

Along the lake in Greentown there are numerous resorts and marinas geared to vacationers who want to spend time on the water.

- **Pine Crest Yacht Club, Inc.,** Route 507; (570) 857–1136. Open May through October. Boat rentals available.

- **Pocono Action Sports,** Route 507; (570) 857–1976. Sailboats, rowboats, fishing, and waterskiing boats available.

- *Spirit of Paupack,* U.S. Route 6 and Route 507; (570) 226–6266. Open daily Memorial Day through October. Dinner, 7:30 to 9:00 P.M. Scenic tours, 9:00 A.M. to 5:00 P.M. daily; $$ for adults, $ for children under twelve. Dinner tours, 7:30 to 9:00 P.M., $$$$ for adults, $$ for children. One-hour scenic cruises: Adults $$, children $. Two-hour sunset cruises: Adults $$$, children $$. Two-and-a-half-hour dinner cruises: Adults $$$$, children $$$. For a sunset dinner cruise or a one-hour sight-seeing tour on the lake, the 48-foot double-decker *Spirit of Paupack* is a great way to see the lake.

Woodloch Pines Resort (all ages) 🛏️🍽️⚠️

Route 590, Hawley; (800) 572–6658 or (800) 272–9428; www.woodloch.com. Open year-round.

If you follow Route 590 east from Hawley, you'll arrive at an excellent family resort, Woodloch Pines Resort named "one of the most exceptionally family-friendly resorts we've seen in many years" by Family Travel Network. Woodloch Pines was established as a small inn back in 1958. Since then, it has grown into a complex with 160 hotel rooms, a nightclub, several restaurants, game rooms, recreation complex, and more family activities and children's programs than you can cram into a seven-day stay.

The resort is located right on Lake Teedyuskung, sixty-five acres of crystal-clear waters with a sandy swimming beach and rowboats, paddleboats, canoes, kayaks, and sailboats for exploring on your own. Woodloch Pines has the space and the layout that allow some families to be quiet and relax with one another while other groups applaud and cheer one another in games and contests. Other seasonal activities include hiking, biking, golf, snowtubing, snowmobiling, ice-skating, bumper cars, go-karts, rifle range, batting cages, and more.

Woodloch Pines rates include three meals a day, activities, and entertainment. For families who prefer a more independent vacation, homes are available for rent at Woodloch Springs, a planned village centered around an award-winning golf course. Rates vary according to package length and accommodation type. Please call for current rates and availability.

ALSO IN THE AREA

Lacawac Wildlife Sanctuary (ages 6 and up), Lacawax Road, Ledgedale; (570) 689–9494; www.lacawac.org. Open year-round. One-mile self-guided nature trail overlooking Lake Wallenpaupack (pick up a trail guide at the parking lot), plus a host of special programs May through October.

Dorflinger–Suvdam Wildlife Preserve, White Mills; (570) 253–1185. Located off U.S. Route 6 between Hawley and Honesdale, this private preserve features hiking and cross-country ski trails and a great series of outdoor concerts in the summer months. The glass museum on the same property is interesting to adults and older children but not a great choice for toddlers and active kids.

Fly-Fishing

Both the Delaware and the Lackawaxen Rivers are known by anglers as prime fly-fishing areas. Licensed guides will take you and your older kids out on the river for lessons. Check the list published by the park service.

Lackawaxen

Route 590 continues east from Woodloch Pines to the state line at Lackawaxen and the Delaware River. This tiny Pennsylvania town was the home of Zane Grey, author of such famous Western novels as *The Riders of the Purple Sage* and more than fifty others. Today the property is owned by the National Park Service as part of the Upper Delaware Scenic and Recreational River, which encompasses a 74-mile stretch of river from Sparrowbush, New York, to Hancock. Rafting is a popular activity in this area.

Zane Grey Museum (ages 8 and up)

River Road; (570) 685–4871; www.nps.gov/upde.zgmuseum.htm. Open seasonally. No park entrance fee. A program fee is charged for the museum. Admission is $; children under 10 are free. Call ahead for museum hours.

This museum, operated by the National Park Service as part of the Upper Delaware Scenic and Recreational River, houses an impressive collection of memorabilia of Grey's life and his passion for the West.

Little ones will be frustrated by the "don't touch" policy of the museum, but school-age and older kids interested in stories of the Wild West will enjoy the twenty-minute guided tour. The paintings on the walls of Grey's study depict scenes from the Southwest.

Also at the museum is a gift shop (many of Grey's novels are on sale for some light vacation reading). The ranger on duty will be able to point out some of the highlights of the park, including Roebling's Delaware Aqueduct and the locks of the D&H Canal. Be sure to ask for the *Junior Ranger Program Activity Book*. Children who successfully complete six of the twelve activities in the pamphlet are awarded a certificate of achievement and a Junior Ranger patch.

Roebling's Delaware Aqueduct (ages 6 and up)

Route 590; (570) 685–4871; www.nps.gov/upde. Information center open seasonally. The bridge operates year-round.

Down the road about ½ mile from the Zane Grey Museum is the Delaware Aqueduct, also known as the Roebling Bridge. Believed to be the oldest existing wire suspension bridge in the Western Hemisphere, it was designed and built in 1848 by John Augustus Roebling, the man who later designed the famous Brooklyn Bridge in New York City. The Tollhouse, on the New York Side, contains historic photos from the canal era (1825 to 1898). It is open seasonally.

Upper Delaware **River Trips**

The Upper Delaware River is one of the last and longest free-flowing rivers in the northeastern United States. There are some rapids here, but most of the river is class I, which means it is safe for beginning boaters and children over five. (Always wear life jackets and exercise caution when on or near the water.)

There are several river accesses along the Upper Delaware, including one in Lackawaxen. If you don't have your own boat to launch here, contact one of the liveries that rent canoes, rafts, and tubes and conduct guided trips down the Delaware. The Park Service publishes a list of liveries and licensed guides. Most outfitters provide boats, life jackets, and drop-off and pick-up service at various river access points. They also have campsites available, although most are located on the New York side of the river. Remember, although the river is open to the public, the land on either side is privately owned. Please respect the rights and privacy of landowners.

Some of the bigger operations on the northern portion of the river include the following:

- **Kittatinny Canoes, Inc.,** 102 Kittatinny Court, Dingmans Ferry; (800) FLOATKC; www.kittatinny.com. Rafting, canoeing, kayaking, tubing, and paintball.

- **Lander's River Trips & Campgrounds,** 5666 Route 97, P.O. Box 500, Narrowsburg NY 12764; (800) 252–3925; www.landersrivertrips.com. Children must be fifty pounds. With landings in Hancock, Hankins, Callicoon, Skinners Falls, Narrowsburg, Ten Mile River, Minisink, Pond Eddy, Knights Eddy, and Matamoras, Lander's has the Upper Delaware covered. In addition to conducting rafting and canoe trips, the company rents equipment for self-guided expeditions. Facilities include campgrounds, motel (Ten Mile River Lodge in Ten Mile River, New York), and large grassy areas for playing near the river.

- **Wild and Scenic River Tours,** 166 Route 97, Barryville, New York; (800) 836–0366.

Honesdale

Honesdale, located at the intersection of US 6 and 191, is in many ways the quintessential American small town. Its Main Street is lined with shops and stores that have been operated by the same families for years. Through a special Main Street program, many of the stores have been renovated to reflect the town's historic architecture. And the Victorian homes and big porches of north Main Street are classic examples of American design.

Wayne County Historic Society Museum (ages 2 and up) 🏛 🔖

810 Main Street; (570) 253–3240; www.waynehistorypa.org. Open year-round; call for current hours. Admission is $; children under 12 are free.

Here you can see a replica of the original Stourbridge Lion, the first commercial steam locomotive to run on an American rail in 1829. (The original is in the Smithsonian Institution in Washington, D.C.) Another exhibit traces the history of the D&H Canal, which connected Honesdale to the Hudson River, 108 miles away. There's also an impressive collection of Native American artifacts found in the Upper Delaware River Valley by a local archaeologist.

Stourbridge Line Rail Excursions (all ages)

303 Commercial Street; (570) 253–1960; www.waynecountycc.com. Call or check the Web site for current schedule. Rates vary according to season and itinerary.

The Stourbridge Line Rail Excursions run on weekends in summer and for special occasions at other times. The excursions follow the Lackawaxen River to Hawley and Lackawaxen. Different themes include fall foliage tours, dinner-theater tours, the Great Train Robbery Run, the Halloween Fun Run, the Easter Bunny Run, and the Santa Express.

The Wayne County Visitors Center, at the same address, will soon house a number of railroad exhibits, and there's a gift shop featuring railroad souvenirs.

ALSO IN THE AREA

Carousel Water and Fun Park, Route 652, Beach Lake; (570) 729–7532; www .carousel-park.com. Open May through October. Go-karts, waterslides, bumper boats, minigolf, and batting cages are among the attractions here. Pay one price or pay by the ride.

Fun and Games, Route 6 Plaza, US 6; (570) 253–9111. A pay-and-play center with indoor minigolf that can be just the ticket on rainy days.

Wayne County Fair, Route 191; www.waynecountyfair.com. The first week in August, the Wayne County Fairgrounds hosts a fairly traditional county fair. There are rides and food, but the best part is watching local 4–H kids with the animals they've raised and trained themselves.

Starlight and New Milford

Head north from Honesdale on Route 191 and you'll find yourself in northern Wayne County. The thick forests of this corner of the state add to the feeling of an escape from civilization.

Inn at Starlight Lake (all ages) 🚫🏊⛺

Lake Road, Starlight; (800) 248–2519; www.innatstarlightlake.com. Open year-round.

One of the best places to enjoy northern Wayne County is the Inn at Starlight Lake, which has been attracting vacationers since 1909. Guests can stay in the inn itself, but families will generally prefer the cottages. Each cottage is a little different: Some have fireplaces, others have sleeping lofts for kids. All have private bathrooms.

The inn, as the name suggests, is located right on Starlight Lake, a pretty little body of water that's great for swimming and exploring by rowboat or small sailboat (no powerboats allowed). There is a tennis court, shuffleboard, and a library and game room for evenings and rainy days. In winter visit nearby Mount Tone and Elk Mountain for downhill and cross-country skiing.

The inn is also the first stop on the four-day self-guided Inn-To-Inn bike tour of Wayne and Susquehanna Counties. For families with older children, this is a great combination of an active vacation and lovely accommodations.

Old Mill Village Museum (ages 5 and up) 🏛

Located 1 mile south of New Milford on Route 848 (exit 223 of I–81) and accessible from U.S. Route 11; (570) 465–3448; www.oldmillvillage.com. Hours vary seasonally. Admission is $ for adults, free for children under 2 with an adult.

Follow the signs from the interstate to this group of historic buildings and artifacts depicting life in the area in the 1800s. During summer artisans demonstrate different crafts, from blacksmithing to quilting. There are also special events and festivals throughout the season, including an Annual Arts and Crafts Day, an antique doll show, Old Time Country Music Contest, and more.

Scranton

Scranton has a lot to offer to family travelers.

Steamtown National Historic Site (all ages) 🏛🚂🚻

Entrance off Lackawanna Avenue, just west of Steamtown Mall; (570) 340–5200 or (888) 693–9391; www.nps.gov/stea. Open daily 9:00 A.M. to 5:00 P.M. (closed major holidays). Museum entrance fee: $$ adults, children free.

Railroad buffs of all ages won't want to miss Steamtown. Occupying fifty-two acres of a working railroad yard in downtown Scranton, Steamtown traces the history of railroading in the region and throughout the country. The structure, opened in 1995, includes a visitor center, a theater, an operating turntable, technology and history museums, a renovated roundhouse, and a museum store.

Watch the eighteen-minute film Steel and Steam to learn about the history of American steam railroading. At the history museum meet the people (actually lifelike statues) who worked, used, and depended on the railroad. Visit the roundhouse to see several examples from the Steamtown collection of locomotives and railroad cars. Learn about locomotive design and railroad communications at the technology museum.

From Steamtown you can board a rail excursion along the Pocono Mainline or ride the Heritage Valley Station Stops on the former D&H Mainline ($$$ for adults, $$ for seniors and children) or to the historic Radisson Lackawanna Hotel (included in general admission). According to one park ranger, children are "glued to the window or fast asleep during these trips. Either way, it's great for parents!" Call the park for current information and train schedules.

The Steamtown site is wheelchair accessible, and there are bathrooms with changing tables. The excursion is accessible, but prior reservations are required. There are chemical toilets on the train, and snacks are available during a brief stop at Moscow.

After touring Steamtown, walk up the long ramp to the mall at Steamtown. (On rainy days, or when little ones are tired, it may be better to drive to the mall and park in the lot there.) There's a food court with fast food for every taste. If you prefer a more leisurely dining experience, head downstairs, or into town where there are many restaurants to choose from.

A Paulsen **Family Adventure**

On a rainy weekend in November, Faith and I took Eli (one and a half years old) and Gideon (two and a half) to Steamtown National Historic Site in Scranton. It is tailor-made for train-loving toddlers who need a chance to run around. The boys loved the roundhouse and climbing up on the trains, as well as the train sounds and the photographs of trains in the museum.

On our way out to the car, the excursion train was pulling into the station. The boys were excited to see the big engine coming closer and closer. We picked them up so they could see better. They waved at the passengers and at the engineer. In reply, the engineer blew the loud train whistle. Both boys immediately burst into tears. It was probably not the reaction the engineer expected!

Lackawanna County Electric City Museum (all ages)

300 Cliff Street on property of Steamtown; (570) 963–6590. Open Tuesday through Sunday. Ride and museum combo tickets are $$; children under 3 are free.

The Electric City Trolley Museum shares a parking lot with Steamtown, making one-stop shopping for kids who love the rails. This museum tells the story of electric traction and trolley systems in northeastern Pennsylvania. Trolley excursions depart regularly from the same platform as the Steamtown trains, and go through the Crown Avenue tunnel. The Children's Gallery teaches "painless geography" through models set on maps of the area. Kids can generate their own electricity, run a trolley system, and build their own model anthracite communities. The trolley excursion has recently been extended to reach the Lackawanna County visitor center.

Radisson Lackawanna Station Hotel (all ages)

700 Lackawanna Avenue; (570) 342–8300; www.radisson.com/scranton.pa.

Sticking with the railroad motif, why not stay in a glorious old railway station? The Lackawanna Station Hotel, a building on the National Register of Historic Places now operated by the Radisson chain of hotels, is just a few blocks from Steamtown. You can actually take the Steamtown Excursion train to Steamtown. The station's waiting area has been transformed into a palatial lobby with two restaurants and complete hotel facilities—including a game room that's a hit with kids.

Houdini Museum (ages 3 and up)

1433 North Main Avenue; (570) 342–5555; www.houdini.org. Open daily Memorial Day through September 15; other times by appointment. Admission is $$.

Featured on the Travel Channel's *Magic Road Trip,* the Houdini Museum is a must-see for budding magicians. The museum takes visitors back to the days of vaudeville, when traveling performers like Houdini frequently visited the Scranton area. There are continuous guided tours, a film, and nonstop magic shows, along with Houdini memorabilia and exhibits about Scranton's vaudeville past. A wonderful magic show is performed by nationally known magicians such as Dorothy Dietrich and Bravo the Great. Lots of laughs, live animals, and audience participation.

The Halloween "Spook-tacular" Theater of Illusion takes place from Columbus Day through Halloween. Appropriate for all ages, this magic show features classic illusions with nothing too scary for little ones.

Lackawanna Coal Mine (ages 3 and up)

McDade Park; (800) 238–7245 or (570) 963–MINE; www.lackawannacounty.org. Open daily April through November. Admission: $$, adults, $ children ages 3 to 12; children under 3 are free.

Coal is a major part of this region's history. One of the best places to gain an understanding of the life of a coal miner is on the Lackawanna Coal Mine Tour at McDade

Park in Scranton. Here visitors ride 250 feet down into a real underground coal mine. Former miners and sons of miners tell the story of what a typical workday was like for the men and boys (as young as seven years old!) of the mines. Children who are afraid of the dark should be forewarned, but most children's favorite part of the tour is when the guide turns out the lights and the group stands in total darkness for a long couple of seconds.

The tour is partially wheelchair accessible, as long as the person can move from a wheelchair to the car. It's chilly and damp down below (fifty-five degrees year-round), so be sure to bring along a sweatshirt.

Montage Mountain (ages 2 and up)

1000 Montage Mountain Road; (800) GOT–SNOW or (570) 969–7669; www.skimontage .com. The summer park is open from mid-June to Labor Day, weekdays noon to 5:00 P.M. and weekends 11:00 A.M. to 5:00 P.M.

Another center of family-oriented activity is Montage Mountain, located right off exit 182 of I–81. Summer activities include waterslides, batting cages, chairlift rides, children's activity park, playground, and more. During the colder months, Montage is home to a top ski resort offering skiing, snowboarding, and snowtubing. Saturday night is Family Night. A new Northeastern Pennsylvania visitor center is located here.

ALSO IN THE AREA

Lackawanna County Stadium (ages 5 and up), Montage Mountain Road; (570) 969–BALL; www.redbarons.com. Home to the Red Barons, an AAA farm club for the Philadelphia Phillies. Call for game information and schedules for the upcoming season.

Everhart Museum (all ages), Nay Aug Park, 1901 Mulberry Street, Scranton; (570) 346–7186; www.everhart-museum.org. Open year-round. Admission is $$ for adults, $ for seniors and children; children under 5 are **free.** Permanent exhibits include a dinosaur hall, rock and mineral display, a bird gallery, and children's gallery, as well as examples of American and European painting, prints, and more. The Everhart often attracts high-quality traveling exhibits, so be sure to call ahead and see what will be there during your stay.

Eckley Miners' Village (all ages), RR 2, Box 236, Weatherly 18255; (570) 636–2070; www.eckleyminers.org. Open daily year-round. Admission: $ per person, $$ for families. Just 9 miles east of Interstate 81, Eckley Miners' Village offers the chance to visit an authentic nineteenth-century "patch" town. The town was originally built in 1854 by the mining firm of Sharpe, Leisenring and Co. for its workers, mostly new immigrants to the States. The town, which was restored in the late 1960s for the filming of the movie *The Molly Maguires,* is now a historic site, administered by the Pennsylvania Historical and Museum Commission. Throughout the summer season the village holds various special events, including Patch Town Days, a Living History Weekend, and Family Sunday, which features a community picnic typical of the 1800s.

McDade **Park**

The Lackawanna Coal Mine may be the main attraction, but there's lots more to do in McDade Park. Next door to the mine is the Anthracite Heritage Museum, which traces the history of coal and its influence on the people of this area, including immigrant workers in the coal mines. Call (570) 963–4804 for more information.

McDade Park is also home to a summer theater festival, a fall balloon festival, and other special events. In addition, it's a great place for a family picnic and outdoor play. For more information and a schedule of upcoming events, call (570) 963–6764.

The Lehigh Gorge and Surrounding Area
(White Haven, Jim Thorpe, Lehighton)

The Lehigh River cuts through the section of the Pocono Plateau south of Wilkes-Barre and creates a gorge that has become a mecca for recreation enthusiasts. A bike path along the river is a dramatic but easy ride (especially going north to south), and the river itself offers challenging white water for boating. There's also great skiing in the area, as well as some terrific resorts for families.

For a family that wants to combine outdoor activities like biking, hiking, and swimming with more urbane pursuits such as museums, shops, and restaurants, the town of Jim Thorpe has a winning combination.

Mauch Chunk Lake Park (all ages)

625 Lentz Trail, Jim Thorpe; (570) 325–3669; www.carboncounty.com/park. Open year-round.

In the late 1800s and early 1900s, tourists flocked to Mauch Chunk (now Jim Thorpe) to ride the famous Switchback Railroad. This 18-mile figure-eight of track was more like a roller coaster than a train ride—at some points on the trip, cars reached speeds of 60 miles per hour. Now, a century later, the Switchback is again attracting tourists. Although the railroad has not operated in many years, its railbed has been transformed into one of the best-known mountain-bike trails on the East Coast.

Much of the Switchback trail is located within or near Mauch Chunk Lake Park, a county park that offers more than a vacation's worth of activities. The park features nice campsites, a sandy beach on a beautiful lake, excellent programs at the environmental center, picnic pavilions, food and refreshment stand, and 18 miles of biking, hiking, or cross-country skiing trails. Trails include scenic overlooks, one of which offers a spectacular view of the Lehigh Gorge and Glenonoko Falls. On weekends during the month of October—peak foliage time—the park offers hayrides along the Switchback Trail.

Other special attractions of the park include wheelchair access to the lake, a wheelchair-accessible fishing pier, bathrooms with changing tables, and a nice playground for kids. Fees are charged for many of the park's activities, including swimming, hayrides, equipment rentals, and camping. Eight camping cottages are available for rent.

Mauch Chunk Museum and Cultural Center (ages 4 and up)
41 West Broadway, Jim Thorpe; (570) 325–9190; www.mauchchunkmuseum.com. Open Tuesday through Sunday year-round. Call ahead for current hours. Admission is $.

Stop here to learn about the history of the Switchback Railroad and the town that grew up around it. An exhibit called *The Story of Mauch Chunk* (the town that changed its name to Jim Thorpe) portrays the history of the coal mining industry in Mauch Chunk (the town's former name), the Lenni Lenape Indians, the life of Jim Thorpe, the Native American Olympic athlete for whom the town was renamed in the 1950s. Although Thorpe was never a resident of the town, his widow heard of the area's efforts to revitalize its economy and offered her husband's memorabilia in exchange for naming the town in his honor.

The museum is housed in a beautiful redbrick Victorian church built in 1843.

The Old Jail Museum (ages 6 and up)
128 West Broadway, Jim Thorpe; (570) 325–5259. Open daily except Wednesday, Memorial Day through Labor Day. Open weekends only in September and October. Admission is $.

Asked what kids like best about his museum, Thomas McBride answers, "It's a real jail and it's spooky. Real 'bad guys' were here!" Indeed, this building served as the Carbon County jail from 1871 to January 1995. It was also the site of the hanging of the Molly Maguires. Purchased by Thomas and Betty Lou McBride in 1995, it has now been preserved as a museum. Tour guides take visitors through the kitchen, cell blocks, and even down to the dungeon, where prisoners were kept in solitary confinement. Yes, it's a bit spooky, but there are lessons to be learned here. Older kids especially seem fascinated. Look for the "mysterious handprint" left by a prisoner in 1871. No matter how many times the room is repainted, the ghostly handprint always bleeds through!

Blue Mountain Sports and Wear (ages 8 and up)
US 209, Jim Thorpe; (800) 599–4421; www.bikejimthorpe.com. Open daily.

According to *Outside* magazine, Jim Thorpe offers the "best biking in Pennsylvania." If mountain biking or other outdoor sports are your pleasure, stop in at the Blue

Mountain Sports and Wear shop for information about the excellent trails in the area. The store offers top-quality bike rentals and shuttle service to various trailheads. Tell the experienced staff your skill level and how much time you want to spend, and they'll guide you to the right trail. In addition to bike rentals, the store has camping equipment, kayaks, rowboats, canoes, cross-country skis, and snowshoes for rent.

Pocono Whitewater Rafting (ages 5 and up)

Route 903, Jim Thorpe; (800) WHITEWATER or (570) 325–8430; www.whitewater rafting.com.

Another option for outdoor enthusiasts is a rafting trip down the Lehigh River. Pocono Whitewater Adventures offers "Family-Style Floatrips" for kids from "five to eighty-five," including riverside barbecue. One child per two paying adults rides **free.**

Rail Tours, Inc. (ages 4 and up)

P.O. Box 285, Jim Thorpe 18229; (570) 325–4606; www.railtours-inc.com. Admission: $$–$$$ for adults, $–$$ for children 2 through 11.

The visitor center in the old Jersey Central Railroad Station is the starting point for a number of special train-ride excursions. The schedule changes throughout the season, but rides take place on most weekends from April to October and the first two weekends of December.

Asa Packer Mansion (ages 8 and up)

Packer Hill, Jim Thorpe; (570) 325–3229; http://asapackermansionmuseum.homestead .com. Open daily Memorial Day through October 31. Call ahead for hours. Admission is $$ for adults and $ for children under 12.

Although not a place to take your wound-up preschooler, older kids will enjoy ogling the opulent furnishings in this Victorian mansion.

Old Mauch Chunk H.O. Scale Model Train Display (all ages)

41 Susquehanna Street, Jim Thorpe; (570) 386–2297 or (570) 325–4371. Open year-round. Hours vary. Admission is $; children under 4 enter free.

Across the street from the visitor center, in the Hooven Mercantile Co. building, head up to the second floor to see the Scale Model Railroad Display. With 1,000 feet of track, 60 cars, 200 miniature buildings, and 100 bridges, it sure is an impressive display.

The Inn at Jim Thorpe (all ages)

24 Broadway, Jim Thorpe; (570) 325–2599; www.innjt.com.

With a restaurant on-site and kid-friendly policies, this is a great place to stay right in Jim Thorpe. You can walk to all the sights. Suites have dining areas, whirlpools, VCRs, refrigerators, microwaves, and coffeemakers—things that make a family vacation much easier.

Pennsylvania **State Parks**

With 116 parks adding up to more than 300,000 acres, Pennsylvania has the largest state park system east of the Mississippi—and one of the best travel bargains anywhere. From the majesty of old growth forests to the drama of waterfalls, from the solitude of fishing to the camaraderie of a multigenerational family vacation, these parks offer something for just about everyone. And, admission is **free**.

But while many families are aware of the recreational offerings of the state parks, many don't know about the cozy cabins and excellent campgrounds that offer an escape from ordinary life. Fifty-five of Pennsylvania's state parks offer camping. Located in the woods, on the edge of a lake, by a babbling brook, or at the edge of an inspiring vista, these accommodations are the stuff vacation dreams are made on—at prices that make wishes come true.

Cabin rentals include tiny rustic cabins for two and modern cabins with living room, bathroom, kitchen, and bunk beds for six. You'll have to reserve a weekday for the best rates, but even on weekends, the cabins are still a bargain. In summer, the cabins are available by the week. Bring your own food, linens, and cooking utensils, and you've got a terrific vacation.

Leave your tent behind and try two new overnight choices in the state park system: yurts and camping cottages. A yurt is a round tent on a wooden deck, equipped with a cooking stove, refrigerator, table, chairs, electric heat and outlets, fire ring, water pump two bunk beds, and other simple amenities. The camping cottages are rustic wooden structures with electric lights and outlets, windows, screened porches, heaters, and mini-fridges. Each cottage sleeps five.

Modern campsites rent for as low as $$$ per night—rustic for even less.

By calling (888) PA–PARKS, you'll be able to make reservations up to eleven months in advance at any of the state parks in Pennsylvania. If one park has no available cabins for the dates you select, the operator will locate another that does. You can also check the Web site at www.dcnr.state.pa.us.

Your best bet is to call the individual parks if you have specific questions. For general park information and for cabin, campsite, or pavilion reservations, the number to call is (888) PA–PARKS.

ALSO IN THE AREA

Big Boulder and Jack Frost Ski Resorts, Lake Harmony; (570) 722–0100 or (800) 468–2442; www.big2resorts.com. Big Boulder and its neighbor, Jack Frost, offer a great vacation deal for families. Families can try skiing (downhill and cross-country), snowtubing, snowboarding, motorsports, and paintball and stay in a vacation home on the property. Even better, kids under five stay **free.** Both resorts also offer babysitting, ski lessons in the winter, music festivals in the summer, and nightlife all year long. Jack Frost has TRAXX, a 15-mile course through the woods with divisions for motocross, ATV, and BMX bikes. This course is available for people ten and up. Bring your own equipment, but you can rent bicycles only. Also at Jack Frost is night-time snowtubing on Saturday nights.

Ashland

Pioneer Tunnel Coal Mine & Steam Train (all ages) 🏛

Nineteenth and Oak Streets; (570) 875–3850; www.pioneertunnel.com. Open April through November. Call ahead for specific times. Mine tour: $$ for adults, $ for children under 12. Steam train: $$ for adults, $ for children under 12.

If you didn't visit the Lackawanna Coal Mine in Scranton—or if you and your kids enjoyed it so much you're ready for another mine tour—then head to Ashland and the Pioneer Tunnel Coal Mine. Like the Scranton mine, this is an actual coal mine. When the coal company shut it down, some local volunteers and former miners transformed it into a fascinating study of a coal miner's life. Visitors enter the mine in open mine cars, just as the miners did when they started their workdays.

After the thirty-five-minute mine tour, take a ride on a narrow-gauge steam loco-motive, the Henry Clay. Along the 1½-mile round-trip, you'll see two other examples of coal mining: a strip mine and a bootleg coal mine, where men snuck past guards to get coal to sell or to heat their own homes. You can see the smoke rising from the ground as a result of the famous Centalia mine fire.

Red Rock

Ricketts Glen State Park (ages 2 and up) ⊗ △ ⊕

Route 487; (570) 477–5675 or (888) PA–PARKS; www.dcnr.state.pa.us. Open year-round. Free.

Ricketts Glen State Park may well be the most beautiful and least well-known of Pennsylvania's many state parks. The park, which spills into Luzerne, Sullivan, and Columbia Counties, covers 13,050 acres with lakes, waterfalls (twenty-two in all!), hiking and cross-country skiing trails, and many opportunities for fishing, boating, camping, horseback riding, and more.

The Glens Natural Area, a registered National Natural Landmark, is the centerpiece of the park. Here, where two branches of Kitchen Creek create deep gorges, there are rare stands of virgin hemlock and other trees, some more than 500 years old. Much of the hiking in the park covers pretty steep territory, but with the help of a park ranger, you can choose trails that may be easier for children. For example, the Evergreen Trail, just ½-mile long, takes hikers through giant hemlocks and pine trees and to a view of several waterfalls. There are 120 tent and trailer campsites available year-round at the park. In summer there are flush toilets and hot showers. In winter, only pit toilets are available.

If camping sounds a bit too rustic, consider staying at one of the ten comfortable family cabins in the park. Each has a living area, kitchen, bath, and two or three bedrooms. Advance reservations are required for the cabins.

Hunting is permitted in parts of the park. If you visit during the hunting season (primarily in late fall), check in with park rangers to find out what safety precautions are appropriate.

Forksville

World's End State Park (ages 6 and up) ⊕ ⊗ △

Route 154; (570) 924–3287 or (888) PA–PARKS; www.dcnr.state.pa.us. Open year-round. Free.

Despite its small size (less than 1,000 acres), it's easy to feel as if you're at the edge of the world in this remote valley. If you're looking for a good place to introduce your children to wilderness camping, this is the spot. There are seventy tent and trailer sites and nineteen cabins, equipped with refrigerator, range, fireplace, table, chairs, and beds. (There's a central shower facility.)

The park includes numerous hiking trails, including the 59³⁄₁₀-mile-Loyalsock Trail, part of which runs through the park. Most of the trails are pretty steep, so this park is a better choice for older kids and more experienced hikers.

Festivals of Forksville

Forksville might as well be called Festiville, with all the annual events planned for the fairgrounds and other locations around town. The fun starts in the winter with the annual Endless Mountains 50 Sled Dog Race. The 50-mile race, which is run in the state game lands near Forksville, attracts six-dog racing teams from as far away as Canada. When and if the weather gets cold enough, folks in the area start calling (570) 525–3255 to find out if the Ice Toboggan Slide has been set up in Eagles Mere.

In February the Forksville fairgrounds is the site of the Sullivan County Sleigh Ride and Rally. Here, horses pull the sleighs. In addition to divisions for men, women, and children, there's a timed obstacle-course race and a "Currier & Ives" class, where contestants are judged on the "postcard" quality of their sleighs. Visitors can get a ride in a bobsled. Labor Day weekend brings the Sullivan County Fair, held at the Forksville Fairgrounds. In October it's time for the Fall Festival, with demonstrations by quilters, woodcarvers, and apple-butter and apple-cider makers. There are wagon rides, draft horses, and lots of activities for children.

For more information: Sullivan County Chamber of Commerce (570–946–4160) or Endless Mountains Visitors Bureau (570–836–5431). Check the Web site www.endlessmountains.org. The calendar portion of this Web site can be searched like a database for events of special interest to you.

Where to Eat

IN THE DELAWARE WATER GAP AND STROUDSBURG AREA

Brandli's Pizzeria & Italian Restaurant, 6A Foxmoor Village, East Stroudsburg; (570) 223–1600; www.brandlis.com. Family-oriented, casual Italian fare.

Brownie's, Main and Oak Streets, Delaware Water Gap; (570) 424–1154.

Brownie's in the Burg, 700 Main Street, Stroudsburg; (570) 421–2200.

The Sarah Street Grill, 550 Quaker Alley, Stroudsburg; (570) 424–9120. Casual dining including steaks, seafood, and pasta. Children's menu offers chicken fingers, grilled cheese sandwiches, and pizza.

IN THE MOUNT POCONO AND EASTERN POCONOS AREA

Memorytown, Grange Road, Mt. Pocono; (570) 839–1680. Shops, snack bar, restaurant, and amusement area all in one.

Smuggler's Cove, Route 611, Tannersville; (570) 629–2277.

IN THE HAWLEY–LAKE WALLENPAUPACK AREA

Ehrhardt's Lakeside Restaurant, Route 507, 1 mile south of Route 6, Hawley; (570) 226–2124. Dining with a view of Lake Wallenpaupack.

Falls Port Inn & Restaurant, Main Street, Hawley; (570) 226–2600. Children's menu, Sunday brunch, historic building.

IN THE HONESDALE AREA

Beach Lake Cafe, Route 652, Beach Lake. Open year-round. The most popular place around for weekend breakfasts, this little coffee shop serves up omelettes and pancakes. Get there early on Saturday to avoid a wait.

IN SCRANTON

Coney Island Lunch, 515 Lackawanna Avenue; (570) 961–9004. *Electric City* magazine's "Best of 2004" readers' poll voted as offering Northeastern Pennsylvania's best hot dogs.

Cooper's Seafood House, 701 North Washington Avenue; (570) 346–6883.

The Mall at Steamtown, Lackawanna Avenue; (570) 343–3400. Food court upstairs and two sit-down restaurants downstairs.

Pat McMullen's Restaurant, 217 East Market Street; (570) 342–3486.

Where to Stay

IN THE DELAWARE WATER GAP AND STROUDSBURG AREA

Ramada Inn, Delaware Water Gap; (570) 476–0000.

Shawnee Inn & Golf Resort, River Road, Shawnee-on-Delaware; (570) 424–4000 or (800) SHAWNEE; www.shawnee inn.com.

Sheraton Four Points, 1220 West Main Street, Stroudsburg; (570) 424–1930 or (800) 777–5453; www.quikpage.com/P/ pocono.

Timothy Lake, RD 6, Box 6627, East Stroudsburg 18301; (570) 588–6631 or for reservations (800) 588–2221. Part of the "Outdoor World" group of camping resorts.

IN MOUNT POCONO AND EASTERN POCONOS

The Britannia Country Inn, Upper Swiftwater Road, Swiftwater; (570) 839–7243. Open year-round. Rates are $$$$ per adult, $$$ for children 4 to 13. Children under 3 stay free. If you can't bear to leave the pooch at home for your family vacation, consider a cottage at the Brittania Inn. Located on twelve acres with an outdoor pool, the inn serves up a taste of England in the Poconos. Modified American Plan (MAP) rates and ski packages available.

Hampton Court Inn, Route 611, Mt. Pocono; (570) 839–2119.

Mount Airy Lodge, Route 611, Mt. Pocono; (570) 839–8811 or (800) 441–4410; www.mountairylodge.com.

Pocono Super 8 Motel, Route 611, Mt. Pocono; (570) 839–7728.

IN THE SCRANTON AREA

Best Western University Inn, 320 Franklin Avenue, Scranton; (570) 246–7061. Near Steamtown National Historic Site.

Holiday Inn Scranton–East, 200 Tigue Street, Dunmore; (570) 343–4771. Indoor pool, newly renovated rooms.

Scotrun, Route 611, Scotrun; (570) 629–0620 or for reservations (800) 588-2221. Part of the "Outdoor World" group of camping resorts.

IN THE HONESDALE AREA

Beach Lake is on Route 652, a great home base for exploring the Upper Delaware Valley and Honesdale.

Central House. Off Route 652; (570) 729–4411 or (570) 729–8341. Open year-round. An on-the-lake location, family-style meals, and on-site swimming pool and volleyball court—a nice spot for a value—priced vacation.

Pine Grove Cabins. Off Route 652; (570) 729–8522. Open May through October. For families who prefer to cook their own meals, these cabins can't be beat. Owners Jerry and Barbara Zimmerman keep this bungalow colony immaculate. Kitchens, small living rooms, bathroom with showers, and two bedrooms are crammed into each cabin. There's a beach for swimming and boats for guest use. Weeklong packages are available.

For More Information

Carbon County Visitor Center, Broadway, Jim Thorpe; (888) JIM–THORPE; www.pavisnet.com/carbon. Open year-round. Stop by to pick up brochures, ask questions, and check out the historic displays.

Endless Mountains Visitors Bureau, RR 6, Box 132A, Tunkhannock PA 18657; (800) 769–8999 or (570) 836–5431; www.endlessmountains.org.

Jim Thorpe Tourist Agency, (570) 325–3673.

Luzerne County Tourist Promotion Agency, 200 North River Street, Wilkes-Barre 18711; (570) 825–1635; www.tournepa.com.

Pennsylvania's Northeast Territory Visitors Bureau, 201 Hangar Road, Suite 203, Avoca 18641; (800) 22WELCOME or (570) 457–1320; www.visitnepa.org.

Pocono Mountains Convention and Visitors Bureau, 1004 Main Street, Stroudsburg 18360; (800) 762–6667; www.800poconos.com.

Schuylkill County Visitors' Bureau, 91 South Progress Street, Pottsville 17901; (800) 765–7282 or (570) 622–7700; www.schuylkill.org.

Upper Delaware Council, Bridge Street, Narrowsburg, New York; (570) 252–3022. An organization of businesses and individuals along the New York and Pennsylvania shores of the river. Contact them for more information about the area.

Central
Pennsylvania

The center of Pennsylvania holds a wonderful array of cultural, historical, and recreational opportunities for families. Two cities, Williamsport and State College, have great museums, cultural events, and a wide variety of amenities, such as accommodations, shopping, and restaurants. Either one makes a good base for exploring the surrounding areas.

Dotted around the region are charming small towns, wonderful state parks, farms, and other rural attractions. Campgrounds are plentiful, and little bed-and-breakfasts often welcome families. The local county tourism organizations and chambers of commerce are great resources for planning your trip. Here are our recommendations.

Faith & Emily's
FavoriteAttractions
in Central Pennsylvania

1. Knoebels Amusement Park and Campground, Elysburg

2. Peter J. McGovern Little League Baseball Museum, Williamsport

3. Mountain Dale Farm, McClure

4. Shaver's Creek Environmental Center, State College

5. Bellefonte Museum for Centre County, Bellefonte

6. Children's Discovery Workshop, Williamsport

7. Clyde Peeling's Reptiland, Williamsport

8. T&D's Cats of the World, Mifflinburg

9. Historic Williamsport Trolleys, Williamsport

10. Walking tour of the Victorian downtown in Lewisburg

CENTRAL PENNSYLVANIA

Williamsport

If you have a child in Little League, then Williamsport—the home of the Peter J. McGovern Little League Baseball Museum—is a required stop on your vacation in central Pennsylvania. Once you get to the city, you'll find that the museum is a great destination. So is a Crosscutters game. To find out more about Williamsport's own minor league baseball team, including schedules and ticket information, visit www.crosscutters.com.

In Williamsport, you can also access the Pine Creek Rail Trail, which stretches for 64 miles from Ansonia in Tioga County to Jersey Shore in Lycoming County.

Peter J. McGovern Little League Baseball Museum (ages 5 and up)

U.S. 15 South; (570) 326–3607; www.littleleague.org. Memorial Day through September 30: Open Monday through Saturday 9:00 A.M. to 7:00 P.M.; Sunday noon to 7:00 P.M. October 1 through Memorial Day: Open Monday, Thursday, and Friday 10:00 A.M. to 5:00 P.M., Saturday noon to 5:00 P.M., and Sunday noon to 4:00 P.M. Closed Tuesday and Wednesday and major holidays. Adults, $$; children 5 to 13, $.

The Peter J. McGovern Little League Baseball Museum traces the history of Little League from its founding in 1939 to the present, when millions of children in scores of countries participate in the program. There are interactive displays and batting and pitching cages with instant replay monitors so that kids can see themselves on "instant replay." You can watch highlights of the Little League World Series—a truly international sporting event that takes place here each August. The Hall of Excellence includes tributes to such famous former Little Leaguers as Tom Seaver, Kareem Abdul-Jabbar, columnist George Will, and former New Jersey Senator Bill Bradley.

Faith & Emily's
FavoriteEvents
in Central Pennsylvania

- **Belleville Farmers Market** in Belleville (Wednesdays); (570) 248–6713.

- **Big Spring Film Festival** in Bellefonte (mid-May); (800) 355–1705.

- **Mifflinburg Buggy Days** in Mifflinburg (end of May); (570) 966–1355.

- **Central Pennsylvania Festival of the Arts** in State College (July); (814) 237–3682; www.arts-festival.com.

- **Ag Progress Days** in State College (mid-August); (814) 865–2081.

Children's Discovery Workshop (ages 3 to 11) 🧩

343 West Fourth Street at Elmira Street; (570) 322–5437; williamsportymca.com. Open September through May, Tuesday through Friday and Sunday 10:00 A.M. to 5:00 P.M., Saturday 11:00 A.M. to 5:00 P.M.; June through August, Tuesday through Saturday 9:00 A.M. to 4:00 P.M., Saturday 10:00 A.M. to 4:00 P.M. Admission: $ per person; children under 2 are free.

Located inside the Williamsport YMCA, the Children's Discovery Workshop is a hands-on museum for children ages three to eleven. The interactive exhibits are designed to inspire children's imaginations, explorations, and discoveries. Features include a toddler area, bricks to build a castle, a pretend ice-cream parlor, and changing exhibits. One of the most popular features is the 129-foot-long "FUNnel," which children can crawl through.

Thomas T. Taber Museum of Lycoming County (ages 5 and up) 🧩

858 West Fourth Street; (570) 326–3326; www.lycoming.org/lchsmuseum. Open year-round Tuesday through Friday 9:30 A.M. to 4:00 P.M. and Saturday 11:00 A.M. to 4:00 P.M. Open Sunday from May to October 31, 1:00 to 4:00 P.M. Adults $$, children 12 and under $.

Model-train enthusiasts will want to stop here to see the Larue Shempp Model Train exhibition, with more than 300 toy trains and two working layouts—reputed to be one of the finest displays of its kind in the country. There's a frontier room, which re-creates the furnishings from the county's first European settlement in 1769; a general store from the turn of the twentieth century; a one-room schoolhouse; a working gristmill; and a collection of farming, blacksmithing, and milling tools from the 1700s to 1900s. You can board the Historic Williamsport Trolley here, too.

Historic Williamsport Trolleys (all ages) 🏛

Downtown Williamsport; (800) CITYBUS or (570) 326–2500; www.citybus. org. Open Tuesday, Thursday, and Saturday during June, July, and August. Tours are $ per person.

The Historic Williamsport Trolleys are run by the City Bus company of the Williamsport Bureau of Transportation. The three trolleys, the *Herdic*, the *Weightman*, and the *Stotz*, are actually replicas of historic streetcars. Each makes a ninety-minute narrated trip around the historic areas of Williamsport. The route takes you past Millionaire's Row (6 blocks of magnificent mansions), the field where the first Little League game was played, and other sights of the city. Riders can get on and off at one of the downtown stops and each of the two outlying stops. On Tuesday and Thursday you can get off the trolley and onto the *Hiawatha* for a cruise—another great way to tour the sights of this city.

Hiawatha Riverboat (all ages) ⚠

Susquehanna State Park; (570) 326–2500 or (800) 248–9287. In season only (570) 326–1221; www.williamsport.org. Cruises operate Tuesday through Sunday, May through mid-October. Public cruises: Adults $$, children 3 to 12 $. Family Night cruises: Adults $$, children 3 to 12 $. First come, first served after tickets go on sale at 10:30 A.M.

The other way to tour the town is aboard the *Hiawatha*, a paddlewheeler that plies the Susquehanna River. The hour-long public cruise includes a narration that relates the history of the area, from the time when the Susquehannock Indians lived along these shores through the European settlements and boom years of the lumber industry. On Tuesday nights in June, July, and August, come aboard for a special cruise just for families, ninety minutes long, with a different featured activity every night. Sunday brunch cruises, for $$$ per person, will sail you to the Antlers Country Club for brunch, then take you back by Historic Williamsport Trolley.

Clyde Peeling's Reptiland (ages 4 and up) 🐘

US 15, south of Williamsport; (570) 538–1869 or (800) REPTILAND; www.reptiland.com. Open year-round daily 9:00 A.M. to 7:00 P.M. Closed major holidays. Admission is $$; children under 4 are **free.**

Don't miss Clyde Peeling's Reptiland, an accredited zoo with a collection of sixty different species of reptiles and amphibians. Poison dart frogs, a giant toad, a gaboon viper, a green tree python, a king cobra, alligators, giant tortoises, turtles, iguanas—they're all here. There are educational programs five times during the day that give visitors a chance to see and touch the animals up close.

The newly renovated indoor exhibit complex allows comfortable viewing of animals year-round. You may dine at a Subway restaurant in the entrance building. And on the third weekend of October, come learn about nocturnal animals at Reptiland's Flashlight Safari.

Although it doesn't offer wheelchair rentals, Reptiland is wheelchair accessible.

Elysburg

Knoebels Amusement Park and Campground (ages 2 and up)
🌊 🎡 🏕

Route 487, about 12 miles south of Bloomsburg; (800) ITS–4FUN or (570) 672–2572; www.knoebels.com. Open weekends in April, May, and September; daily in June, July, and August. Admission **free** to park; camping and cabins are $$$$. Individual ride prices are $. Pay-One-Price plans available Monday through Friday during the in-season.

If you've ever wondered what happened to the traditional amusement parks you remember from your own childhood, head to Knoebels (pronounced with a hard "k"). This park got its start at the turn of the twentieth century, when Henry Hartman Knoebel charged 25 cents to water, feed, and brush the horses that brought groups to swim on his property. After a few years he added picnic tables and sold ice cream and other snacks to the visitors. A pool, overnight cottages, and a carousel were added in 1926. By the 1940s Knoebels had graduated to an amusement resort.

At present Knoebels offers fifty rides (including two world-class roller coasters, the Phoenix and the Twister), a huge swimming pool, and many rides, especially for the younger set. There are several restaurants, snack bars, and picnic areas as well as a collection of shops and regularly scheduled entertainment. All of this is nestled among natural streams and shady hemlock trees that keep the temperatures here a good ten degrees lower than elsewhere in the area.

If this sounds like too much for a day trip, stay the night—or longer—at one of 500 campsites and log cabins. Cabins sleep six and have electricity. Call (570) 672–9555 for campground information.

Lewisburg

A pretty Victorian town that is home to Bucknell University, Lewisburg is a good place to stop and stretch your legs or grab some lunch. There are some great historic homes in town that are open for tours. Although not geared for small children, older ones enjoy the tours.

Slifer House Museum (ages 6 and up) 🏛

1 River Road; (570) 524–2245; www.slifer.albrightcare.org. Open April 15 through December 31, Tuesday through Sunday 1:00 to 4:00 P.M.; January 1 through April 14, Tuesday through Friday 1:00 to 4:00 P.M. or by appointment. Admission is $; children under 10 are free.

House tours aren't on most kids' top ten list, but the Slifer House has several exhibits that children six and older enjoy. An artifact quiz is designed to stimulate minds, both young and old. Among the favorites are the children's bedroom and old toys, a Regina music box, and the doctor's office, with antique medical tools. A sure hit with kids. Slifer House also hosts family activities such as Civil War encampments, storytelling, and workshops. The house is wrapped in Victorian excess for the Christmas holidays, including a floor-to-ceiling tree with nineteenth-century ornaments and garlands of roses over the dining-room table.

Packwood House Museum (ages 6 and up) 🏛

15 North Water Street; (570) 524–0323; www.packwoodhousemuseum.com. Open Tuesday through Saturday 10:00 A.M. to 5:00 P.M. Admission is $; children under 6 are free.

One of the oldest log-built structures in Pennsylvania, the Packwood House was originally constructed between 1796 and 1799. Christmas is a special time for children at the Packwood. Even younger children love seeing the decorations and lights. The rest of the year, the museum is more geared for school-age children. There is an impressive collection of antique furniture, glass, ceramics, textiles, and more at the Packwood.

Mifflinburg

In addition to the following sights, Mifflinburg serves as the headquarters for no fewer than four Pennsylvania state parks: McCalls Dam State Park (known for its fishing); R. B. Winter State Park (with lake swimming, environmental education, and camping); Ravensburg State Park (fishing, hiking, and camping); and Sand Bridge State Park (known for snowmobiling trails). For information on any one of these parks, call (570) 966–1455 or (888) PA–PARKS.

Mifflinburg Buggy Museum (ages 3 and up)

598 Green Street; (570) 966–1355; www.lycoming.org/buggy. Open May through October, Thursday through Saturday 10:00 A.M. to 5:00 P.M., Sunday 1:00 to 5:00 P.M. Visitor center open November through April, Thursday through Saturday 10:00 A.M. to 5:00 P.M. Admission is $$ for adults and $ for children 6 to 17. Children under 6 enter free. Free parking.

The Mifflinburg Buggy Museum gives you a chance to see horse-drawn buggies up close. Through the late nineteenth century, Mifflinburg earned the nickname "Buggy Town" by producing roughly 5,000 horse-drawn vehicles a year, more per capita than any other town in Pennsylvania. Over an eighty-year period, the town was home to seventy-five separate buggy makers. Only one of these factories remains, the W. A. Heiss Coachworks, now part of the museum. The Mifflinburg Buggy Museum is the only known preserved nineteenth-century carriage shop, and it has all its original contents.

First, stop at the visitor center to view the seven-minute introductory video and self-guided exhibit. The hands-on workbench includes a wheel that can be disassembled, tools to handle, a buggy engraving, coloring and word-find sheets kids can complete at the museum or take home, and more.

Then, take a guided tour of the original factory, complete with tools and supplies; the Repository (showroom) with vehicles on display; and the family home. Recently reopened after restoration, the museum has also upgraded accessibility for wheelchair users and for the visually and hearing-impaired. Each May the museum hosts the annual Mifflinburg Buggy Day Festival, featuring craft vendors, antiques dealers, live entertainment, food, activities for children, demonstrations, and buggy rides.

Christkindl Market (ages 2 and up)

Downtown Mifflinburg; (570) 966–1666; www.mifflinburgchristkindlmarket.com.

Another Mifflinburg traditional celebration is Christkindl Market, held Thursday through Saturday, the second week of December. The festival re-creates a traditional

German Christmas Market, with authentic food, seasonal music, and handmade gifts for sale. At 6:00 P.M. on Friday night, children participate in a beautiful Children's Lantern Parade. There's also a Santa's Workshop with crafts and games.

T&D's Cats of the World 🐘

Penn's Creek; (570) 837–3377; www.tdscats.com. Open weekends May through September noon to 6:00 P.M. Admission is $$; children under 2 enter free. Group tours can be arranged throughout the year.

According to the Web site, the purpose of T&D's Cats of the World is "to rescue wildlife, especially exotic felines, from situations of abuse, mistreatment, and abandonment, when they are no longer wanted as pets." This effort began as a labor of love when the Mattive family (Terry, Donna, Jennifer, and T. J.) discovered how many exotic animals are abandoned when they outgrow the baby stage. Today, the entire Mattive family is involved in the care of eleven Bengal tigers, one Siberian tiger, eight African lions, nineteen cougars, five bobcats, and three leopards, twelve servals, plus smaller mammals such as skunks, coyotes, raccoons, river otters, and more.

McClure

Mountain Dale Farm (all ages) 🐘 🍽

Rural Route 2, Box 985, 17841; (570) 658–3536; www.pafarmstay.com. Open year-round.

If your family wants to experience farm life firsthand, then a vacation at Ken and Sally Hassinger's Mountain Dale Farm is just the ticket. This 175-acre farm is surrounded by state forest and game land, making it a complete getaway from civilization. But you don't have to rough it completely. The farm offers accommodations in a variety of cabins and efficiencies. Children under twelve are half price, and those under two years old stay free. Meals are provided at an extra cost upon request, but most visitors enjoy cooking in their own kitchens or in the common kitchen.

Kids love helping out with the barn chores and getting to know the sheep, goats, cattle, horses, geese, ducks, chickens, and dogs. Other activities include boating, fishing, swimming, or ice-skating on three ponds; cross-country skiing or hiking in the woods; or just relaxing on the front porch of your cabin. Come before Christmas and choose your own tree from the Christmas tree farm.

New Bloomfield

Little Buffalo State Park (all ages) 🏕 👥 🏛

Off Route 34; (570) 567–9255; www.dcnr.state.pa.us/stateparks/parks/littlebuffalo .aspx. Open year-round. Free for most activities.

In Perry County 830-acre Little Buffalo State Park has both historic and natural attractions. There's an eighty-eight-acre lake, a brand-new swimming pool (fee charged), hiking trails, fishing, and picnic areas. But there are also a covered bridge, a working gristmill from the 1800s, an old farmhouse, and a narrow-gauge railroad trace with an original railroad car. In winter there are 7 miles of cross-country trails, a sledding and tobogganing area, and a skating area on the lake (the rest of the lake is open for ice fishing in winter). There is no camping in the park, but the park ranger can furnish names of other campgrounds in the area.

Box Huckleberry Natural Area (all ages) 🏕️ 🚶

Route 34; (570) 536–3191; wwww.dcnr.state.pa.us. Open year-round. Free.

Just a few miles south of Little Buffalo State Park and technically part of Tuscarora state Forest, on Route 34 is the Box Huckleberry Natural Area, a special reserve for a box huckleberry plant estimated to be 1,300 years old. A short interpretive nature trail around the area is a favorite of small children. This is a good place to teach your kids about the importance of preserving our natural resources. Trail maps and a written history of the plant are available on-site.

New Germantown

Tuscarora State Forest (all ages) 🚶 🅰️ 🚲

Route 274, southwest of New Germantown; (570) 536–3191; www.dcnr.state.pa.us/ forestry/stateforests/tuscwild.aspx. Open year-round. Free.

Traveling southwest on Route 274 from New Germantown, you'll come upon the entrance to the Tuscarora State Forest—90,512 acres of amazing vistas, undisturbed areas, trout streams, state parks, hiking, snowmobiling, and more. The forest roads are well maintained, making a great route for a mild "off-road" driving experience. The Bureau of Forestry has developed a brochure that will guide you on a 26-mile auto tour of the forest. The dirt roads are in good shape, so you shouldn't need four-wheel drive to navigate the route in good weather.

Highlights in and around the state forest include: Hemlocks Natural Area, a 120-acre area of virgin hemlock forest with 3 miles of hiking trails; the Iron Horse Trail, a rails-to-trails project that provides 10 miles of hiking with only moderate climbing necessary; the Tuscarora Trail, a 22-mile side trail of the Appalachian Trail; Fowler Hollow State Park, with eighteen campsites and fishing in the creek; and Colonel Denning State Park, with fifty-two trailer and tent sites, excellent hiking, and an extensive environmental education program during summer months. For more information about the state forest and natural areas, contact the Bureau of Forestry, RD 1, Box 42–A, Blain 17006. For more information about the state parks within the forest, call (888) PA–PARKS.

Belleville

Everyone loves a farmers' market: rows of fresh vegetables, home-baked goods, handmade crafts, and the chance to meet the people who produce them. The town of Belleville may have the ultimate farmers' market.

Belleville Farmers Market (all ages) 🔒
South Penn Street, Route 655; (717) 935–2146. Open March through December, Wednesday during daylight hours. Free admission.

The Belleville Farmers Market takes place every Wednesday from six in the morning to six at night. The ten-acre Amish market has livestock yards, auction barns, and 400 flea-market stalls. It's a popular event, so be prepared to walk a ways from your car to the auction areas. For more information about the area, call the Juniata Valley Area Chamber of Commerce at (570) 248–6713. For information on this and other farmers' markets, check www.ams.usda.gov/ and select "Farmers Markets."

ALSO IN THE AREA
Mifflin County Trout Hatchery (ages 4 and up), Route 655, between Belleville and Reedsville; open Wednesday and Saturday. While you're in the area, check out the Mifflin County Trout Hatchery, where children can fish for trout and pay only for what they catch. Fishing poles and bait are provided.

A Paulsen **Family Adventure**

The first rule of traveling with children should be, if possible, get a hotel with a pool.

Most kids love the water. At the Holiday Inn in State College, Eli (eighteen months) learned how to jump from the edge of the pool into our arms. He thought this was great fun and jumped and jumped until his lips turned blue.

Eli was totally wound up from a day of sightseeing and visiting with his grandparents. He wanted to run around, but the confines of a small hotel room, the car, or a restaurant didn't allow this. The pool let him get his ya-yas out.

Which leads to the third benefit of a pool: It wears kids out. After playing in the pool, we put him in his pajamas and put him in his por-tacrib. He was out like a light in a matter of minutes. No mean feat for a kid who was bouncing off the walls earlier in the day.

State College

A visit to a college campus is a great way to inspire a child's educational dreams. The home of Penn State University, one of the country's best public universities, State College has much to offer families.

Bolstered by the university population, State College is a thriving town with many hotels, shops, and restaurants. Many of the area's attractions are within an easy drive, making the town an ideal base for your explorations.

Central Pennsylvania Festival of the Arts (all ages)

Downtown State College; (814) 237–3682; www.arts-festival.com. Five days in July. Free admission.

State College is the site of the Central Pennsylvania Festival of the Arts, a five-day celebration that takes place in July each year. The first day of the festival is traditionally Children and Youth Day, featuring the creations of local children ages eight through eighteen and a wonderful procession through town in which children wear masks and carry their works of art. Life-size puppets also take part in the procession. Storytelling, marionette performances, concerts, and more round out this not-to-be-missed event. Organizers have made special attempts to include people with special needs, including those with visual impairments.

Frost Entomological Museum (ages 5 and up)

Headhouse 3, halfway between Shortlidge and Bigelar Roads; (814) 863–2865; www.ento.psu.edu/home/frost/index.html. Open Monday through Friday 9:30 A.M. to 4:30 P.M. Free.

The Insect Zoo features a functional beehive plus a variety of insects and other arthopods such as scorpions, tarantulas, and cockroaches. Kids will get a kick out of it; parents may or may not.

Earth and Mineral Sciences Museum (ages 5 and up)

122 Spiedle Building, Pollock Road; (814) 865–6427; www.ems.psu.edu/museum. Open year-round Monday through Friday 9:30 A.M. to 5:00 P.M. Closed holidays. Free.

The halls of the Spiedle Building are lined with crystals, gems, carvings, and fossils. Kids especially like the ultraviolet light room that highlights minerals invisible under normal incandescent lights. The shrunken heads also get an enthusiastic reception from most kids.

Penn State Ice Pavilion (ages 2 and up)

Pollock and McKean Streets; (814) 865–4102.; www.psu.edu/deptice_pavilion. Open to the public for part of most days. Call ahead for current hours. Admission is $. Skate rental is $.

After checking out the museums, you might want to take a spin around the indoor ice-skating rinks at the Ice Pavilion, in the Greenberg Indoor Sports Complex. The complex offers two rinks with superior surfaces.

Beaver Stadium (ages 5 and up)
University Drive and Curtin Road; (814) 863–1000 or (800) 833–5533. Various prices.

Of course, for many people the most famous aspect of Penn State is its football team. The Nittany Lions play in the Big Ten College Football League, and sports fans come from around the country to see a game at Beaver Stadium. For current schedules and tickets, call the aforementioned phone numbers or log onto www.psu.edu.

Bryce Jordan Center (ages 5 and up)
University Drive and Curtin Road; (814) 865–5555 or (800) 863–3336; www.psu.edu/ sports/tickets.

Men's and women's basketball as well as a variety of special events take place across the street from Beaver Stadium at the Bryce Jordan Center. Call for schedules and tickets.

College of Agricultural Sciences (all ages)
Agriculture Administration Building, University Park; (814) 865–4433. Open 9:00 A.M. to 4:00 P.M. Free.

Check out the animals at the agricultural facilities of the College of Agricultural Sciences, near Beaver Stadium. See white-tailed deer, sheep, cattle, horses, and pigs. There's also an exhibit of flowering plants and vegetables.

Throughout the year special events are scheduled for the nearby Ag Arena. Check the marquee outside to see what's scheduled or call ahead. Children especially enjoy the shows of horses or dairy cattle. Around Christmas, the Festival of Trees features more than one hundred different trees, decorated by area businesses and organizations.

AG Progress Days and Jerome K. Pasto Agricultural Museum (all ages)
Russell E. Larson Agricultural Research Center, Route 45; (814) 863–1383; http://apd .cas.psu.edu (for information on AG Progress Days) or http://pasto.cas.psu.edu (museum information). Free.

Penn State's Ag Progress Days is one of the largest agricultural shows in the country. It takes place in mid-August each year and features live animal exhibitions, a petting zoo, computer-based games, demonstrations of the latest farming technologies, and displays of antique farm equipment. The Family and Youth Building has special programs just for kids.

On the same site as the Larson Agricultural Research Center, the Jerome K. Pasto Agricultural Museum traces the history of farming in America with displays of old tools and appliances from the days before electricity. It's open April 15 to October 15. Call ahead for scheduling information (814–865–8301). Admission is free, but donations are encouraged.

Millbrook Marsh Nature Center (all ages) 🏵

614 Puddintown Road, State College; (814) 231–3071. Open year-round. Call ahead for current hours. Free admission.

A cooperative venture of many local educational organizations, this is the site for several nature programs conducted by the Shaver's Creek Environmental Center. The mission of the center is to educate and inspire people about the natural world and to instill a passion for the environment through science, history, culture, and art. Call for updated information and a schedule of events.

Stone Valley Recreation Area (all ages) 🏵 ⏶ 🌐

Route 1029, off Route 26 South; (814) 863–1164; www.psu.edu/Stone_Valley. Open year-round sunrise to sunset. Free.

After the hubbub of the active campus, this is a great place to come and wind down. Administered by Penn State, the Stone Valley Recreation Area has a wide variety of activities for all ages. Depending on the season you can enjoy boating (canoes, rowboats, or sailboats—all of which are available for rent), fishing (trout and bass), hayrides, hiking, ice-skating (rentals available), sledding, ice fishing, or cross-country skiing (lessons available). There are eleven wheelchair-accessible cabins for overnight accommodations. The one-room cabins are equipped with bunk beds, refrigerator, electric range top, electricity, and gas heat. There are central bathroom and shower facilities nearby. Bring your own linens and cooking and eating utensils. Call for rates and reservations.

Shaver's Creek Environmental Center (all ages) 🏵 🐘

Route 1029 (Charter Oak Road) off Route 26 South; (814) 863–2000; www.shavers creek.org. Open mid-January to mid-December. Call ahead for current hours. Visitor and Raptor Center admission is $ per person; children under 3 are free.

At the Environmental Center, learn about the local wildlife and how injured eagles, hawks, owls, reptiles, and amphibians are cared for at this lovely environmental center. There's a bookstore with a good selection of books for children; you'll also find other wildlife accessories there. Special gardens attract butterflies, bees, and hummingbirds.

Shaver's Creek is the site of a wonderful day-camp program for children six and up. For children six to eleven, the Discovery and Explorer Camps run from Tuesday through Friday and end up with a family overnight at the camp.

Children twelve and up can choose from several different camp experiences, including Raptor and More Camp (in which campers work with rehabilitated birds of prey), which is for campers ages fourteen to seventeen.

Boalsburg

Looking for a special way to spend an upcoming three-day weekend? The town of Boalsburg has several claims to fame that make it a good destination any time of year. For Memorial Day weekend, how about visiting the place where the holiday got its start? Boalsburg has been commemorating this day since 1864, and today there are community picnics and parades to enjoy.

In July Boalsburg is the site of the **Peoples' Choice Festival of Pennsylvania Arts and Crafts.** The weekend of activities includes free museum tours for children, a petting zoo, and a stuffed-animal vet.

Columbus Day weekend coming up? What better place to get in touch with the discoverer of the New World than at the **Christopher Columbus Family Chapel,** part of the Boal Mansion and Museum. And, for Veterans Day, learn the history of our nation's veterans at the Pennsylvania Military Museum across U.S. Route 322.

Boal Mansion and Museum (ages 6 and up) 🏛

300 Old Boalsburg Road; (814) 466–6210; www.boalmuseum.com. Open Tuesday through Sunday noon to 5:00 P.M. summer to Labor Day; 1:30 to 5:00 P.M. in spring and fall; closed Monday. Admission is $$$ for adults and $$ for children 7 to 11; children under 7 enter free.

This historic house has an added attraction: original objects belonging to Christopher Columbus. Originally part of the Columbus family castle in Spain, the chapel contains heirlooms that date back to the 1400s. The *Wall Street Journal* called the collection "a strong tangible link to Columbus in the New World." Kids especially enjoy looking at the antique weapons and dresses and hearing stories about nine generations of the Boal family, across 210 years in the same house, continuing today.

Cave Exploration

Woodward Cave and Penn's Cave may get most of the attention, but Central Pennsylvania actually has hundreds of fascinating caves and caverns. If you're interested in doing some cave exploring that's a bit off the beaten path, contact the Nittany Grotto, headquartered in State College. This group of enthusiastic cave explorers encourages safe and responsible cave exploring. Its members are pleased to arrange Beginner Trips. In order to take advantage of this service, families may be asked to join the group at a cost of $10 a year. For more information contact the group's Web site at www.clubs.psu.edu/nittanygrotto.

Pennsylvania Military Museum and Twenty-eighth Infantry Division Shrine (ages 7 and up)

Route 45 and Business US 322; (814) 466–6263; www.psu.edu/dept/aerospace/
museum. From April through October, open Tuesday through Saturday 9:00 A.M. to
5:00 P.M. Closed Monday except for Memorial Day, July 4th and Labor Day. Call ahead
for hours November through March. Admission fee charged. Senior citizen, youth, and
group discounts available.

Built on the site of the Pennsylvania National Guard's shrine for service in the two
World Wars of the twentieth century, the Pennsylvania Military Museum commemorates the service and sacrifice of Commonwealth veterans from the Spanish American War through Desert Storm. Pennsylvania citizen soldiers, sailors, airmen,
marines, and industry are honored with exhibits on technology, tactics, and service.
The shrine and museum are situated within a sixty-seven-acre parklike setting that
includes walking/bike paths and a covered picnic pavilion, only a short walk away
from historic Boalsburg. On-site public programming includes "Celebration of Service:
Honoring Pennsylvania Veterans" on the third Sunday in May; "World War Two Revis-
ited" with re-enactors bivouacking on the ground on Memorial Day Weekend; and the
People's Choice Arts Festival in July. For more information on these and other events,
go to www.boalsburgcentral.com/specialevents.html. This museum is one of twenty-
six sites administered by the Pennsylvania Historical and Museum Commission
(www.phmc.state.pa.us).

Tussey Mountain Ski Resort (ages 3 and up)

301 Bear Meadows Road; (800) 733–2754 or (814) 466–6810; www.tusseymountain
.com. Open year-round.

Heading east from State College on US 322 is Tussey Mountain Ski Resort, a
great place for family skiing and snowboarding. At the Kid's Mountain
Learning Center, children ages three to six can ski in a specially
designed learning area. They can even join a Paw Prints group and
enjoy instructed play and an introduction to skiing. The Mountain
Lion group, for children six to ten years old, is aimed at building
children's skiing skills. Both classes run two hours and are scheduled twice a day on weekdays and three times a day on weekends.
Tussey Mountain also offers Avalanche Canyon, a snowtubing area.
There's a Winter-Break Camp for kids six and up when they're off
from school for the holidays.

Summer activities include concerts, batting cages, go-karts,
fishing, and more.

Eastern Centre County

Just east of State College are several small towns with worthwhile attractions for families. Here are a few of the best.

Penn's Cave (ages 4 and up) 🐘 ⚠️
Route 192, 5 miles east of Centre Hall; (814) 364–1664; www.pennscave.com. Open 9:00 A.M. to 5:00 P.M. February 15 to December 31 (weekends only in December). Admission is $$$ for adults and $ for children 2 to 12.

Penn's Cave has been attracting visitors for centuries, since the Seneca Indians discovered it. It has been a tourist attraction since the late 1800s, when a hotel was built on the site.

A Paulsen **Family Adventure**

We weren't sure how eighteen-month-old Eli would react to being in a small boat, let alone how he would like being in a cave. But at Penn's Cave, the country's only water-filled cave, we got to try both.

There was just one other family and a couple on the tour with us. The other children were about eight and ten—the perfect age for looking for bats and spooking each other. Eli, on the other hand, wasn't so sure about this darkness stuff. He whimpered a bit as the driver pushed off from the dock.

He squirmed out of my lap and into my husband's, then back to mine, as if searching for a place where he might feel safe. I wondered to myself if they've ever had to turn a boat back when a child got scared of the dark.

Once the light show started, Eli started to calm down. He wasn't exactly enjoying himself, but he wasn't complaining either.

At the end of the cave, the driver gave us the option to pull out onto the lake that borders the Penn's Cave Wildlife Sanctuary. Even though it was drizzling, the group gave unanimous approval. As we pulled into the daylight, Eli perked up. At the sight of a group of very ordinary ducks, his eyes lit up, and he pointed and started making quacking sounds. He smiled and laughed.

Even though we were outside maybe five minutes, that glimpse of the the ducks and the daylight was all he needed to reassure him as we headed back into the cave. On the way back, he stayed interested, turning around to see what the guide was talking about. I guess the dark isn't so intimidating once you know it's not forever.

Penn's Cave is the country's only water-filled cave, and tours are given by motorboat. Along the hour-long ride you'll see amazing stalactites and stalagmites in a series of "rooms." Colored lights illuminate formations with names like the Statue of Liberty, Chinese Dragon, and Niagara Falls. If you're lucky, you'll spot some of the bats that live in the cave.

No matter what the temperature outside, it's always fifty-two degrees inside the cave, so bring a jacket in summertime. Some children are initially scared by the dark and the idea of being underground; however, most become more comfortable as they get involved in spotting the formations and enjoying the colored lights. According to tour guides, the temperament of the child is more of a factor than age.

But there's more to Penn's Cave than the cave. There's also 1,000 acres with an operating farm and a wildlife sanctuary with elk, mountain lions, deer, wolves, and mustangs. Professional guides take you through the park in four-wheel-drive vehicles, pointing out animals and telling about their habits. Tours last about one and a half hours. The sanctuary is open daily March through November. Call ahead for rates and reservations.

In September Penn's Cave is also the site of the Nittany Antique Machinery annual show. Model trains, tractor parades, demonstrations of antique machinery, toy tractors, and a children's pedal pull are among the attractions.

Woodward Cave and Campground (ages 4 and up) 🧗 ⛺

Route 45, Woodward; (814) 349–9800; www.woodwardcave.com. Open daily 9:00 A.M. to 6:00 P.M. in summer, 10:00 A.M. to 4:00 P.M. in spring and fall. Closed November through March. Admission is $$ for adults, $ for children 3 to 12, and free for children 2 and under.

If Penn's Cave has whet your appetite for spelunking, head back to Route 45 and continue east to Woodward Cave and Campground, one of the largest caverns in Pennsylvania. A sixty-minute tour takes you through the five rooms of the cavern, each filled with rock formations. The Hanging Forest features a large collection of stalactites. In the Hall of Statues, see one of the largest stalagmites in the United States: the Tower of Babel. If you're planning to camp in the area, inquire about the nineteen-acre campground with sites for tents as well as RVs. Cabin rentals are also available.

Bellefonte

About 12 miles north of State College on Route 26, you'll find Bellefonte, the county seat for Centre County. This lovely Victorian town celebrated its bicentennial in 1996, and things are hopping still. In 2004, the Bellefonte Garden Club set a goal to plant 30,000 daffodil bulbs per year for the next five years. If their dream comes true, by spring 2009, Bellefonte will be breathtaking to behold! For information, go to www.bellefonte.com/gardenclub.

With a historic district of more than 300 buildings, taking a walking tour through this town is like taking a walk back in time. The town is especially beautiful when decked out for a Victorian Christmas each December (call 814–353–8074 or check www.bellefonte.com for more information).

Bellefonte Museum for Centre County (ages 5 and up)

133 Allegheny Street; (814) 355–4280; www.bellefonte.org/museum. Open year-round. Admission charged. Call for schedule and rates.

The goal of the Bellefonte Museum is to promote appreciation of the area's heritage, especially among children. The hard-working volunteer staff visits schools and has set up exhibits around town. The museum is now housed in the historic Benner–Linn House, donated to the town by the Omega Bank next door. The exhibits change at least three times per year and are designed for both children and adults.

Bellefonte Historical Railroad (all ages)

Train Station, High Street; (814) 355–0311. Various excursions throughout the year, mostly on weekends. Call (814) 355–2917 for schedules and prices or check www.bellefontetrain.com.

When you're tired of walking, climb aboard one of the rail excursions offered by the Bellefonte Historical Railroad. The train station is located across the High Street Bridge. On weekends from Memorial Day to Labor Day, the railroad offers trips to Curtin Village (described below), Sayers Dam (a nice place for a picnic), the town of Lemont, or the gliderport at Julian. In fall the route takes you to Bald Eagle Ridge, aflame with autumn leaves. The Santa Claus Express in December features a visit from you-know-who. Other excursions are offered throughout the year.

Eagle Iron Works and Curtin Village (ages 4 and up)

Route 150, 2 miles north of I–80; (814) 355–1982; www.boggstownship.org. Open weekends in May, September, and October; daily during summer. It is also open in mid-December for Christmas at Curtin. Call for current hours and rates.

Heading north on Route 150 from Bellefonte, stop off at Eagle Iron Works and Curtin Village, a historic site that gives a glimpse of life in the 1800s. Or, take an excursion on the Bellefonte Historic Railroad to Curtin. There's a restored iron furnace, the iron master's mansion, and a worker's log cabin. Throughout the year the museum holds special events, including craft shows, Civil War encampments, and antique tool demonstrations.

Garman Opera House (ages 4 and up)

Across the street from the County Court House; (814) 355–7884. Call for schedule and ticket prices.

This restored former vaudeville house now offers live theater, concerts, and other events, including performances for families and children.

Bellefonte **Festivals**

The Victorian Christmas is the biggest festival in Bellefonte's schedule, but there are several more that are worth checking out. In mid-May come for the Big Spring Festival, which celebrates the spring that supplies the town with water. For more information and this year's schedule, call (814) 355–1458.

In June the streets of Bellefonte fill with antique and vintage automobiles as the town re-creates a Historic Cruise, that lapping-the-block ritual favored by teens in the 1950s. August brings the annual Bellefonte Arts and Crafts fair, with area craftspeople exhibiting and selling their creations and with special events for children.

Where to Eat

IN WILLIAMSPORT

Bonanza Steak House, 1503 East Third Street; (570) 326–7114.

Chi-Chi's Mexican Restaurant, 2502 East Third Street; (570) 321–9208.

Heavenly Pasteria, 135 West Third Street; (570) 327–9035. Casual Italian food. Children's portions of pasta and pizza.

Hoss's Steak and Sea House, 1954 East Third Street; (570) 326–0838.

Manhattan Bagel, 1790 East Third Street; (570) 322–4500; e-mail: yrgyo3@prodigy.com.

Olive Garden, 1825 East Third Street; (570) 321–9250.

Peter Herdic House, 407 West Fourth Street; (570) 322–0165. A little more formal but family-oriented, offering a variety of traditional meats, seafood, pasta, and salad.

Red Lobster, 1951 East Third Street; (570) 323–0423.

Vinnie's Italian Eatery, 44 West Fourth Street; (570) 326–1998.

IN STATE COLLEGE

Backstage at Michael's, 240 South Pugh Street; (570) 238–8454. Breakfast and family dinner daily.

Chili's Grill & Bar, 139 South Allen Street; (570) 234–5922. Mexican fare.

The Tavern Restaurant, 220 East College Street; (570) 238–6116. Offers a variety of steaks, seafood, chicken, and salads. Children's menu has chicken nuggets, burgers, etc., and side dishes. Relaxed atmosphere.

Whistle Stop Restaurant, Pennsylvania Avenue; (570) 364–2544. "Meat and potatoes and nothin' fancy." Children's menu.

Where to Stay

IN WILLIAMSPORT

Genetti Hotel, 200 West Fourth Street; (717) 326–6600 or (800) 321–1388. Located in downtown Williamsport, this full-service historic hotel offers suites as well as standard guest rooms. An on-site pool and restaurant make it a good choice for families.

Holiday Inn & T.G.I.Friday's Complex, 1840 East Third Street; (717) 326–1981 or (800) 36–WILPA; www.holiday-wilpa.com. This hotel complex offers some great features for families—an outdoor pool, free Disney channel, on-site restaurants—plus kids stay and eat free. In summer a "Poolside King Room" may be the best choice for families. Features include a king-size bed plus pull-out sofa just steps from the pool.

Sheraton Inn, 100 Pine Street; (800) 325–3535 or (717) 327–8231. The Sheraton has two clinchers that make this hotel a hit with kids: an indoor pool and Nintendo-equipped televisions. And the hotel's kids-eat-free policy at the on-site restaurant makes it a hit with parents, too.

IN LEWISBURG

B/W Country Cupboard Inn, Route 15 North; (717) 524–5500. Hotel, restaurant, and gift shop all in one complex.

Days Inn–Lewisburg, Route 15; (717) 523–1171. Perkins Family Restaurant on premises.

IN THE STATE COLLEGE AREA

Many of the major hotel/motel and restaurant chains have facilities in and near State College. Here are a few to check out:

Bellefonte/State College KOA Campground, 2481 Jacksonville Road, Bellefonte ; (814) 355–7912 or (800) KOA–8127. Full-service campground with cabin rentals available.

Best Western State College Inn, 1663 South Atherton Street, Business US 322, State College; (814) 237–8005 or (800) 635–1177. Breakfast is included, and there is a twenty-four-hour restaurant on premises.

Courtyard by Marriott, 1730 University Drive, State College; (814) 238–1881. An indoor pool, suites, and an on-site restaurant make this a good choice for families.

Days Inn Penn State, 240 South Pugh Street, State College; (814) 238–8454 or (800) 258–DAYS. Just blocks from campus, the Days Inn has on-site parking, a restaurant/sports bar, and an indoor pool. Continental breakfast is included.

Holiday Inn State College, 1450 South Atherton, State College; (814) 238–3001 or (800) HOLIDAY. Two outdoor swimming pools make this an especially good choice in the summer.

The Nittany Lion Inn, 200 West Park Avenue, State College; (814) 231–7500 or (800) 233–7505. Colonial-style inn on the Penn State campus.

For More Information

Bellefonte Tourism Commission, c/o Chamber of Commerce, Train Station, Bellefonte 16823; (814) 355–2917; www.bellefonte.com. Call ahead for recommendations on accommodations, train schedules, and other events in the area.

Central Pennsylvania Convention and Visitors Bureau, 800 East Park Avenue, State College 16803; www.visit pennstate.org or www.centralpacvb.org.

Columbia–Montour Visitors Bureau, 121 Papermill Road, Bloomsburg 17815; (800) 847–4810 or (570) 784–8279; www.itourcolumbiamontour.com. Call for more information about accommodations, restaurants, and the twenty-four covered bridges in the area.

Lycoming County Tourist Promotion Agency, 454 Pine Street, Williamsport 17701; (800) 358–9900 or (570) 326–1971; www.williamsport.org. Call or write for more information about things to do and see in Williamsport, as well as a list of restaurants, motels, and other accommodations.

Susquehanna Valley Visitors Bureau, 81 Hafer Road, Lewisburg 17837; (800) 525–7320 or (570) 524–7234. Call for more information about attractions, accommodations, and upcoming events in Northumberland, Snyder, and Union counties.

Pennsylvania's
Northern
Tier

Pennsylvania has the largest rural population in the country. That means there are more people living in towns of fewer than 2,500 people here than in any other state. Although all of the regions covered in this book have many towns that meet that description, along Pennsylvania's Northern Tier, it's hard to find towns that don't. There are large stretches of this region that remain wilderness—and provide wonderful opportunities for camping, boating, hiking, skiing, and more.

Scenic U.S. Route 6 traverses the Northern Tier of Pennsylvania, passing some of the region's best-loved sights and towns. For information about scenic US 6, call 1–87–PAROUTE6 or check the Web site www.paroute6.com. Pine Creek Gorge, billed as Pennsylvania's Grand Canyon, is a spectacular achievement of nature. Allegheny

Faith & Emily's
FavoriteAttractions
in Pennsylvania's Northern Tier

1. Splash Lagoon Indoor Waterpark, Erie

2. Pine Creek Gorge, Ansonia

3. Ole Bull State Park, Cross Fork

4. Crook Farm and Country Fair, Bradford

5. Knox Cane Railroad, Marienville

6. expERIEnce Children's Museum, Erie

7. Heart's Content National Natural Landmark, Allegheny National Forest, Warren

8. Cook Forest Sawmill Center for the Arts, Cooksburg

9. Presque Isle State Park, Erie

PENNSYLVANIA'S NORTHERN TIER

National Forest is one of only fifteen national forests in the eastern United States and harbors some of the last remaining virgin stands of northern hardwoods left in the East.

This is a big area. Our advice would be to keep your ambitions within limits. Pick a state park, a town, or a sight that interests you most, and build your vacation around it. Try to see more than a portion of this region, and you'll spend more time in the car than enjoying its many offerings. You can always come back to see more at another time.

Troy

We start our tour of Pennsylvania's Northern Tier in the town of Troy, located on US 6 just west of the Susquehanna River. Please note that the town of Bradford is *not* in Bradford County, but Troy is. This leads to some confusion.

Bradford County Heritage Farm Museum (all ages) 🏛 🖢

Route 14 North, ½ mile from Troy; (570) 297–3410 or (570) 297–3405 during the off-season; www.pavisnet.com/troy/farmmuseum. Open late April through October, Friday to Monday and holidays 10:00 A.M. to 4:00 P.M. Admission is $; children under 6 are free.

Young and old alike will enjoy "The Farm Museum," established by the Bradford County Heritage Association on the Troy Fairgrounds. Local resident and dairy farmer Wilmer Wilcox's impressive collection of farm antiques is on display. The displays work together to tell the story of rural farm life in Bradford County. There's a kitchen and antique clothing and an old country store. The association has recently begun work to restore the oldest house in Troy Township, built in 1822, adjacent to the current museum. Formerly an inn on the stagecoach route, it houses period furniture, glassware, and antique toys and clothing. Portions of this house are open for tours.

Faith & Emily's
FavoriteEvents
in Pennsylvania's Northern Tier

- **Pennsylvania State Laurel Festival** in Wellsboro (June); (570) 724–1926.

- **Teddy Bear Weekend** in Cooksburg (end of July); (814) 744–9670.

- **We Love Erie Days** in Erie (August); (570) 454–7191.

- **Fabulous 1890s weekend** in Mansfield (end of September); (570) 662–3442.

During the Fall Carriage, Wagon, and Sleigh Festival in mid-September, children six and older enjoy the flax demonstration, blacksmithing, carpentry, tinsmithing, and stories of how chores were done in the past—from butter making with a dog-treadle butter churn to laundry with washboards and wringers. Throughout the season the heritage gardens display heirloom varieties of vegetables, plants used to make dyes, herbs, and perennials.

The museum is open daily during the Troy Fair, a typical country fair with farm animals, agricultural displays, and amusements. The fair has usually been held each year, for more than one hundred years, toward the end of July. For more information about the Troy Fair, call (570) 297–3648.

Towanda

Not to be confused with the Bradford County Heritage Farm Museum, the Bradford County Historical Society and Museum recently opened in the newly renovated jail building in Towanda.

Bradford County Historical Society and Museum 🔖
109 Pine Street; (570) 265–2240. Open Thursday through Saturday.

The new Bradford County Historical Society and Museum houses many interesting exhibits that preserve the history of Bradford County and the building's role as the local jail. Portions of the jail were left in their natural state to preserve a sense of the building's past. You can peek at the jail cells through a peephole actually used by the guards.

Greater Mansfield Chamber of Commerce
Celebrates the Fabulous 1890s

Every September, the town and university team up to host the Fabulous 1890s weekend. The event commemorates the first night football game, in which Mansfield University played Wyoming Seminary on September 28, 1892. The entire Mansfield community comes out to celebrate with a motorless parade, a balloon rally, a football reenactment, and fireworks. For more information on other events and festivals in Mansfield, call (570) 662–3442 or check www.mansfieldorg.com.

Wellsboro Area

Located on scenic US 6 in Tioga County, Wellsboro is an ideal base for adventures in Pine Creek Gorge, Pennsylvania's Grand Canyon. Forty-seven miles long with a maximum cliff height of 1,450 feet, this majestic canyon is surrounded by four state parks and hundreds of thousands of wilderness acres to explore by boat, foot, horseback, snowmobile, cross-country skis, mountain bike, and more. For information check www.visittiogapa.com.

Colton Point State Park (ages 8 and up)

Five miles south of US 6 at Ansonia; (570) 724–3061; www.dcnr.state.pa.us/stateparks/parks/coltonpoint.aspx. Open year-round.

Perhaps the easiest way to get a glimpse of the Pine Creek Gorge is to head south from US 6 at Ansonia. There's a sign there that directs you to the park. The drive follows the rim, with short trails that lead to views over the canyon. Although there are guard rails at official overlooks, make sure children don't run ahead or rough-house near the edge.

In addition to great views, Colton Point offers family camping, hiking trails, snowmobiling, and picnic areas. Most of the trails involve steep terrain and are recommended for experienced hikers aged eight and up.

Leonard Harrison State Park (ages 8 and up)

Route 660, 10 miles west of Wellsboro; (570) 724–3061; www.dcnr.state.pa.us/stateparks/parks/leonardharrison.aspx. Open year-round.

Leonard Harrison State Park is on the east rim of the canyon. It offers one of the best views of the canyon anywhere. Stop at the visitor center to learn about the history of the canyon. Camping is available, and there are hiking trails of varying length and difficulty. Experienced family hikers (ages eight and up) won't want to miss the Turkey Path, a steep, 1-mile journey that takes you from the rim of the canyon down to Pine Creek.

Pine Creek Trail (all ages)

Trailheads at US 6 in Ansonia and at Route 414 in Blackwell. Open year-round. Bathrooms at trailheads. Call (570) 724–3061.

In an ongoing rails-to-trails project, 22 miles of the abandoned ConRail Railway along Pine Creek have been converted into a trail for hiking, biking, horseback riding, and other nonmotorized transportation. The relatively flat, groomed trail is wonderful for family hiking. The trail is wheelchair accessible and perfect for all-terrain strollers. The less strenuous Ansonia access is recommended for families.

If you'd like to tour Pine Creek Trail on a covered wagon, call Mountain Trail Canyon Wagon Rides (570) 376–5561 or (877) 376–5561 or go to www.mountaintrail horse.com.

Pine Creek Outfitters (ages 6 and up) ⚠️ 🚶 🚲
RR4, Box 130B, Wellsboro 16901; (570) 724–3003; www.pinecrk.com.

Whether you're looking for trail maps, equipment rentals, shuttles to trailheads, camping permits, guide service, or you-name-it, the folks at Pine Creek Outfitters are the ones to talk to. From kayaking to canoeing, biking to hiking, if they can't provide it themselves, they'll point you in the right direction. For families with young children, they particularly recommend their Upper Pine half-day trip, which navigates a calm section of the creek. There is no minimum age on this trip; others have a minimum age of seven. Pine Creek also rents bikes. Pine Creek Outfitters offers several useful guidebooks to the canyon.

Tioga Trail Rides (ages 8 and up) 🐎
RD 106, Route 105, 536 Broughton Hollow Road; (570) 724–6592; www.pavisnet .com/ttr.

Tioga Trail Rides offers western riding on day rides or overnight trips. Children without experience must be at least twelve years old; younger children are allowed on shorter rides if they can control their horses and have an inseam of at least 21 inches (gotta be able to reach the stirrups!). Sunset and supper rides are also available. During winter Tioga Trail Rides offers bobsled rides.

Mountain Trail Horse Center (ages 8 and up) 🐎
Wellsboro; (570) 376–5561; www.mountaintrailhorse.com; e-mail: maier@epix.net. Open spring, summer, and fall.

Mountain Trail Horse Center offers a wide variety of horseback rides designed as wilderness adventure. Covered-wagon rides are good for families of varying ages and abilities. There's no age minimum on the rides through the gorge. During the twice-yearly Family Vacation Horseback Adventures, the minimum age for overnight trips is dropped to eight (from the usual twelve). Longer trips are available. Rates go down per person with groups of more than four people.

Storms Horse Drawn Rides (all ages)
RR 4, Box 1031, Little Marsh 16950; (570) 376–3481; www.stormshorsedrawnrides .com. Open spring through fall. Groups of ten to twelve people or more.

Scenic views, a comfortable horse-drawn wagon, home cooking over a campfire—this is a backcountry adventure with style!

Geocaching in Pennsylvania

It's the latest thing! Geocaching is a new kind of outdoor adventure for the 21st century. All you need is a GPS receiver, a set of coordinates, and some friends. GPS refers to Global Positioning System, a handheld electronic device that monitors your approximate position by satellite. The satellite determines your coordinates in latitude and longitude. Today more than two hundred countries have caches hidden. In Pennsylvania, so do towns such as Allentown, Bethlehem, Easton, Harrisburg, Lancaster, Philadelphia, Pittsburgh, Punxsutawney, Scranton, St. Marys, Williamsport, and York.

The goal of the game is to use your GPS to locate a "cache"—a "treasure"—hidden somewhere, using your GPS unit to navigate from your original position to the cache. Usually the cache turns out to be a strongbox containing surprises like small toys, CDs, or objects hidden by other geocachers. Some contain a disposable camera, but that isn't one of the prizes; it's so that the finder can take a picture of him or herself and leave it behind for the owner of the cache. After opening the cache, leave something behind for the next geocacher to find.

If you'd like to see what all the fuss is about, go to www.geocaching .com and type the name of the area you want to visit.

Tioga Central Railroad (all ages)
P.O. Box 269, Wellsboro 16901; (570) 724–0990; www.tiogacentral.com. Various rates.

Take the 24-mile round-trip excursion from the station near Wellsboro to the north end of Hammond Lake, near the New York State border. The trip takes about an hour and twenty minutes and runs three times a day on weekends.

ALSO IN THE AREA

Hills Creek State Park, East of Wellsboro; (570) 724–4246; www.dcnr.state.pa.us/ stateparks/parks/hillscreek.aspx. One hundred ten campsites, cabins available, 137-acre lake.

Little Pine State Park, Waterville; (570) 753–8209; www.dcnr.state.pa.us/stateparks /parks/littlepine.aspx. One hundred four campsites; ninety-four-acre lake; hiking, biking, and cross-country ski trails; nature programs and swimming in summer.

Galeton Area

Home of the Pennsylvania Lumber Museum and headquarters for four state parks, Galeton has a full roster of events and activities for families.

Pennsylvania Lumber Museum (ages 6 and up) 🎒

5660 US 6 West, P.O. Box 239, Galeton 16922; 12 miles west of Galeton; (814) 435–2652; www.lumbermuseum.org. Open daily April through November 9:00 A.M. to 5:00 P.M. Closed major holidays. Admission is $; children under 6 are free.

From Wellsboro head west on US 6 to the Galeton area to enjoy a visit to the Pennsylvania Lumber Museum. Antique tools and other logging artifacts tell the story of this area's logging history. Tour a real logging camp and sawmill. A restored Barnhart Log Loader also included in the display. The museum is the site for several unusual special events throughout the year, including the Bark Peeler's Convention the weekend closest to July 4th.

Lyman Run State Park (all ages) 🚶 🎣 🅰

454 Lyman Run Road, Galeton 16922; (814) 435–5010; www.dcnr.statepa.us/stateparks/lymanrun.aspx. Open year-round.

Lyman Run acts as the headquarters for three other state parks in the area: Cherry Springs, Patterson, and Prouty Place. Lyman Run offers trout fishing, ice fishing, swimming, and camping. Cherry Springs has picnic areas, hiking trails, hunting, snowmobile trails, and a campground. It's also the site of the Woodsmen's Carnival in early August. Patterson State Park offers picnicking, hiking, and camping. Prouty Place State Park is known for its picnic areas, cold-water fishing, hiking, and camping.

Ole Bull State Park (all ages) 🚶 🚲 🏊

Off Route 144, Cross Fork; (814) 435–5000 or (888) PA–PARKS for reservations; www.dcnr.state.pa.us/stateparks/parks/olebull.aspx. Open year-round.

About 20 miles south of Galeton is the Lodge at Ole Bull State Park, voted by *Condé Nast Traveler* magazine as Pennsylvania's top getaway. The lodge is actually a three-bedroom log cabin built by the Civilian Conservation Corps in the 1930s. It sleeps ten comfortably and is well equipped with everything you need for a woodsy adventure. It even has a playground out back for the kids. The first floor is wheelchair accessible. Book your reservations early (up to eleven months in advance). This is the kind of place where people come back each year.

Even if you're not lucky enough to book a week at the lodge, Ole Bull is still a great place for a family adventure. There are eighty-one tent and trailer sites along Kettle Creek, some with electrical hookups. Swimming, hiking, fishing, and biking also are all available in the secluded 125-acre park. During summer weekends there's a full schedule of environmental education programs.

Penfield

Parker Dam State Park and S. B. Elliot State Park (all ages)

Off Route 153, Penfield; (814) 765–0630 or (888) PA–PARKS for reservations; www.dcnr.state.pa.us/stateparks/parks/packerdam.aspx. Open year-round.

There are some great family programs available at Parker Dam State Park and S. B. Elliot State Park. Parker Dam offers a variety of naturalist programs for families, starting with Maple Sugar Weekends in March all the way through Apple Cider Sundays in the fall. During summer there are bat programs, evening campfire talks on the weekends, and even a guided trip to see the elk herd. In summer you can swim in the twenty-acre lake.

The camping here is class A, which means hot showers are available. There are also rustic log-frame and stone cabins available for rent year-round. There's no running water in the cabins, but there's a separate building with showers. A big fireplace supplies the heat, a refrigerator stores your perishables, and you can cook with an electric stove.

S. B. Elliot State Park offers a quieter setting on top of a hill. There are six cabins here and some class B campsites, but no flush toilets or showers.

Bradford

Please note that the town of Bradford is *not* in Bradford County. It's in McKean County.

Penn–Brad Oil Museum (ages 6 and up)

U.S. Route 219; (814) 362–5984; www.pennbradoilmuseum.com. Open daily Memorial Day through Labor Day. Monday through Saturday 10:00 A.M. to 4:00 P.M. and Sunday noon to 5:00 P.M. Admission is $$ for adults and $ for seniors; children under 12 are free.

Just as eastern Pennsylvania has coal, the northwestern part of the state is oil country. This museum traces the state's involvement in oil drilling and includes a working example of the 1890s-style wooden oil rig that once dotted the countryside.

Crook Farm and Country Fair (all ages)

US 219, third exit north of Bradford; (814) 362–6730 in spring, fall, and summer, or (814) 362–3906 in the off-season. Open Tuesday through Friday afternoons during May through September and various times throughout the year. Call ahead for hours and admission prices. $

The Crook Farm is a collection of restored buildings from the 1800s, including a farmhouse, a one-room schoolhouse, barn, herb garden, tool house, train depot, and outbuildings. At the end of August, join the celebration at the Crook Farm Country Fair with crafts, food, entertainment, and special events for children. For information, contact the Bradford Chamber of Commerce at www.bradfordchamber.com.

Zippo/Case Visitors Center (ages 6 and up)

1932 Zippo Drive, off US 219; (888) 442–1932; www.zippo.com and www.wrcase.com. Open Monday through Saturday 9:00 A.M. to 5:00 P.M. and Sunday 11:00 A.M. to 4:00 P.M. On Thursday, open until 7:00 P.M. Admission is free.

Here's something you don't see every day: a collection of antique and rare Zippo lighters and cases. For the uninitiated, Zippo Manufacturing has been making "windproof" lighters with a lifetime guarantee since 1932. The company also makes steel tape measures, knives, money clips, pens, and key holders. Zippo products are popular among collectors, with swap meets and collector's clubs around the world. The Zippo/Case Visitors Center is the most-visited museum in Pennsylvania's Northern Tier.

Since its opening in 1997, the Zippo/Case Visitors Center has attracted thousands of visitors from over 120 nations. More than 2,000 Zippo products are on display. New exhibits include "ZAC" (the Zippo/Case audio kinetic sculpture) and a 14-foot flag made entirely of Zippo lighters. Definitely not just another roadside attraction.

ALSO IN THE AREA

Holgate Toy Store and Museum (all ages), Wetmore Avenue, Kane; (814) 837–7600; www.holgatetoy.com. Open daily year-round. Windows and a video allow you to see these charming toys being made at the toy factory. Kids love the trolley cars based on Mr. Rogers's Village of Make-Believe.

Sights of **St. Mary's**

From Bradford head south on 219 into Elk County, home of one of the two free-roaming elk herds east of the Mississippi—and the only one in Pennsylvania, now numbering more than 800. One of the best places to spot the herd is near the airport in St. Marys. The Dent's Run viewing area is located near the town of Benezette, near Elk State Forest on Route 555. Early morning or late afternoon are the best times to see them. For information check the Web site www.pagreatoutdoors.com and click on "Elk Herd." You can download an Elk Scenic Drive map. You can even view the elk live via webcam. For a free elk viewing guidebook, call Northwest Pennsylvania's Great Outdoors at (800) 348–9393. Remember, feeding the elk is against the law.

Allegheny Arms and Armor Museum (ages 5 and up), Route 46, Smethport; (814) 362–2642; www.armormuseum.com. Open daily, 365 days a year, 10:00 A.M. to 6:00 P.M. Wheelchair accessible. Kids love this military museum with its changing displays of helicopters, tanks, vehicles, armor, and more. Living History Days, during the third week in June, offers the chance to see actual encampments and reenacted battles.

Warren

Allegheny National Forest (all ages) 🏕️ 🎣 🏕️

P.O. Box 847, 222 Liberty Street 16365; (814) 723–5150; www.fs.fed.us/r9/forests/ allegheny. Open year-round.

With more than a half million acres, there's room for many a family adventure within the boundaries of Allegheny National Forest, the only national forest in Pennsylvania. You will find a working forest when you visit the Allegheny. Congress mandates that national forests be managed for a variety of uses, using techniques that ensure future generations will be able to enjoy the benefits of these lands. Recreation, wood production, and wildlife habitat improvements are just some of the many activities going on in Allegheny National Forest.

Several towns act as good bases for explorations of the forest, including Warren, Marienville, Bradford, Ridgway, Tionesta, and Kane. Warren serves as the headquarters for the forest, but there are information centers in Marienville and Marshburg. Before planning your trip, be sure to get a copy of the **free** outdoor recreation map of the Allegheny National Forest Region, available at tourist information centers or by calling ahead. It displays the small roads of the forest much more clearly than most road maps.

The forest has just about everything a family adventurer looks for: camping (developed and backwoods), fishing, hiking, ATV trails, horseback riding, snowmobiling, cross-country skiing, and hunting. There are nearly 200 miles of hiking trails, 700 miles of streams, two Wild and Scenic Rivers, and several lakes and reservoirs within the forest.

But if you only have a few hours to explore the park, head to **Heart's Content,** a National Natural Landmark that harbors one of the last stands of old-growth forest in the eastern United States. The turnoff from U.S. Route 62 is easy to miss (it's just before the bridge to Tidioute). Stop at the Tidioute Overlook, where an easy path leads to two vistas over the river gorge. Look carefully; it's not unusual to see a bald eagle circling over the river. At Heart's Content, there's a 1-mile interpretive trail. White pines and hemlocks that are hundreds of years old reach high into the sky.

Although no motorized vehicles are allowed in the old-growth forest, there are several excellent scenic drives through other parts of the forest. US 62 follows the Allegheny River from Tionesta to Warren; the Allegheny Reservoir Scenic Drive circles the large lake formed by the Kinzua Dam, and the Longhouse Scenic Drive starts at the Kinzua Dam and includes other area highlights.

A Paulsen **Family Adventure**

What do you do with a baby on a trip to a place like Allegheny National Forest? Well, lots of things. My husband and I have realized that, although having a child changes many aspects of our lives and our travel habits, there are still a lot of outdoor activities and adventures we can include Eli in.

Hiking: We started hiking with Eli soon after he was born. We put him in a front pack facing out. He insisted on this fairly early on, even if it meant we had to hold his head up for him. Most of the time, he would fall asleep fairly quickly. But at the Heart's Content section of the Allegheny National Forest, he stayed awake for a 2-mile hike through the old-growth forest. He seemed aware that it was a rare treat to see trees hundreds of years old.

Cross-country skiing: By the time Eli was nine months old, he graduated from the front pack to the back pack. We bought a top-of-the-line model with all sorts of straps and supports. Snapped into the pack, Eli accompanied us not only on hikes, but also cross-country ski trips. We made sure he was dressed very warmly, and we didn't stay out as long as we did without him, but he loved getting outside, even on a winter's day. As Martin headed down a gentle slope, Eli said "WEEEE" and clapped his hands in the air.

Driving long distances: Lots of people dread taking their kids on long car trips, but (knock on wood) so far so good. Our secret: get on the road early; I mean really early. We usually take off on a long trip by 4:30 in the morning. We just move Eli from his bed to the car seat. Although he wakes up for a bit, he's usually back to sleep within a half hour and stays asleep until 6:30 or 7:00. Entertain him for an hour, and we've done half of a six-hour drive before stopping for breakfast.

Marienville

Knox Kane Railroad (all ages)

P.O. Box 422, Route 66 16239; (814) 927–6621; www.kkrailroad.com. Various schedules June through October. Rides cost $$$$ for adults; $$$ for children 3 through 12.

One way to enjoy the beauty of the forest without expending too much energy is a ride on the Knox Kane Railroad. But just because you aren't hiking or biking doesn't mean you're not going to have an adventure on this 96-mile ride from Marienville to Kinzua Bridge and back. The train is pulled either by a diesel engine or a steam locomotive. If you're lucky enough to ride when the steam engine is used, don't sit in the open-air car unless you don't mind water and soot from the stack ending up on you. Riders have a thirty- to forty-minute break to picnic or walk around while the engine is switched to the opposite end for the return trip.

Mount Jewett

Kinzua Bridge State Park (all ages) 🏕️ 👫
Off US 6, Ormsby Road, Mount Jewett; (814) 965–2646; www.dcnr.state.pa.us/state parks/kinzuabridge.aspx. Open year-round.

Even if you can't take the Knox Kane Railroad, stop at the state park and take a look at the bridge. It's an engineering feat that will take your breath away. The brave can walk across the bridge. Others can just gawk from the overlook.

Tionesta

Flying W Ranch (all ages) 🛶 🏇 🏕️
Tionesta; (814) 463–7663; www.flyingwranch.com. Children must be 4 feet, 6 inches tall.

Another highlight of the Allegheny National Forest is the Flying W Ranch, west of Marienville in Tionesta. This 500-acre working ranch sits within the boundaries of the national forest and offers countless opportunities for adventure. Spend an hour or a week here taking western riding lessons, canoeing on the Allegheny River, hiking, fishing, and more. In July come for the professional Allegheny Mountain Championship Rodeo. For a real adventure go on one of the overnight horseback trips into the national forest.

Accommodations range from bunkhouses to cabins, or you can bring your RV and hook up at the campground. In summer the ranch offers a western riding camp for children ages six to fourteen.

Cooksburg

Not only does this area harbor one of the largest stands of virgin hemlock and pine forests in the East, it is also home to a thriving arts center. The combination is unbeatable for a family vacation.

Cook Forest Sawmill Center for the Arts (ages 6 and up) 🎵

Breezemont Drive; (814) 744–9670 or (814) 927–6655; www.sawmill.org. Open summer and fall. Admission free**. Ticket prices for live theater and special events and fees for classes vary. For information on classes or festivals, call (814) 927–6655.**

Cook Forest Sawmill Center for the Arts has two buildings full of crafts, art and craft classes, various special events, and more. (Site I, which offers crafts, is open only in the summer.) Festivals include a Herb Festival in June, Wood Competition and Show in July, Forest Fest and Quilt Show in August, and Dulcimer and Folk Music Gathering in September. In the summer, children ages six to twelve can participate in a morning arts program. There's also Creative HeARTS, for the mentally and physically challenged, and a young people's drama workshop and dance camp.

Cook Forest State Park (all ages) 🎒 👫 ⛺

Exit 8, 9, or 13 off Interstate 80 (P.O. Box 120 16217); (814) 744–8407; www.dcnr.state .pa.us/stateparks/parks/cookforest.aspx.

Named one of the nation's top fifty parks, Cook Forest contains one of the last remaining old-growth forests of 200- to 350-year-old white pine and hemlock that reach 200 feet into the sky. At the Log Cabin Inn Visitor's Center, check out the Historical Room, which displays logging and rafting tools as well as models and other artifacts of the logging industry.

There are 27 miles of trails that are wonderful for hiking, cross-country skiing, and more. Many of the trails are less than a mile in length—a distance that's just right for little hikers. During the summer season nature programs are offered on Friday and Saturday nights, and guided walks are conducted regularly. The easy-flowing Clarion River is a great way to introduce yourself and your family to tubing or canoeing.

The twenty-three rustic cabins in the forest are a popular vacation option. The cabins are grouped in two areas. There are eleven small, one-room cabins in the Indian area, located by the park office and near the accessible fishing pier. Flush toilet and shower facilities are nearby. The thirteen River cabins are located on a hillside overlooking the Clarion River. Twelve of these are some of the largest models built by the Civilian Conservation Corps (CCC), with a living room, kitchen, and two bedrooms. Recently the park has completed work on two cabins to make the doors and kitchen appliances accessible to people in wheelchairs. Another bonus of these larger cabins: cold running water. But you'll still have to use the composting toilets.

Pine Crest Cabins (all ages)
Cook Forest; (814) 752–2200; http://users.penn.com/~pinecrest/pinecrest.html.

For families who want to combine horseback riding with their vacation, one of the best choices is Pine Crest Cabins. Don't let the name fool you: There is a campground on the property as well as stables. There are also canoes, go-karts, bumper boats, and long-putt golf—all on a seventy-five-acre family-oriented resort. More than half of the land has been preserved in its natural state and provides great hiking territory for families. Log cabins sleep eight to ten people and have indoor and outdoor fireplaces and two or three bedrooms.

Double Diamond Deer Ranch (all ages)
Route 36, south of Cook Forest; (814) 752–6334; www.doublediamonddeerranch.com. Open year-round. Call for current hours and admission prices.

If you want to see your wildlife up a little closer, check out the Double Diamond Deer Ranch, near the entrance to the state park on Route 36 South. Here a herd of twenty-five deer have been raised since birth. The deer are tame, so they'll come right up and greet you, eat from your hand, and enjoy a good scratch behind the ears. Fawns are born each spring, and during June through August they are bottle-fed. Children are welcome to hold the bottles. A Whitetail and Wildlife Education Center offers a chance to learn about the animals you've seen in the woods. The "Buck Barn," added in 2003, houses ninety taxidermy displays in naturalistic dioramas.

Punxsutawney

On Groundhog Day each year, the world focuses its attention on the little town of Punxsutawney and on a groundhog named Phil. If he climbs out of his burrow on Gobbler's Knob and sees his shadow, the story goes, winter will be sticking around for a while longer. Phil's an old hand at this prediction stuff: He (or his ancestors) has been doing it every year since February 2, 1887. You can watch Phil on the webcam at http://visitpa.com/visitpa/webcams.do?wc=zoo.

Punxsutawney Groundhog Zoo (all ages)

124 West Mahoning Street; (800) 752–PHIL; www.groundhog.org or www
.punxsutawneyphil.com. Open year-round. Admission **free.**

You don't have to wait until February to get a glimpse of Phil. He can be found living with his family at the Punxsutawney Groundhog Zoo at the Civic Complex in town. Each summer the town celebrates its favorite son with a weeklong Groundhog Festival in July. Parades, dances, contests, flea markets, and lots of food are all part of the festivities.

This is also the site of the Punxsutawney Chamber of Commerce, (124 West Mahoning Street; 800–752–PHIL or 814–938–4303; www.punxsutawney.com), your source of information on accommodations, restaurants, attractions, and, of course, all things groundhog.

Franklin

Franklin is a great area for biking, hiking, and camping. Here are a couple of outfitters to help you plan your trip:

- **Outer Limits (ages 8 and up),** U.S. Route 322 East, Franklin; (800) 707–6520; www.bikeandfloat.com. Outer Limits offers customized outdoor adventures for families and other groups. From hiking, biking, and backpacking to canoeing and fishing, the guides provide everything you need, including equipment, meals, and transportation. All tour guides are certified in first aid and CPR.

- **Country Peddlers Recreational Rentals and Sales (ages 8 and up),** US 322 East, Franklin; (814) 432–8055; www.bikeandfloat.com. Located on the Allegheny River at the trailheads for two excellent family adventure trails: the Samuel Justus Recreational Trail (5%₀-miles) and the Allegheny River Trail (14 miles). Country Peddlers rents the bikes, skates, or canoes you need to enjoy this beautiful area.

ALSO IN THE AREA

Dandy's Frontier Family Fun Park (ages 2 and up), US 322, Cranberry; (814) 677–5278. Open Friday 4:00 to 11:00 P.M., Saturday 11:00 A.M. to 11:00 P.M., and Sunday 11:00 A.M. to 7:00 P.M. during the school year; open daily 11:00 A.M. to 11:00 P.M. during summer. Admission is **free.** From the easygoing tyke train to the exhilarating Rodeo Raceway, this family fun park has something for everyone in the family. There's an indoor play area and video arcade for rainy-day amusement.

Oil City and Titusville

To get a better picture of the history of oil in this area, head to Oil City and Titusville.

Oil Creek & Titusville Railroad (all ages)

7 Elm Street, Oil City; (814) 676–1733; www.octrr.clarion.edu. Open mid-June through October. Call for current fares.

You can board the Oil Creek & Titusville Railroad through "the valley that changed the world." The two-and-a-half-hour narrated trip describes the world's first oil boom. Stations are at Rynd Farm, 5 miles north of Oil City, as well as the Drake Well Museum, Petroleum Centre, and Perry Street Station in Titusville. Wheelchair accessible.

Oil Creek State Park (all ages)

Off Route 8, between Oil City and Titusville; (814) 676–5915; www.dcnr.pa.state.us/ stateparks/parks/oilcreek.aspx. Open year-round.

The 9½-mile paved bicycle trail through Oil Creek Gorge is the main attraction here. Bike rentals are available from the concession at the Old Egbert Oil Office. Hikers and, in winter, cross-country skiers are also welcome to use the trail.

Drake Well Museum (ages 6 and up)

Off Route 8, south of Titusvi6lle; (814) 827–2797; www.drakewell.org. Open year-round. Adults $$, children 6 to 12 $.

Heading up Route 8 toward Titusville, stop at the Drake Well Museum, where Edwin Drake drilled the first oil well and launched the petroleum industry in 1859. Here you'll find exhibits, videos, historic buildings, and operating oil machinery. Kids can make plastic, enjoy the fire-engine display, and blow the steam whistle in the full-size replica of Drake's engine house. Have fun "feeding" the horses in the oil transportation exhibit, but watch out for the nitro explosion! Trails in adjacent Oil Creek State Park provide great hiking, and there's a picnic pavilion.

Casey's Caboose Stop (all ages)

221 South Monroe Street, Titusville; (814) 827–6597 or toll-free (866) 275–9821.

Got a train lover in your family? Stay at this twenty-one-caboose motel, where cabooses have been converted into accommodations complete with cable TV, heat, air-conditioning, telephones, and computer data ports. Pretty cool. It is adjacent to Molly's Mill, a renovated mill, which has family dining.

Greenville

There are a couple of museums worth a look-see in Greenville. For information try Mercer County Tourism at www.mercercountypa.org.

The Canal Museum (ages 6 and up)
60 Alan Avenue; (724) 588–7540; http://members.tripod.com/~greenville/canal.html. Call for hours and admission.

This museum traces the history of the Erie Extension Canal. You can see a full-size replica of a packet boat and a working model of a canal lock.

Greenville Railroad Park and Museum (all ages)
314 Main Street; (724) 588–4009; http://members.tripod.com/~greenville/rrpark.html. Open weekends only in May, September, and October 1:00 to 5:00 P.M. Open Tuesday through Sunday during summer months, 1:00 to 5:00 P.M. Admission is free, but donations are gladly accepted.

Here your kids can climb aboard the largest steam switch engine ever built in the United States. There are also railroad cars, a 1914 Empire automobile, and the world's first parachute on display.

Greenville Farmers' Curb Market (all ages)
Corner of Penn Avenue and Main Street. Open Wednesday and Saturday 7:00 A.M. to 2:00 P.M.

If you're in town on a Wednesday or Saturday, check out this outdoor market that features the produce of farmers within a 20-mile radius of town.

Brucker Great Blue Heron Sanctuary (all ages)
Route 18, south of Greenville; (724) 589–2117. Open year-round. Admission is free.

More than 400 of these majestic birds nest at this wildlife reserve—the largest colony of herons in the state.

Conneaut Lake Area

You'll find lots of family fun around Pennsylvania's largest lake.

Conneaut Lake Area (all ages)
12382 Center Street, Conneaut Lake; (814) 382–5115; www.conneautlakepark.com. Open daily early summer to late fall. Admission is free—you pay only for the rides you want.

For more than one hundred years, families have come to Conneaut Lake Park to enjoy the lake, ride the rides, and just plain have fun. There is a 167-room historic hotel, a

105-site modern campground with camping cabins, and a full range of rides and amusements. The classic Blue Streak wooden roller coaster is sure to thrill, and the Waterpark is a hit with most kids. When you've had enough of the rides, relax on the lake beach or take a ride on the stern-wheeler *Barbara J.*

Pymatuning State Park (ages 5 and up)

Route 58, Jamestown; (724) 932–3141; www.dcnr.state.pa.us/stateparks/parks/ pymatuning.aspx. Open year-round.

With the 27-square-mile Conneaut Lake as its centerpiece, the park offers boating, hiking, fishing, camping, and winter sports.

Pymatuning Deer Park (all ages) 🐘

Route 58, Jamestown; (724) 932–3200; www.pymatuning.com/deerpark.htm. Open weekends in May and daily Memorial Day through Labor Day. Call for current admission prices.

This small zoo offers train and pony rides as well as an opportunity to pet and feed the animals. Small children especially seem to enjoy this stop. The park has over 200 animals, including lions, tigers, bears (oh my!), wallabies, kangaroos, and camels in addition to the favorite farm animals.

Erie

Erie is the area's largest population center, the state's only Great Lake port, and the home of former governor Tom Ridge. The city celebrated its bicentennial in 1995, and things have been booming ever since. With Splash Lagoon Indoor Waterpark, Erie Otters hockey, Erie SeaWolves baseball, and so much more, Erie has never been better. For information on the Otters, go to www.ottershockey.com; for the SeaWolves, www.seawolves.com.

Presque Isle State Park (all ages) 🧗🚴🌊

Peninsula Drive (P.O. Box 8510 16505); (814) 833–7424; www.dcnr.state.pa.us/state parks/parks.presqueisle.aspx. Open year-round. Free admission.

Presque Isle State Park is one of the most remarkable aspects of Erie. This narrow spit of sand (*presque isle* literally means "almost an island") juts out into Lake Erie, providing an unusual environment for wildlife and a beautiful retreat for humans. To plan your day at the park, stop at the interpretive center, where there is a wonderful nature gift shop and bookstore as well as exhibits about local wildlife.

Choose the calm waters of Presque Isle Bay for boating or the almost oceanlike waves of Lake Erie for swimming. Water enthusiasts can rent canoes, rowboats, or motorboats to explore the waters on their own, whereas landlubbers can enjoy 13 miles of hiking trails. Bring your binoculars; Presque Isle is touted as one of the best bird-watching sites in the country. More than 300 species live in or pass by the park.

B.O.A.T. (Best of All Tours, Inc.) runs the forty-nine-passenger *Lady Kate* from the Perry Monuments at Presque Isle. There's also a thirty-six-passenger water taxi, Presque Isle Express, that runs between Presque Isle and Dobbins Landing in downtown Erie. It's a great way to pack in a full day of Erie sights and fun.

Although busiest in summer, there's something to do year-round at the park. In winter hiking trails turn to cross-country ski trails, and Presque Isle Bay provides great ice fishing.

Waldameer Park and Water World (ages 3 and up)

220 Peninsula Drive; (814) 838–3591; www.waldameer.com. Open Tuesday through Sunday, mid-May through Labor Day. Individual-ride and combo tickets available. **Free** parking and admission.

Right outside the entrance of Presque Isle State Park is Waldameer Park and Water World. If you don't spot it, your kids definitely will. There are five body slides, three double-tube slides, the Wild River tube slide, free-fall slide, speed slide, Endless River ride, three "tad pool" areas, and a heated pool. The amusement park has sixteen major rides and ten rides for children, including the fantastic log flume ride, Thunder River. Use of tubes and life jackets is **free,** and there is a variety of gift shops, snack bars, and midway games at the park. Or you can bring your own picnic. Puppet shows and musical shows are offered throughout the day.

Erie Maritime Museum (ages 6 and up)

150 East Front Street; (814) 871–4596 or (814) 452–BRIG; www.brigniagara.org. Open seven days a week year-round. Open Monday through Saturday 9:00 A.M. to 5:00 P.M., Sunday noon to 5:00 P.M. Last tickets sold at 4:00 P.M. Call for winter hours January 1 through March 31. Admission: adults $$, family ticket $$$, youth 6 to 12 $; children under 6 are **free.** Reduced rates when the Niagara is underway.

The maritime attractions of downtown Erie have been united in the Erie Maritime Museum. This state-of-the-art facility features exhibits about the ecology of the Great Lakes; Lake Erie; Pennsylvania's North Coast maritime history's *Wolverine* and interactive Fighting Sailing Deck; several video displays about the *Niagara*, the Battle of Lake Erie, reconstruction of the *Niagara;* and a live fire exhibit. In addition, when it is in port, tour O. H. Perry's flagship, the U.S. Brig *Niagara*.

You can take a look at the *Wolverine*—at least what's left of it. The ship, originally christened the USS *Michigan,* was the first iron-hulled ship ever built. Now the bow is all that remains of this impressive part of maritime history.

When it's in port, you can tour the flagship *Niagara,* a brig built to fight the naval battles of the War of 1812. To avoid disappointing children with their hearts set on seeing this boat, call ahead.

Bicentennial Observation Tower (ages 3 and up)

Dobbins Landing; (814) 455–6055 or (814) 455–7557; www.visiteriepa.com/bicentennial_tower.shtml. Open year-round. Call for current hours and days. Admission is $; children under 6 are free. Admission is free for all ages on Tuesday.

This 185-foot-tall tower gives an amazing view over Presque Isle, downtown Erie, and Lake Erie. Take the 210 stairs to the top observation deck or take the elevator. If you take the stairs, follow the sixteen stations that point out historic, geographic, and other landmarks.

Splash Lagoon Indoor Waterpark Resort

Interstate 90 Exit 24, (866) 3–SPLASH, www.splashlagoon.com. Splash Lagoon opens every day at 9:00 A.M. Closing hours vary seasonally. Day passes are sometimes available on a first-come, first-served basis, but to be guaranteed admission to the park, an overnight package is strongly recommended. Call (814) 217–1111 for day pass availability.

Brand new in spring 2003, Splash Lagoon is an all-inclusive resort featuring accommodations, entertainment, restaurants, and more, but its highlight is its indoor waterpark—over an acre of indoor water fun! Attractions include four twisting and turning body slides, a swirling body coaster for one or two riders, an 80,000-gallon activity pool, and two twenty-five-person whirlpools, one for kids and one for adults.

The newest cutting-edge waterslide in the country, Hurricane Hole is a one-person body slide, 125 feet long. Riders fly down a dark tunnel at speeds exceeding 40 miles per hour, then spin in the Hurricane Bowl before taking a mid-air plunge into the warm water below. Or you can try the Lazy River/Crazy River, a lazy river ride with an adventurous difference. Moms and dads can relax in the adults-only Paradise Cove hot tub, with beautiful murals on the walls, a waterfall, and massaging water jets to take the knots out of your muscles.

Erie Art Museum (ages 8 and up)

411 State Street, Discovery Square; (814) 459–5477; www.erieartmuseum.org. Open Tuesday through Saturday year-round. Admission is $. Free admission on Wednesday.

The Erie Art Museum offers changing exhibitions, concerts, classes, and children's activities. During the first weekend of August the museum hosts the Erie Art Museum Blues & Jazz Festival, which draws 10,000 people to Frontier Park for the Free event.

expERIEnce Children's Museum (ages 2–12)

420 French Street, Discovery Square; (814) 453–3743; www.eriechildrensmuseum.org. Open year-round Wednesday through Saturday 10:00 A.M. to 4:00 P.M., Sunday 1:00 to 4:00 P.M. Closed Monday year-round and Tuesday during school year. Call or check Web site to inquire about special holiday hours. Admission is $. Children under 2 enter free.

For small children the highlight of Erie is the expERIEnce Children's Museum, housed in an old livery stable. The museum is aimed at kids ages two to twelve, but those under age eight seem to enjoy it the most. According to one of the museum's curators, "This is a hands-on museum, which means that kids can come in and break things, and after they leave, we fix them."

There's a Gallery of Science on one floor and a Gallery of the Human Experience on the other. You can also see a simulation of a cave, in which children learn about cave painting, cave exploration, and fossils. At the Wegman's Corner Store, children can shop in a re-creation of a supermarket, complete with scanners, shopping carts, and very real-looking groceries. Youngsters may want to pick out a funny outfit from the costume closet and put on a show on a real stage.

Watson–Curtze Mansion and Erie Planetarium (all ages)

356 West Sixth Street; (814) 871–5790; www.eriecountyhistory.org. Open Tuesday through Sunday afternoons year-round. Call for current hours. Museum admission is $.Planetarium admission is $. Children under 2 are admitted free to both exhibits.

Kids of all ages love planetarium shows. Even toddlers will point out the moon and the stars. Call ahead for schedule of shows.

Erie Zoo (all ages) 🐘

423 West Thirty-eighth Street; (814) 864–4091; www.eriezoo.org. Open year-round. Call for admission prices and hours.

More than 500 animals representing nearly one hundred different species live in this fifteen-acre park. There's a children's zoo and a train ride around the zoo.

ALSO IN THE AREA

Wooden Nickel Buffalo Farm and Shop (all ages), 5970 Koman Road, Edinboro; (814) 734–BUFF; www.woodennickelbuffalo.com. Open year-round. **Free** admission. A herd of more than fifty buffalo roam on this fifty-acre ranch outside Erie. It's quite a sight to see. Who knows, you might get inspired to get into buffalo farming yourself.

North East

About 20 miles east of Erie on U.S. Route 20 is the historic village of North East. Take a walking tour of the historic district (brochures are available at local stores and museums).

Hornby School Museum (ages 4 and up) 🏫

11573 Station Road; (814) 725–5680. Open Sunday 1:00 to 5:00 P.M. or by appointment. Admission is free, but donations are accepted.

If you call ahead and make arrangements, your children can experience what it was like to learn in a one-room schoolhouse built in the 1870s. Even the books and slates are original equipment.

Lake Shore Railway Historical Society Museum (ages 2 and up) 🏫

Corner of Wall and Robinson Streets; (814) 825–2724 or (814) 725–1191; http://lsrhs .railway.museum. Open Wednesday through Sunday afternoons from Memorial Day to Labor Day. Call for exact hours and admission.

Here, you can see a variety of train equipment, including a Pullman car, a caboose, and a dining car. Located on a busy stretch of railroad track, the site practically guarantees that your children will get to see several modern trains pass by during your visit.

Where to Eat

IN THE COOKSBURG AREA

Americo's Italian Restaurant, Cooksburg–Vowinckel Road, 1¼ mile north of Sawmill Theatre, Cook Forest; (814) 927–8516. Open April through October for lunch and dinner. Children's menu. Near attractions.

Cook Forest Country Inn, Cooksburg–Vowinckel Road; (814) 927–8925 or (800) 830–6133. Home-style cooking, homemade rolls, and pies.

The Farmer's Inn, Two miles north of Sigel on Route 949, near Clear Creek State Park; (814) 752–2942. Restaurant, ice cream, bakery, gift shop, Amish furniture, horse-drawn wagon and pony rides, miniature golf, animal exhibits, petting zoo.

Gateway Lodge Country Inn and Restaurant, Route 36 in the heart of Cook Forest; (814) 744–8017 or (800) 843–6862. Dine by kerosene light. Staff dressed colonial-style. Breakfast and lunch daily. Dinner daily except for Monday.

Mama Doe's Restaurant, Shiloh Ranch Resort, Route 36, Cook Forest; (814) 752–2361. Fine dining and Italian cuisine. Breakfast, lunch, and dinner; daily specials, Sunday buffet. Also campground, cabins, and lodge.

Sawmill Restaurant, Intersection of Routes 36 and 66 at the blinker light, Leeper; (814) 744–8578. Soft ice cream, fresh baked goods, home of the Sawdustburger. Open daily, year-round, 7:00 A.M. to midnight.

The Trails End, Cooksburg–Vowinckel Road, near Cook Forest State Park; (814) 927–8400. Steaks, seafood, sandwiches. Near theater and park attractions.

Vowinckel Hotel, corner of Route 66 and Cooksburg–Vowinckel Road, 5 miles from Cook Forest; (814) 927–6610. Homemade bread and pizza dough. Voted "Best Wings in Clarion County." Fireplace.

IN ERIE

Applebee's Restaurant, 7790 Peach Street; (814) 866–8210.

Backstage Grill, 2025 Peach Street; (814) 452–1356.

Bagel Basket, 3 East Eighteenth Street; (814) 452–2435.

Bob Evans Restaurant, 8041 Peach Street; (814) 864–5444.

Calamari's Restaurant, 1317 State Street; (814) 459–4267.

The Carriage House, 1535 West Twenty-sixth Street; (814) 623–1174.

China Garden Restaurant, 6801 Peach Street; (814) 868–2695.

Chuck E Cheese, 7200 Peach Street, Summit Towne Center; (814) 864–3100.

Connie's Ice Cream, 6032 Peach Street; (814) 866–1700. Take-out homemade ice cream made with the freshest ingredients.

Hoss's Steak & Sea House, 3302 West Twenty-sixth Street; (814) 835–6836.

Italian Oven, 2709 West Twelfth Street; (814) 835–6836.

Julio's Family Restaurant & Pizzeria, 29 South Jared; (814) 455–6301. Family-friendly bar and restaurant serving sandwiches, burgers, wings, and more. Children's menu; high chairs available.

Old Country Buffet, 7200 Peach Street; (814) 866–5671.

The Olive Garden, 5945 Peach Street; (814) 866–1105.

Pio's Italian Restaurant & Pizzeria, 815 East Avenue; (814) 456–8866. Pastas, pizza, and other casual Italian-style choices. Children's menu.

Porter's Taproom, 123 West Fourteenth Street; (814) 452–2787.

Smuggler's Wharf, 3 State Street; (814) 459–4273.

Where to Stay

IN WELLSBORO

Comfort Inn Canyon Country, 300 Gateway Drive, Mansfield; (717) 662–3000 or (800) 822–5470. Conveniently located for events in Mansfield as well as touring nearby Pine Creek Gorge.

IN BRADFORD

Howard Johnson Lodge and Restaurant, 100 Davis Street South; (800) 344–4656. Open year-round. A good base for Bradford- and Allegheny Forest-area explorations. Outdoor pool, special combination packages for the Knox Kane Railway excursions, skiing, and golf.

IN THE ALLEGHENY NATIONAL FOREST AREA

Kane View Motel, US 6 East, Kane; (814) 837–8600. The Allegheny National Forest is in the backyard of this convenient motel.

IN WARREN

Super 8, US 6 and US 62 North; (814) 723–8881. Near major attractions and downtown. Continental breakfast.

Holiday Inn–Warren, 210 Ludlow Street; (814) 726–3000. On-site restaurant, indoor pool, and a three-diamond rating from AAA make this a good choice for families exploring the national forest and other area attractions.

IN THE COOKSBURG AREA

Clarion River Lodge, River Road in Cook Forest; (814) 744–8171 or (800) 648–6743. Magnificent view of Clarion River. Guest rooms available. Open year-round.

IN PUNXSUTAWNEY

Pantall Hotel, downtown; (814) 938–6600. Beautifully restored Victorian hotel; restaurants on-site.

IN FRANKLIN

Inn at Franklin, downtown; (814) 437–3031 or (800) 535–4052. Free continental breakfast; restaurant, tavern, family plans.

IN OIL CITY

Holiday Inn–Oil City, 1 Seneca Street; (814) 677–1221 or (800) HOLIDAY. Kids stay free. Full-service restaurant, lounge, entertainment.

IN THE CONNEAUT LAKE AREA

Days Inn–Meadville, just off exit 36A off Interstate 79, Meadville; (814) 337–4264. Minutes from Conneaut Lake. Family restaurant on-site.

IN CLARION

Comfort Inn, I–80 exit 9, north on Route 66; (814) 226–5230. Free continental breakfast, outdoor pool.

Holiday Inn of Clarion, Route 68 and I–80, exit 9; (814) 226–8850 or (800) 596–1313. Free breakfast buffet. Tropical courtyard with indoor pool and saunas, restaurant, and lounge. Kids stay and eat free.

Super 8 Motel–Clarion, I–80, exit 9; (814) 226–4550. AAA-rated, first-floor, and nonsmoking rooms. Free continental breakfast and local calls, cable television, outdoor pool.

IN ERIE

Erie has an impressive array of hotels and motels—with just about all the major chains represented. Most of the big-name places are equipped with indoor pools, definitely good news for families traveling in winter or when bad weather interrupts sightseeing plans. Here are a few highlights:

The Glass House Inn, 3202 West Twenty-sixth Street (US 20); (814) 833–7751 or (800) 956–7222; www.velocity.net/~ghilel. A family-friendly, family-run, colonial-style inn with outdoor pool and lots of room to play.

Marriott Residence, 8061 Peach Street; (814) 864–2500; www.ncinter.net/~erie inns/. This all-suite hotel has kitchens in the rooms, an indoor pool, and a breakfast buffet. (Web site serves three other big hotels, so do some online comparison shopping.)

Presque Isle Cottage Court, 320 Peninsula Drive; (814) 833–4956. Located close to Waldermeer Water World and Presque Isle State Park.

For More Information

Allegheny National Forest Vacation Region, with visitor centers in Bradford (80 East Corydon Street, Suite 14), Lantze Corners (3183 US 219), and Marshburg (Route 321 and Route 59); (800) 473–9370; www.allegheny-vacation.com. Call ahead or drop by for information about things to do and see and places to stay and eat in McKean County.

Erie Area of Chamber of Commerce, downtown office: Scenic Route 5, the Pennsylvania Seaway Trail. Mailing address: 1006 State Street, Erie 16501; (800) 542–ERIE or (814) 454–7191; www .eriepa.com. Visit the extensive Web site, write, or call ahead for information, or stop by one of several information centers along major routes for up-to-the-minute details on attractions, accommodations, and events in the Erie area. Some major festivals in the area include the Erie Summer Festival of the Arts (end of June) and We Love Erie Days (August). Both feature special events for children.

Northwest Pennsylvania's Great Outdoors Visitors Bureau, 175 Main Street, Brookville 15825; (814) 849–5197; www .pagreatoutdoors.com.

Endless Mountains Visitor Bureau, 712 US 6, East Tunkhannock 18657; (800) 769–8999, (570) 836–5431; www.endless mountains.org.

Mercer County Convention and Visitors Bureau, 835 Perry Highway, Mercer 16137; (800) 637–2370 or (412) 748–5315; www.mercercountypa.org. Your source for information on accommodations and attractions in Greenville, Sharon, Hermitage, Grove City, and all of Mercer County.

Northern Allegheny Vacation Region, 315 Second Avenue, Warren 16365; (800) 624–7802 or (814) 726–1222; www.northernalleghenies.com. Tourist information for Forest and Warren Counties.

Oil Heritage Region Tourist Promotion Agency, Inc., National City Bank Building, Third Floor, 248 Seneca Street, Oil City 16301; (800) 483–6264 or (814) 677–3152; www.usachoice.net/oilregion tourist. Write or call ahead for an information packet with brochures about attractions and accommodations in Venango County.

Potter County Recreation, Inc., P.O. Box 245, Coudersport 16915; (888) POTTER–2 or (814) 274–3365; www.potter countypa.org. Provides information on recreational opportunities in Potter County.

Tioga County Tourist Promotion Agency, 114 Main Street, Wellsboro 16901; (570) 724–0635 or (888) 846–4228; www.visittiogapa.com. Contact from home or stop by for area information.

Wellsboro Chamber of Commerce, 114 Main Street, Wellsboro 16901; (717) 724–1926; www.wellsboropa.com. For more information about festivals, accommodations, and other attractions in Wellsboro, this is your source.

General Index

Activities Index

Living-History Sites

Museums

Trolleys

Zoos & Animals